Matthew Harrison

UNRAVELING
WRONGFUL
CONVICTION
AND MISCARRIAGE OF JUSTICE

True Story Transforming Despair to Hope

Contents

PREFACE

I knew it would be a challenge to write a history of my life from prison. I did not have a computer or word processor, only a tablet that allowed me to send emails to my family who helped me with editing and grammar. Add my lack of writing experience, and I knew that I would need the Lord's help if I were to write things that would be of greatest worth and importance.

My goal in writing my history was twofold: First, I wanted to share with others the circumstances that took place in my life—the trials and challenges I faced—because none of those things were unique to just me. By writing my experiences, I hoped to help others who will or are now going through similar difficulties learn from my mistakes and avoid the painful and destructive outcomes I faced. Second, I wanted to share the miracle that took place to bring me back to the Lord and His church. As lost as I was, I feared there was no way I could ever come back to the church. All the mistakes that I made over the years had me feeling that not even God could forgive me for the sins I had committed. But through a series of events over time that were orchestrated by the Lord, I was humbled to the point that I was ready to do whatever was necessary to come back.

It was amid this anguish I felt for sins committed that the Lord softened my heart and led me to read my patriarchal blessing given years before. In that blessing I was reminded that my family and the Lord loved me, that repentance was possible, and that all hope was not lost. I felt a powerful witness that day that my Heavenly Father loved me dearly and wanted me to come back to Him. I chose with all my heart to do just that; and in that moment, my entire life changed. It did not immediately change the outcome because the Lord will not remove the consequences of the choices made. But with His help, I was able to get through some of the hardest trials I have ever experienced.

While during these difficulties, I also had some of the most powerful and sacred experiences I have ever had. I gained a strong testimony of the reality that God truly lives and that through His Atonement, I could change my desires and my heart to become a new person. My hopes and prayers are that when others read about my experiences, they will see just how much the Lord has blessed and directed my life—not just while in prison but also during other times when I was protected and blessed. It was the Lord who enabled me to get to this point, to be spared from harm, and also to receive the necessities I could not provide for myself. The Lord blessed me in ways that were miraculous and could only be explained by divine intervention. These are the things I wanted to share because they show how God's hand has always been present in my life.

Perhaps more importantly, as bad as I thought I was at times, the Lord never gave up on me and provided a way for me to come back if I put my trust in Him with all my heart. So I decided that I would focus more on the things that were more impactful and had the greatest effect on my life because those things set the stage for what I experienced later in my life.

I was surprised at first how difficult it was to go back to my childhood years and recount the experiences that were so traumatic and painful. Though I had many happy memories in my formative years, the more painful and difficult memories were the ones that had the most dramatic effect on what would happen later in my life because of unresolved feelings and anger. Though I was not aware at that time how traumatized I was, and would yet be, the effects of those early experiences and feelings were not easily forgotten or overcome. Even as I write about them now, tears well up in my eyes as I relive those experiences once again. Being an inexperienced writer, I struggled to express my feelings and emotions in coherent ways when I wrote about my childhood. I felt I could never quite express the emotions I was feeling at that time, as well as the intensity of the pain I felt.

Reliving those difficult moments in my childhood, I could not help but think of the trauma my imprisonment had on my children. I will never forget my daughter's screams as officers came to our home and arrested me. Knowing that I was the cause of so much pain and suffering in their lives is a painful reminder of how much my choices impacted them. The very thing I swore I would not do to them, I ended up doing, just as my Father did to me. This history, I hope, will provide them with some answers and some hope that no matter how difficult their lives are, they can overcome their feelings, pain, and circumstances to be happy and successful.

The key to rising above feelings, pain, and circumstances is to follow the only path that can lead to successful outcomes—the Savior. He has the power to heal broken hearts, to heal the innocent who did no wrong but were hurt by the choices of others, and to overcome any obstacles or pain in our lives. After all that I experienced in my life, He was able to help me overcome challenges against all odds. I know that all who believe and turn to the Lord can be healed. That is the message I hope people receive as they read about my life and how I was able to turn it around. Though my life was never easy, and I blamed others for many years for my mistakes, it was only when I turned to the Lord and accepted personal responsibility that the Lord helped me to change and overcome my weaknesses.

The greatest benefit that I and hopefully others will take away from reading about my life and the experiences I had is the reality that our choices matter—every single one of them. Also, the Atonement of Jesus Christ is real, and it has the power to change and help those who use it to become new people. No matter what your circumstances in life, you can overcome them by trusting in the Lord and keeping his commandments. This will enable Him to bless you with the strength and determination to overcome all obstacles you face. I know that the Lord lives, that He loves us, and that all I have experienced has brought me to this knowledge. I sincerely hope that those who read my story will have the desire to gain that knowledge for themselves also and that it will change their lives as it has mine.

As you read my story, you may not be familiar with some of the religious terms I use from my Church of Jesus Christ of Latter-Day Saints, To help you better understand these terms, a list of terms is included after the conclusions to my story. Given in alphabetical order, I encourage you to read the definitions to better understand my faith and how it has affected my life.

Chapter 1

Childhood

OVERVIEW

My childhood was pretty typical of life growing up in the 80s. We lived in a large Latter-Day Saint community, and our neighborhood was filled with children my age. I had three brothers—two older and one younger—and an older sister. My family and I were all active members of The Church of Jesus Christ of Latter-Day Saints. I was involved in scouting and sports, and I also enjoyed being outdoors and hunting with my brothers and Father.

I was always out being active or jumping from trees or on trampolines; consequently, I became a frequent visitor to the emergency room for stitches in various body parts. I think at one point, I had to get stitches three times in the same spot on the back of my head. As a result of my frequent injuries, the emergency room hospital staff knew me on a first-name basis and would ask what I had done this time!

Summers were fun because I loved being outdoors and playing with friends or catching insects or reptiles. We would go sledding in wintertime, build snow forts, and have snowball fights. But that fun, carefree life changed drastically at age nine as I became aware of and witnessed firsthand some of the marital problems my parents were having. Little did I know I would be right in the middle of some of the difficulties that ended my parents' relationship.

EARLY CHOICES BRING PROBLEMS

All relationships have ups and downs; my parents' relationship was no exception. As a child, I never realized my parents had some significant issues they had been dealing with long before I was born. It was not until I was much older that I learned what had occurred when I was younger, even before their marriage. Through conversations with my parents, I came to realize their struggles seemed to begin when they were dating. Because of certain choices they made and the circumstances at the time, they felt compelled to get married. Once married, my parents made mistakes that hurt one another deeply. I was not born when my Mom made some terrible mistakes. But I was nine when my Father made some life-changing choices; unfortunately, I remember it most because I witnessed some of it firsthand. Some of what I witnessed had a grave effect on me and on my parents' relationship that, I believe, ultimately led to divorce.

Dad enjoyed going to the gym to work out or play racquetball with clients or friends and would often take me with him. My friends and I would swim, play basketball and foosball, or run around and watch people. I occasionally saw my Dad with a woman I did not recognize when with my friends. Later that night when looking for my Dad to get money for a drink, I found him playing racquetball with this woman. My friend and I were in the windows above the courts, and just when I was about to ask him for some money, she scored a point and then put her arms around him and kissed him. My friend and I were stunned, and not knowing what to do, we just left. When I got home from the gym, I told my Mom what I saw because I felt something was wrong. It upset her, but she maintained her composure and asked me to tell her everything I could remember about this woman.

Later that same night my parents had a horrible argument. As I lay in my bed and listened to them scream and fight, I regretted ever saying anything to my Mom about what my friend and I saw. I was so scared because I had never heard them fight like they did that night. The fighting escalated to breaking dishes and, finally, physical contact. I began to cry and prayed that they would stop. My room was directly below my parents', so I could hear everything that happened. At first, I was afraid my Father would come downstairs and yell at me next. Then I remember being scared that my Mom would be hurt and regretted saying anything to her. I thought it was my fault for all that took place that night. It would never have happened if I had not said anything—I kept thinking to myself. The fear and anxiety I had that night have never been forgotten, and it is something I still remember like it happened yesterday. That day, I began thinking that some things are better left unsaid—something I had to unlearn later in life. After that incident, my Mom increasingly asked me if I had seen this woman again at the gym or anywhere else. During this time, my Father began to be gone a lot and would work late into the evenings. I often remember playing games at night when my Dad would drive in after working late. My friends commented how weird it was that my Dad, who sold insurance, would be out sometimes until 11:30 pm. I was too young to understand what was happening.

My parents became increasingly distant, and I knew things were not good between them. At this point, I started to worry my parents might not stay together, and I tried my best to be as good as possible. If I behaved well and made them happy, their relationship would improve. I also wondered if my Dad ever found out I told Mom what happened at the gym. He probably knew and was mad at me but could not say anything about it. Nevertheless, I blamed myself for their failing marriage because I told my Mom about the kissing incident and things only deteriorated from that day forward. That left only one conclusion in my mind, and that was because of what I told my Mom: my parents were now getting divorced.

Others in our neighborhood and ward called my Mom telling her they had seen my Dad with this woman and thought she should know. Then, one evening, my Mom and my older brother somehow found out my Dad was at this woman's house and went there to confront him. I cannot recall how they knew he was there, but after that confrontation, it was not long before my Dad decided to leave.

THE SEPARATION

My Dad decided to leave one afternoon when my friends and I were playing football in our backyard. He said he had to drop something off up the street and would be back later. A couple of hours passed, and it was dark outside, yet my Father had not returned. My little brother and I were watching television when my Mom came home and asked where my Father was. She immediately ran up the stairs to their room when I told her he had not returned from dropping something off a few hours earlier. There she found a note telling her he was leaving us. I still remember the feeling I had that night when I saw my Mother's face and knew my Dad had gone and was not coming back, or so I thought. I did my best to be strong for my Mom because she broke down and began sobbing. I remember feeling so guilty and helpless because I thought I was the reason my Dad decided to leave.

My Mother called my aunt, who came to be with her, and I went to my room and just lay on my bed and cried. It was so hard to see my Mom so hurt, and also to be abandoned by my Father. I felt discarded, unloved, and confused about why he would leave us. I had so many questions: Did he not love us anymore? Was he mad at me? Would I ever see him again? Being only nine, I could not fully understand what this all meant. I tried to be strong for my Mom, and I also began to believe that I needed to stop telling her the truth because so far in my life, it seemed to lead to only bad outcomes.

After some time, my Father came back to live with us while my parents went to a counselor and tried to work things out. During this time, I was determined to keep my family together. I did everything I could to make my parents happy and proud of me. I thought I was the problem, so if I behaved better, helped around the house, and did anything else I could to please them, maybe the situation would change for my parents. I asked my Dad if he would ever leave us again. He promised me he would not and was sorry for leaving the first time. He seemed sincere and determined to work things out with my Mom, so I felt relieved hearing his words and thought things would return to normal. But his coming back to us did not last very long.

One Saturday afternoon a short time after my Dad came back to live with us, my Mother told all the children to get in the car for a ride. While we were driving around, my Mom told us that my Dad had decided to leave us again, but this time for good. She told us she was taking us for a drive so he could pack his things and leave before we returned. We were all heartbroken and upset over this news. We all cried and tried to figure out how he could leave his five children. I have never forgotten the sinking and heartbreaking feeling I had as we all cried and tried to console one another and figure out why my Father no longer wanted to be with us. I did not know what we were going to do without him. Looking out the window and feeling completely rejected and abandoned, I thought my Dad loved me; however, at that moment, I felt like I truly did not know if he cared at all.

When we pulled into the garage after driving around for a while, my Father loaded his things into his car. With tears in our eyes, we all got out of the car and begged him to stay. I remember standing in the driveway devastated, as I watched him get into his car and drive away while we all stood there sobbing. He left all of us standing in our driveway completely crushed and heartbroken. How he drove away that day, I will never know or understand. Nothing we said or did changed his mind. I cried and begged my Father not to go. But that was not enough. That was the day my heart broke.

All the promises I can remember my Dad making to me he broke—every single one. I questioned over and over why he would leave us. The only thing that made sense to me was that he did not love us anymore. After telling my Mom what I saw, I decided he especially did not love me.

After he left, I was insecure that my Mom might leave us, too. Though she assured us she would never leave, my Dad had promised me that, too, and now he was gone. I did not realize it then, but later, I realized how much I started to doubt people and not trust them— especially those who were supposed to love me but not enough to be with me. Looking back now, this is when my abandonment fears began. From that day on, I wondered if the people I loved would one day leave, too.

I lost more than my Dad that day, I lost my faith in people. During my parents' separation, my younger brother and I would spend weekends with my Dad. One particular place we stayed was an old, run-down, and scary-looking motel that allowed people to stay for a cheap price. That night, we ate food and watched television programs before bed.

Later that night, I woke up to use the bathroom and realized my Dad was gone. I ran to the window to see if the car was there, but it was gone, too. I began to get scared and wondered why my Dad had left us there and if he was coming back to get us. I did not know what to do. I returned to bed and prayed my Dad would come back for us. I could not figure out where he would go or why he would leave us there. I was only ten then, and my little brother was three, and the place where we were staying was not very nice. I thought about calling my Mom but was afraid of my parents fighting again so I decided not to call. I climbed back into bed and hoped my Dad would be there when I woke.

The next morning, when I awoke, my Dad was there in bed with us, and I was so relieved yet confused about where he went that night. I debated whether to tell my Mom what had happened but feared telling her the truth would again lead to problems and fighting. When we got home, the fear of being left overnight again by my Dad persuaded me to tell my Mom what had happened. That led to a big fight with my Mom saying hurtful things about my Dad, and my Dad doing the same. I felt like I again made a mistake by telling the truth about what happened because it seemed only to make things worse—not better. I was finding that telling the truth only leads to fights and more problems, so I stopped telling my parents things I believed would lead to more fighting and arguments. I just kept things inside and only shared the good things. It was another behavior I had to fix when I got older.

Because I was now afraid of my Dad leaving us at night to visit his girlfriend, I was hesitant to visit. Between my fear of abandonment and the war of words my parents engaged in each time I left and came back, I dreaded seeing my Dad. I hated feeling like I was in the middle. Both parents tried to convince me that the other was at fault for the problems in the marriage. I only wanted them to stop hurting me by putting me in the middle and using me to relay negative and mean messages back and forth.

During this time of not knowing how to feel or what to do, I began having trouble in school and acting out. I would yell at my Mom to stop asking questions and leave me alone. I threatened to run away because I was hurting, and no one seemed to care. I got into trouble because when I did, this was one of the few times I was asked how I was doing. All the anger and bitterness that my parents had for each other was replaced with concern for how I was doing. My Mom had me see a counselor at this point, but I never told the counselor what was going on in my head. I feared what would happen if I did. So, when the counselor would tell me what she thought was going on with me, I went along with her to get her to stop asking questions. I didn't particularly appreciate going to the counselor because I felt that doing that was admitting I was the problem. This just compounded the guilt I already felt for my parents' deteriorating relationship.

Chapter 2

Divorce

COPING BEHAVIOR CHANGES

After my parents separated, they ultimately divorced. As a result, my behavior changed. Instead of the happy-go-lucky kid I had been up to that point, I turned into an angry and combative kid who did all he could to cause problems. I was acting out because I was insecure and felt unloved and unwanted. That is an inevitable outcome for many children who experience divorce.

As a result of my behavior changes, my parents decided to come to my school to speak to my teachers about what was going on and how it might be affecting me. My teachers were very kind and understanding, but I was mad and did not want to hear one more person tell me they understood what I was going through. When anyone said those words to me, I shut them down. Once I shut down, I would rebel to protect myself from further pain and heartache. I did not let others get close to me, including my teachers. It was a coping mechanism I learned to keep from getting hurt again. I realized the less I trusted people and opened up to them, the less likely I would be hurt or disappointed by them. Though I consciously did not know what I was doing at the time, I have since realized that was exactly what I was doing. My Father's leaving hurt me more than I ever realized or admitted to at that young age, and I coped with that hurt by preventing others from getting close to me or to my heart. I was determined never to have it crushed again like it was when my parents divorced.

In my rebellious state of mind, I started to get in trouble at school as a way to bring my parents together to speak to my teachers. I was going to show them how angry and hurt I was by their divorce. I thought if my parents could see how I was hurting, then maybe they would get back together again, and things would be like they were before. But when that failed, I no longer cared, and my behavior deteriorated. I began to get into fights at school. I threw rocks through the school windows. I also mooned the hall monitor from the bathroom window on the second floor and gave her the accompanying hand gesture. If I remember correctly, I also stole candy bars and sodas from the teachers' lounge. As a result, my friends and I had to stay after school many nights to clean the school with the janitor. I cannot remember his name now, but he was a returned missionary and greatly impacted me and my friends. He would play basketball with us and talk to us. He genuinely seemed to care and asked us why we were doing the things we did. The fact that he cared made all the difference for me. We liked being around him so much that we got into trouble to spend time with him after school. However, because the janitor cared and I respected his advice, I stopped getting into trouble at school.

Even though life was better at school, I struggled at home. I took out my frustrations on my Mom and threatened her often with running away. I would intentionally fight my Mom as a way to let out all the hurt and frustrations I had built up inside me. Many times, I packed a bag and just left. Sometimes, I just walked around with no destination in mind. I was angry, unsure how to express my frustrations, and felt no one would understand. The truth was I wanted my Dad back, even though I felt unloved and abandoned by him. But she would have been crushed if I said those things to my mom. She was barely hanging on, and I did not want to add any more pain or heartache to her plate, so I kept all those things to myself. Instead, I would go to our neighbors' playhouse next door, sit there, cry, and wish things could return to how they were. I just hated life without my Dad in it, and ever since he left, my wounded heart never seemed to heal.

This was a very difficult time emotionally and spiritually for us all, but especially for my Mother. I do not remember my family being overly spiritual growing up, but during this time, my Mom changed and started looking to the Lord for help. I remember her telling me that after reading many self-help books and not finding the answers she needed, she felt impressed to turn to God instead. The results were obvious. She seemed to have a greater strength and capacity to manage things, much more than when my parents first separated. She also went to the bishop and sought a calling. We all spent more time praying together and seeking the Lord's help. It taught me a valuable lesson at an early age: when life gets hard and seems overwhelming, we must turn to the Lord because He can strengthen us in our weakest moments. It was a lesson I remembered later in my own life when I had a circumstance I felt I could not handle. But I did as my Mom had done years before, leading to the greatest spiritual experience in my life. Her example during this hard time in our lives laid the groundwork for me to do the same.

DIVORCE AND FINANCIAL CHALLENGES

The divorce also brought financial challenges. My Father struggled to stay current on his child support, and with five children to care for, my mother began working multiple jobs to make ends meet. That left me often caring for my younger brother, who was three then. Many times, he and I would be home alone until late in the evening because my Mom was working. Despite this, she could not always make ends meet and had no choice but to ask the church for help. During this time, I wore clothing from thrift stores and discount centers. My friends at school would make fun of me because my clothing was not new and not always stylish. I became very self-conscious of this and started wearing my older brother's clothing, which he ordered from a catalog. He, of course, caught me wearing his clothes several times and forcefully made sure I did not do it anymore. But it was a challenging time for all of us, and we all suffered in different ways because of the circumstances we had been forced into.

FRIENDS' INFLUENCES

Because home was depressing in many ways, I began spending more time with friends and going to their houses. This led to an experience with a friend I never shared with anyone. He was a good friend, at least I thought so, and had never said or done anything to make me uncomfortable. Then, one afternoon, while I was over at his house, he suggested we do something I was shocked he would ever propose. He told me he and a neighbor girl from our ward had done some things together that were sexual, and he wanted to show me what they did. I was so stunned he asked me to do something like that; I had no idea what to do. At that time, because of my poor self-esteem and my need to have people like me, I gave in and allowed him to show me. I never felt right about it and wished it had never happened. Sadly, this led to my self-esteem being further diminished because I knew it was not right, and I was not strong enough to say no. I could have and should have, but I did not. It happened a few more times after that, and then I moved away.

About this same time, I encountered some pornographic material in our house, and that, too, aroused feelings that were hard for me to figure out. I did not really like girls then, but somehow, I wanted to go back and look at the pictures. This became a problem for me on and off in my life until just these past six years and led to choices and addictions that ruined the life I once had. If I had to do it all over again, I would never look the first time because once I did, it became hard for me not to go back for more.

To deal with all of the confusing feelings of anger, disappointment, and guilt with which I struggled, I turned to music. From my earliest memories, I have loved to listen to music. It always seemed to have a way of relaxing me and allowing me to express emotions through song. Music gave me the courage to express things in ways words could not, so I would hear songs and then want others to listen to them because the music and lyrics expressed my feelings. Several times, when I liked a girl in my school, I would record a song I heard on the radio for her. Then,

I would dub her name into the song, replacing whatever name was there originally. I would call the girl on the phone and play the tune while she listened. Most of the time, it went over well, but other times, when the song was over, the girl was not on the other end of the phone!

Music was also an escape and a release for me. When I heard songs I liked, they let me think about how I felt. Sometimes, I would open up and cry. Music became an outlet for me to express my feelings by myself in a safe way. I needed that a lot back then, and I still find music to be therapeutic in helping me to open up and express my feelings today when I am struggling or feeling vulnerable.

FAMILY EFFECTS OF DIVORCE

The overall divorce experience was really hard on my entire family. Each of us handled it differently, and we all struggled in our own way. For me, the feelings of abandonment and feeling rejected or unloved were hard to overcome.

Before my parents were divorced, I was accidentally left at a McDonald's in California, and the experience terrified me. They returned for me, but the fear never left me after that experience. So, when my Father left, it only exacerbated that already-established fear. I used to tell myself that I was okay and that it did not bother me anymore after a while—but I was lying to myself and everyone else. I went from being happy and unconcerned about most things to wondering when I woke up if my Mom or family would still be there. Sometimes, I tried to convince myself that those feelings were crazy and irrational fears. However, they seemed all too real to me.

Another challenging thing for me to reconcile was the guilt that I felt from the things I shared with my Mom. I was convinced that her knowing those things had led to their divorce. No matter what people told me or how they reassured me it was not my fault, I still felt responsible. I carried that guilt forward until my incarceration. All those years, I blamed myself for my Dad not having a relationship with me and the reason he gave my little brother and me up for adoption. Surely, they told me, it was because of the money he owed and other things. But for me, it was because of what I did when I was nine that made my Dad not want to have a relationship with me.

MOM BEGINS DATING

Unfortunately, these and other experiences I had in my teenage years helped reinforce my fears from early childhood. Those set the stage for a difficult struggle with self-esteem and doubt in my relationships moving forward. So, when my Mom began dating again, it was hard to accept at first. Of course, I wanted my Mom to be happy and have someone to help and love her. But I worried about how that would affect my relationship with my Father. Would he be mad if I wanted my Mom to date again? Would I still see him if my Mom married again? Too young to fully grasp how it would affect things, I worried that it would make things worse and that I might not see my Father again if my Mom remarried.

Another issue I struggled with during this time was whether I could trust someone new. At this point, I was pretty skeptical of anything I was told. Too often, what I was told and what happened were two quite different things. I knew my Mom was lonely and, at times, overwhelmed trying to raise a family of five children, but I was also afraid of having someone new around. It was a challenge for me to open up to people I did not know, and I protected myself by acting out and being rebellious. I did not know what else to do at this point in my life.

Chapter 3

New Family

POTENTIAL STEPFATHER

Until now, I had never thought about my Mom dating anyone else. I was having a hard enough time with my Dad being gone, let alone having someone new in my life. So when my Mom came to me and said she was having someone over for dinner that night, I was unhappy. She also told me to be sure I was home by six that evening. She said he had a son my age and wanted me to meet him. So, in my rebellious state, naturally, I made sure I was late that night and well past 6:30 pm.

To emphasize my displeasure, I also ignored my Mom when she reprimanded me when I arrived. It made her date uncomfortable, so I acted indifferent and belligerent to my Mom. If he hated me, I thought he might not come back. He had brought us a load of firewood, and I was tasked with helping his son unload it. I was not at all friendly to him or his Dad. I did my best to be a nuisance the entire evening by ignoring him and saying little at dinner.

After they left, my Mom told me about embarrassing her in front of him. I did not care, though; I hoped not to see him again. Instead, they continued to date, and he did his best to befriend me and say and do all the right things.

Over time, I began to think I might be wrong about him, so I eased up a bit. Then, one evening, when I was out in my Mom's car listening to music, as I was prone to do, he got in the car with me to talk privately. He said he was not there to replace my Father and would not interfere with that relationship. He also said I would still be able to visit my Father even if he and Mom were to marry. He also assured me that I could take my time getting to know him and call him whatever was most comfortable for me. It all sounded good, and I wanted to believe him so much that I decided to try.

Later, when my Mom asked me how I felt about her marrying him, I told her I wanted her to because she seemed so much happier. Because of all he had promised me, that put my mind at ease about my Dad and my friends. He seemed like a good man, and I was okay if my Mom wanted to marry him. I had no idea how different things would be once they were married.

NEW STEPDAD AND TWO NEW BROTHERS

When my Mom announced she was getting remarried, I realized I would now have two additional brothers. One was about the same age as my oldest brother, and the other was six months older than me. The oldest seemed cool, outgoing, and fun to joke around with and talk to. He also liked cool music, so I was excited to have him in my family.

The younger brother, my age, did not have a good relationship with me at first. Being so close in age, everything was a competition, and we tried our best to beat or undermine one another every chance we got. That led to my parents doing all they could to ensure things were fair between us—meaning getting the same things for Christmas each year, simply different colors. Even if we did not want what the other received, we would still get one regardless. The same thing happened on birthdays. I thought giving us the same things was silly when we were very different and had different interests. My stepbrother enjoyed reading books, watching movies, playing in the band, and associating with his friends. He did not date in high school. As for me, I played basketball and ran track for one year, and I liked to date and go to football games, dances, and socials. But because we were different, and he did not always want to go to games and dances, I was often limited in being able to go as a result. We also had to invite one another to play with each other's friends, or we could not have friends over. It was awkward because my friends did not know him, so he became a third wheel. When he had friends over, I was a third wheel, too.

I know my parents meant well by doing this, but it tended to backfire more than it helped. An unintended consequence was that it caused us to resent each other more because some of the things I wanted to do I could not because of my stepbrother, and vice versa. This led to increased animosity between us. As a result, we would write mean things about one another at night in our journals, knowing the other would read them. We also left little warnings on each entry to further emphasize our dislike of each other! Later, as we got older, we laughed at how much we fought and competed in grades, sports, and everything in between since then; however, at the time, it was game on!

My stepbrother also had a big advantage over me when we moved in. He had been there for a while and had already made friends in the ward and in school and was comfortable. I was the new man and he did his best to make it hard on me. I will talk about that more when I talk about moving to our new home, but the rivalry continued until we both went on our missions.

MOM REMARRIES

After a brief dating period, my Stepfather proposed on Christmas Eve, and my Mom said "Yes." That year, my Stepfather ensured we had the biggest Christmas I can ever remember. We had more gifts than ever before, and so far, in my 11-year-old mind, the whole thing seemed pretty good. He had been nice to me and ensured we had a nice Christmas. He promised to let me go at my own pace and call him dad when convenient. He seemed to love my Mom and treated us all respectfully and kindly. For an 11-year-old, he checked all the boxes, and I looked forward to having two additional brothers and thought maybe life was starting to look up for us after all. The only downside to my Mom remarrying was leaving the friends I had grown up with to that point. On my last day of school, they all signed a shirt for me, hugged me, and said goodbye. It was really hard to say goodbye to them. Though I did not move that far away, I ended up seeing my friends only a few times before I stopped visiting and they did, too.

NEW HOME—NEW WARD

Because my Stepfather was a former bishop, I expected to be heavily involved in the church when we moved. When my Mom began to date, she said she set out to find someone strongly rooted in the gospel. This ensured we had a good example to learn from and provided her with a loving companion who honored his commitments. She felt she had lacked that before and wanted to do things right this time for us all. So, with my stepfather being a bishop, she thought he would be good for her and us.

Just a few years previously, my Stepfather lost his wife and daughter in a terrible car accident, and later, he shared with me a very personal spiritual experience he had as a result. This led me to believe he was a good man and in tune with the Spirit. The bishops I remember growing up had been good men people could trust and rely on. My Stepfather often talked about when he was a bishop while he and my Mom were dating and how he learned a lot from that experience. Being a former bishop, we all expected him to be strict in living the gospel because, so far, that was the impression he had given us, and so we expected nothing less.

However, after my parents came home from their honeymoon, things changed completely. My new Stepfather first came to my room and told me I had two weeks to start calling him Dad and getting used to it. I remember feeling hurt and confused about what had just happened and why. He had promised that he would let me decide what I felt comfortable calling him and allow me to go at my own pace.

Now, suddenly, he was breaking his promises to me, and that was not the only thing that changed once we all lived under the same roof. My Stepfather also began to have arguments with my Mom about money, what she could buy, and how much he was having to spend to take care of us. I remember feeling like nothing more than an expense to him and began to resent how he characterized us as takers and users. He had asked to marry my Mom, not the other way around. So, I took offense at how he blamed us for all the new expenses that our large family now incurred. I also became very self-conscious of how much money people had to spend on me for any reason. The way my Stepfather treated us like we were using him for his money affected how I was with asking for help from others in my life in the future. I never wanted to be labeled as a user and tried my best not to be a burden to others. It is something I still struggle with today.

There were other things we all noticed early on as well, and one of those things was that he was not the righteous man he portrayed himself to be while dating Mom. He went through the motions but lacked the Spirit and did things not aligned with the church doctrines. These changes that happened once my Mom married my Stepfather again destroyed the trust I had given to him when the promises he made to me were broken. Once we lived under the same roof, we all realized very quickly that he had only pretended to be something that, in reality, he was not.

The move to a new town also changed the ward we attended. Most people were friendly and accepting of us when we moved in. The ward had great leaders in scouting and young men's programs that encouraged me as a teenager and adult. There was also a large group of young men my age, quickly enabling me to make new friends. Most lived close by, so we could get together often to play basketball, football, board games, or jump on the trampoline. The warm welcome made the transition easier for all of us, and it was a great blessing to have strong friends who were rooted in the gospel during this time of my life.

GOSPEL IN HOME—GOSPEL IN CHURCH

To this point in my life, the church had been something we went to each week, but an element of spirituality was missing. It was not until I moved to our new ward that I became aware of this spiritual dimension in the gospel that had been missing in our home. We would read scriptures and pray. We went to church and sang in the choir. Yet we lacked that spiritual element that I had begun to notice in my friends, their families, and my young men's leaders. When they prayed, it seemed so sincere. When they fasted, it had meaning and purpose. When they bore their testimonies, I felt a Spirit I did not feel in my home. I wanted to be around these families and leaders increasingly because they seemed genuinely happy and loved one another. They also had genuine love and concern for the young men they were responsible for. I began to realize that the Spirit was missing in my home. We loved one another, but our home also had tension and anger.

After my parents married, they had many arguments about money and other things that led to this feeling of contention. I also struggled to trust my Stepfather because of those things that had happened shortly after my parents were married, thereby making it uncomfortable for me, too. We all felt the tension at times, making the home unhappy and often leading to more fights or tension among family members. As I got older, I noticed other things leading to our home's spiritual void. I began to realize our actions were contrary to the church's standards. For example, we were allowed to watch R-rated movies as long as they had no nudity or sex. But violence was okay. We could drive at a noticeably young age without a driver's license. When I brought a girl over to my house, instead of commenting on how kind or good she was, I would instead be told she had some physical deficiency, and I should not date her as a result. These things contributed to my lack of growth and spiritual development because I was being led to think and do things that were not right. I was not getting the guidance and direction at home that someone would hope to get growing up in the church with parents who knew better and were responsible for teaching us these things. These things were not happening with my friends in their homes.

Often, when confiding in my youth leaders because I felt I could not share these things with my Stepfather, they encouraged me without being critical of my parents. In our conversations, they recommended I avoid things contrary to church standards as much as possible. I profoundly respected and admired these men because they lived what they believed, were humble, and truly loved the Lord. They helped me to feel loved and took the time to teach me about the gospel and life through scouting and church meetings. It was the first time I had felt loved by a Father figure in a long time, and I wanted them to be proud of me. Consequently, I would come to them throughout my teenage years for help, counsel, and sometimes safety. They were men whom I respected and admired. Because of their influence, I avoided many pitfalls and mistakes that some of my friends made in high school. They were the ones who taught me the gospel and helped me to develop a testimony of it through their examples of Christlike living and love. They were put in my life at that time to help me get through some of the most challenging years of my life ahead.

Neither my Dad nor my Stepfather had been good examples of living the gospel. Unfortunately, neither of us presided over the home in love nor through righteous example. It took moving to our new ward to finally have priesthood leaders who taught me correctly and lived their beliefs, not just professing to do so. Because my parents could not fully live the gospel as instructed, I relied heavily on those men in my youth leadership to help me do what was right and learn the correct principles.

Chapter 4

Adoption

After my Mom remarried and we moved, my little brother and I continued to see my Father every other weekend. Visits were hard for many reasons: I was often quiet about what took place when I came home. I could not share things that happened because I feared it would cause problems at home. My Stepfather, on several occasions, made mention of the fact that he cared little for my Dad and seemed to be searching for reasons to keep me from seeing him. When I came home upset or quiet, he would use that as an excuse to keep me from going to visit the next time. He also began to question if I should see my Father because it seemed to him that it did more harm than good. The truth was it was extremely hard for me to visit my Father because his new wife never treated us well. I felt uncomfortable around her, and she did her best to let me know she disliked me.

When we visited, we slept in the cold, unfinished basement with little to keep us warm, and she would lock us in until morning. When we left, she was all too happy to see us go. I loved my Dad, and when I had to say goodbye and leave him, it hurt all over again. Then I came home to ask questions about what had happened and why I was so quiet. Was everything okay? Did something happen? However, I had learned that telling them of problems or how I felt was the quickest way to create more problems and threats to end my visits with Dad. So, I buried my feelings and pretended to be okay. But I was not okay; I was trapped in the middle. My Mom and Stepfather disliked my Dad, and my Dad felt the same way about them. Both sides spoke negatively about the other, and it hurt to hear those things because I loved my parents. This left me feeling like I was a burden everyone had to deal with—not because they wanted to but because they had to.

These difficult visits with my Dad continued until my Father's back child support to my Mom reached over $20,000. At that point, my Stepfather suggested that we be adopted, and in return, the money that my Dad owed would be forgiven. My Dad agreed that in place of child support, he would give up visitation rights with us. I was too young to appreciate the situation my Dad was in fully, or if he had any other options than to give us up for adoption. But I was hurt that he chose that option.

I do not remember having a say about wanting to be adopted. All I knew for sure was that my Dad agreed to allow us to be adopted. I believe the reason my Stepfather adopted us was to limit our time with my Dad. He said it was because I acted out when I came home from visiting him. It was not easy having two completely different father figures and having so much pressure put on me to say and do certain things. For example, who was I to call Dad? How was I supposed to feel when I came home from leaving my birth father? Should I be happy to be home when I missed him so much? Having already experienced the dishonest and manipulative behaviors of my Stepfather, I did not feel I could share these feelings openly. My Stepfather used my silence and withdrawal as his excuse to get my Dad out of the picture. By blaming these behaviors on my visits with my Dad, he convinced everyone it was for the best if I just stopped seeing him.

Because my younger brother was too young, I alone was forced to take the stand in front of my Dad and lie to the judge that I wanted to be adopted. I was instructed beforehand what I would tell the judge, but it was not what I wanted to say. I never wanted to stop seeing my Dad, and already knowing that my Stepfather was not genuine in his intentions made it that much harder to go through with it. Looking down at my Dad as I told the judge I wanted to be adopted was one of the worst moments of my childhood. Not knowing when I would see my Dad again, and knowing that my Stepfather hated me, the feeling of abandonment came rushing back all over again. Once we returned home,

I remember going to my room and questioning if anyone loved me. This was just one of many times I asked myself that question growing up.

After the adoption, my Dad would send birthday and Christmas gifts and even tried to call on birthdays. The only problem was I never knew that he had tried to stay in touch or send us anything until I discovered a large bag of gifts in the garage addressed to my younger brother and me. They had been hidden in the rafters of the garage. Previously, when I asked if my Dad had sent any birthday cards or gifts for my birthday or Christmas, I was told he had not. That just reaffirmed the fears I had about my Dad—that he must not love me and had forgotten about me. When I stumbled upon the presents and cards, I was confused and hurt that they were kept from us. I immediately called and asked my Stepfather about the gifts, and he claimed he did not know what I was talking about. Interestingly, later that evening when I went to show my Mom the gifts hidden in the garage, the bag had already been taken and disposed of. When she asked my Stepfather about the gifts, he claimed he knew nothing about them. I could not believe he would hide gifts from my Dad and lie about them! To make matters worse, he then claimed I was making things up and convinced my Mom I made up the story. At that moment, I lost trust or respect for my new Stepfather.

My Stepfather not only broke all of his previous promises to give me time to call him Dad and not keep me from seeing my Father but also hid or destroyed the gifts my Dad had been sending. His lying to my Mom about hiding them and then accusing me of lying made it impossible for me to trust or respect him going forward.

From then on, he and I had a contentious and distrustful relationship. This impacted me as I got older because I had to be careful about what I told him for fear of him twisting and distorting them to make me look bad. The arguments and confrontations escalated until they crossed over into abuse. Because I would call him out on the lies and the abusive behaviors he engaged in with me, he would try to intimidate me by being increasingly aggressive. When I would tell anyone about the way he treated me, he would do his best to convince others I could not be trusted, was manipulative, and that he had to do what he did to keep me in line. The truth was that I was scared to tell the truth around him for fear of being hurt or humiliated; I was not manipulative but instead felt unloved and unwanted. He abused me because I was not his biological son, and he did not love me. Those were the ugly truths he spent my entire teenage life trying to cover up, and in the process of doing so, he ruined my life in many ways.

Chapter 5

School Problems

We moved in the spring after I finished my sixth-grade year, which gave me the entire summer to enjoy and get to know my new friends; however, soon, it was time to start school again. In my new town, the sixth and seventh grades were part of what they called middle school. I was just beginning my seventh-grade year and was nervous about attending a new school and being the new kid in town. The city I had grown up in was much larger, and people seemed more open and friendly than those I had met thus far in my new town. It seemed like the smaller town made it harder because everyone knew each other or was related, and new people were perceived as a threat for some reason.

My first day was stressful because I was learning where my classes were, meeting new teachers, and trying to make new friends. Then, as the week progressed, I noticed a boy I recognized from where I had lived before. Unfortunately, he and I had fought before he moved. My friends and I had also teased him and made fun of him. Little did I know that the tables would soon be turned, and I would be bullied.

It all started one afternoon not long after school began when this boy recognized me, and he and his friends started following me home, taunting me and throwing rocks at me. They also threatened to beat me up and do anything they could to make my life at school difficult. At first, I just ignored the bullying thinking they would get bored and find someone else to pick on. They persisted, however, and being outnumbered, I thought getting into a fight would not be a good idea. So, I finally went to my parents to tell them I was getting bullied at school and threatened on the way home. My Stepfather dismissed it at first, saying I was probably exaggerating and that everything would be fine. But my Mom said she would start picking me up after school to avoid encountering the boys on the way home. That helped after school, but during school, I would get pushed in the hall, laughed at, and called names. They also spread rumors to make people cautious of me. The result was that people stopped talking to me and I was alone. Living in a small town, people were already hesitant to get to know new people. Now that false rumors were going around about me, it made it that much harder. The bullying got so bad that I finally went to the principal, and he called my parents and asked to have a meeting with them. Again, my Stepfather downplayed the threat. He said I could manage it alone if it were only one or two boys—but five or six was too much. Consequently, the principal said he would talk to the boys involved and help diffuse the situation. That only fueled the fire and gave them additional things to make fun of about me. They also knew I was scared, and that emboldened them even more.

Eventually, it became so bad that I did not want to attend school. As a result, I began to fake illnesses to stay home to avoid dealing with the constant badgering and name-calling. Once I stayed home for a week with a "stomach bug." I was not sick but did anything to avoid going to school. I lived in fear the entire school year, and I hated every minute of it. So, when summer came, I was more excited than ever to have a break and not worry for a few months. But after summer, I was headed to junior high. As August approached, I again started to dread going back to school.

One good thing that happened during that seventh-grade year and subsequent summer was that I started to grow. I grew an inch or more every year from that point on until my senior year. When I started my eighth-grade year, I was still getting harassed, but not as much as I had been the previous year. The previous kids were not bullying the biggest problem I had in the eighth grade, but having my stepbrother tell the people bullying me embarrassing stories about me. Then those people he told the stories to began to spread the rumors around the school to embarrass and humiliate me. My stepbrother was one year ahead of me, and now we were in the same school together—which made for another tough year.

Another reason I struggled that year was because my Stepfather came into a school dance in his bathrobe and slippers in search of my stepbrother and me. We were told to be outside by 10:30 pm, but he came inside fifteen minutes early to embarrass us. He had threatened he would come inside to get us—and he did. As 10:30 pm approached, I decided to have one last slow dance with a girl I liked because it was only 10:15 pm. I thought I had plenty of time. As the slow dance began, my stepbrother came up to me crawling on his hands and knees, and said we had to go because my Stepfather was at the door asking for us. Sheer terror overcame me as I turned and looked at his silhouette in the doorway. I could not believe what I was seeing. He was standing in the doorway in his pajamas, with no shirt on and his robe loosely tied. It exposed his chest, and his chest hair stood on end as he asked others nearby where he could find us. It was probably the most embarrassing thing he could do to us in junior high. We did the only thing we could think of: running! We took off to the other side of the gym through the exit doors and ran home.

When we got home, my Stepfather was pulling into the driveway with a big smile. My stepbrother and I were livid and asked why he did it—especially because we were not late. He said he just thought it would be funny. It was anything but funny to us. At school the next Monday, people all over the school were asking who the crazy drunk man was who came in looking for his kids.

My Stepfather did not stop there at embarrassing us. Whenever he picked us up for any reason, he would roll down the windows and play Barbara Streisand songs at full volume. We could not cover our faces, dive into the car, and yell for him to go before someone saw us! He thought it was hilarious, but for me, it wasn't very comfortable. Not only was I trying to fit in, but I was also trying to avoid coming across as weird!

My ninth-grade year was better because my stepbrother moved up to high school, and I finally got established with some good friends. I also started to compete in sports. My athletic ability helped me make friends with some of the more popular people in school, and when that happened, the bullying stopped as fast as it had begun.

Chapter 6

Teenage Years

THE ABUSE

Upon entering my teenage years, I struggled in many aspects of my life. The previous four years were a lot to deal with, and I had many unresolved feelings and emotions inside me. I felt responsible for my parents' divorce. I had been sexually abused by a friend and had moved to a new town where I was bullied and picked on in school. I had been in the middle of the war of words my parents had engaged in and felt unloved and unwanted by my Dad and new Stepfather. Then, I had just recently been forced into being adopted and could no longer see my Dad. I also missed my friends from the town I left. If all that was not enough, my Stepfather began to be abusive to me in many ways.

My being overwhelmed with different emotions and feelings led to my poor behavior. Being told constantly that I would be just like my Dad, that I was not good enough, or that I was the reason why bad things happened took its toll on my emotions and self-esteem. I made mistakes just like most kids my age, but I was treated like I did horrible things, but I never did. When we first moved in, he would yell at and threaten me. But as time went on, his punishments became more severe, and instead of just taking away privileges, he abused me also.

The physical abuse began after I was adopted and had confronted my Stepfather about the lies he told and the hidden gifts and the coverup that resulted from it. My lack of respect for him came out in our arguments,

29

leading to him becoming increasingly more physical as I got older. When I did something that he felt warranted hitting me, at first he would use his hand or a wooden spoon, then he progressed to a belt. But as the animosity between us increased, and I was more defiant, it escalated to things like a tennis racket or other objects. That is when he began to cross the line. He used things to cause me harm, not just to punish me. The first time this happened, he used a tennis racquet across my arm, which caused a deep bone bruise and required a hospital visit to ensure the arm was not broken.

The day he hit me with the tennis racket, we had an intense argument for reasons I do not recall. We were upstairs near my bedroom door when I said something he did not like. He reacted by picking up a wooden tennis racket and hitting me on the elbow so hard it swelled up to the size of a softball. It hurt so badly; I thought it was broken. I told him that I needed to go to the hospital, but he ignored me and just turned and went downstairs. I followed him down the stairs and said again my arm was broken, but he refused to take me. So I went to my young men's leader, who lived around the corner and asked him to take me instead. He looked at my arm and could tell I was in a lot of pain, so he agreed to take me.

On the way to the hospital, he asked me what happened. I told him about the argument and that my Stepfather had hit me with a tennis racket and refused to take me to the hospital. He was careful not to pry but was obviously concerned about what had occurred. When we arrived at the hospital, I was told I needed a parent or guardian to be seen, so he brought me home. He ensured I was okay to return home and then dropped me off.

I waited for my Mom to come home to take me back to the hospital. When she arrived, I told her I needed to go to the hospital, showed her my arm, and explained what had happened. She immediately took me to the hospital. The doctor said I had a deep bone bruise, but it was not broken. The doctor asked how I hurt it, and I do not remember what I told him, but it was not that my Stepfather hit me. The doctor seemed unconvinced by what I said but did not press the issue. When we came home, my Mom confronted my Stepfather about the giant bruise on my arm, and he denied ever hitting me. He said I did it to myself. As he did with the gifts, he was dishonest and denied ever hitting me and instead placed the blame on me. After he hurt me, the fear of him hurting me again drove me to find ways to protect myself in the future. I was tired of getting hurt physically and emotionally.

That was not the only instance or type of abuse that happened. There was also a time when I was sexually abused. When I was twelve, I had just begun to discover what masturbation was and engaged in it fairly regularly. At that point, I did not know it was wrong to do. My Stepfather seemed to sense something like that was going on and would follow me into the house when I went to use the bathroom. After I entered the bathroom, he would stand outside the door or near the bathroom waiting for me. He even opened the door to see what I was doing if I took too long. I figured he was trying to catch me to let me know it was something I should refrain from doing.

Finally, one time, he opened the door after I went into the bathroom and caught me engaged in inappropriate behavior on the floor. Without a word, he came and picked me up and put me in his lap, exposed and completely embarrassed. I felt ashamed as I waited for him to explain that it was wrong to engage in that behavior, but that speech never came. He never said a word but sat there with me in awkward silence for how long I do not remember. But it was too long. Finally, he let me go, and I pulled my pants up and left, but I never felt right about what happened. Only as I got older did I realize that incident was not normal and was wrong to do to a child. I do not know exactly why he did that to me, but I felt it was wrong even then. I feared saying anything for years because I felt ashamed that it happened. Thankfully, I do not recall any other incidents in particular that were like that.

As a result of being abused in many ways and numerous times, I continued to withdraw from people. I had been harmed physically, sexually, and emotionally and closed off to protect myself. I also felt responsible for all the bad things people did to me—like I somehow deserved the abuse. This made it hard for me to feel good about myself, especially when those who were supposed to love and protect me were the ones hurting me in many ways.

DATING

Once I turned sixteen, I started attending school dances and taking girls out on dates with friends. At first, I did not have a serious or steady girlfriend, so most of my dates were group dates to dances and football games. However, before I began to date, my Stepfather began setting limitations on things, seemingly in anticipation of me making mistakes before I even began. When a girl called me on the phone, he would get on and listen to my call, then say someone needed to use the phone to get me to hang up. Nobody needed the phone; he did not like me talking to girls. He went through my clothing to find notes that girls would give to me at school and would share them with the family to embarrass me. He also commented about me doing things with girls I had never done, and I often wondered how he thought of these things. When I asked him about his comments, he referred to his time as a bishop and emphasized that young people in his ward would do the things he mentioned. So he just assumed I would, too. It was unfair to assume I would make mistakes before I started dating, especially since he never sat down to talk and prepare me for dating.

Treating me as though I had already made those mistakes and denying me privileges based on fears rather than reality was hard for me to accept. His philosophy was to prevent me from making mistakes by choosing for me. Instead of teaching me what I needed to do, and why I should avoid certain things, he just tried to keep me from going out as much as possible. I did not get much chance to choose and learn for myself; he did not allow me the opportunity. He gave me very few chances to make decisions on my own.

One example of this was a school date when I asked to use the car to drive my friends and me to the dance. I had given my parents all the details, including with whom I was going, where we were eating, and where we went after the dance. Because my Stepfather was paranoid when I went on dates, I had to give full details, or I could not go. Ironically, up to this point, I was still new to dating, had not even kissed a girl or had any relationship, and had always been a perfect gentleman. But after I came home from my first date and he checked my lips to see if I had kissed the girl, my clothing, and my breath, I knew then how hard dating would be.

So on this group date, I went and picked up my date and friends and started heading toward the restaurant. While driving, I noticed a car I recognized following behind us a few cars back. I asked my friend to look at the driver to confirm what I had already suspected. Sure enough, it was my Stepfather following us to the restaurant. At first, I thought maybe it was just a coincidence that he was behind us and had an errand to run near where we were eating. But as we neared the restaurant and parked, I noticed he pulled in across the street from the restaurant and also parked. The restaurant had large floor-to-ceiling windows overlooking the street where my Stepfather parked, and they seated us in the window overlooking his parking spot. I sat with my back to the window, but I went from being mad to uncomfortable having him follow us on our date. My friends also gave me a hard time because they could all see him watching us as we ate. It was embarrassing, and I had to answer questions about why he would follow us all night. I was more than a little upset and frustrated by the end of the evening.

After we left the restaurant, I thought he might leave, but he followed us to the dance and afterward to my friend's house. About 20 minutes before I was home, I noticed him pull away and leave. I took my date home and arrived about fifteen minutes later. His car hood was still warm because I checked it before entering. My Stepfather had changed into his robe and was watching television from the sofa when I walked in. Normally, he would ask me about my dates when I got home, but interestingly, this night, he did not. When I asked him what he had done that night, he said he had been home. I, of course, knew this was not true and went to ask my Mom what she knew. I asked her if my Stepfather had been there the entire evening, and she said he had gone home teaching and had just arrived home not long before I had. I asked her if she thought he had been out home teaching until 11:30 pm. Then I told her we had seen him follow us the entire evening and that he had left a few minutes before I did to come home.

After speaking to my Mom, I asked my Stepfather why he had lied about not leaving that night. I told him my Mom said he had been gone all evening home teaching. I also mentioned we had seen him following us the entire night and asked him why he needed to do so. Only then did he admit he had followed us because he did not trust we would do what we said we would do. This was how my Stepfather did things. He lied to try to catch me in lies. He would arbitrarily keep me from doing things because he thought I might do something wrong if he allowed me to do them. He would hide, listen to calls, follow me, and lie about it all to catch me doing something wrong. Instead of letting me make decisions and dealing with the consequences, he made the decisions for me.

Parents who never let their children fall have children who never learn to walk. Without the chance to make and learn from mistakes, it was harder to learn those things until later in life. This had a crippling effect on me and my self-esteem because he had no faith or confidence in me. Later in life when I was able to decide for myself, and because of being so limited in my decision-making growing up, I made some poor decisions just because I finally could.

SPECIAL GIRL

In my junior year, I met a girl I thought was my school's most beautiful girl. Before cell phones and social media, we started exchanging notes between classes, talking before and after school, and occasionally talking at lunch.

Finally, I decided to ask her out on an official date to a school dance with a group of my friends. She told me her Dad would probably want to talk with me and gave me the rundown on what he wanted to ask. When I arrived to pick her up, I was not surprised to see her Dad open the door and invite me in. After we sat down, we began to talk. He asked me what our plans were for the evening. He also said his daughter was leaving one way and needed to return the same. I caught on to his hint and said she definitely would. He then asked when she would return, to which I responded by midnight. He agreed, and then she came into the room, and we left. She asked what I thought of her Dad, and I told her she was lucky to have a Dad who loved her and cared about her that much. I meant what I said with all my heart.

As a result, I was very careful to do just as I had said I would and had her home by 11:50 pm that evening. Her Dad was very happy that I brought her home early, and both parents encouraged us to continue dating moving forward. She had a very different relationship with her parents than I did. She told them everything, and they loved to hear about our dates, the notes we wrote, and even if we disagreed. That gave them a sense of security regarding what we did and did not do, and it helped us build an elevated level of trust between her parents and me. They would suggest I come over when they went on dates so I could help watch the kids with my girlfriend. They knew we did not do things we should not, so they trusted us to be together whenever possible.

As I became more familiar with her family, they supported me at my basketball games. Her Dad would shoot baskets with me and talk about life. In turn, I would occasionally go to her swim meets and practices. We were best friends, and I truly believe I loved her and her family.

I was not excited for her to meet my Stepfather, but I knew it would happen eventually, so I invited her over to watch a movie. When she arrived, my Stepfather immediately pulled me aside and told me I could no longer date her. When I asked why, he said, "She has no bosoms." I was unsure if he was serious, but I did not appreciate the comment. I could not believe he had said that! That was the last thing I was concerned about, and I never dated anyone based solely on physical attributes alone. However, I ignored the comment, and we watched the movie on the couch, with my Stepfather finding a reason to walk into the room every five minutes to monitor us. Little did I know then he would eventually find a way to break us up for good in the not-too-distant future.

Later in the year, my girlfriend invited me to our Sadie Hawkins dance where the girls invite the boys. We went with a group of her friends to eat, then to the dance, and afterward to complete a scavenger hunt around the city. After the dance, we changed clothes and divided up into two teams and cars to do the hunt. I was to be home by 1:00 am and it was only 11:00 pm when we started, so I thought I would have plenty of time. It was close to 1:00 am, so I realized we would not be done in time. Instead of ruining the scavenger hunt for my team, I waited until we finished before I had them drop me off at home. I knew I was going to be in trouble when I got home because my Stepfather would be up waiting for me and would never understand or care why I was late. I was late and that equaled trouble.

I told him we had a flat tire when I arrived, so I was late. As I suspected, he did not care why I was late—I was late, and he would make sure I did not see her anymore. He called her parents the next day and told them I was not to be trusted and that he thought my girlfriend would distract me from serving a mission, so he did not want us to date anymore. Her family were devout church members and would have encouraged me to serve a mission. She would have insisted, too. But my Stepfather liked to make assumptions on fears rather than facts, and he ruined the best thing I had going for me. It had not been easy for me to care for her because I struggled with opening my heart to people. Now that I had, the hurt from this was something I never fully recovered from for years, if ever.

I found out he had called her parents on Monday when my girl-friend told me she was no longer allowed to see me. I did not feel this was warranted at all, and it was done to hurt me and gain control over my life. I would have been happy to tell my Stepfather what had happened and why I was late if he had ever been willing to listen to me lovingly and encouragingly. But the minute I walked into the house, he was yelling at me and worked up into a frenzy about me being twenty minutes late. There was no explaining or talking to him, and I was told he did not want to hear excuses.

That sums up my dating life throughout my teenage years. I was not allowed to get close to anyone, nor them to me. Though my Stepfather said it was because I lied that he ended the relationship, it was more about being able to control my life. He regained that control with her gone and had an excuse to end it. He never seemed happy that I had a girlfriend and instead made remarks discouraging me from seeing her. Most of his remarks were about her physical appearance and lack of superficial features he thought should concern me. The reality was that she was beautiful inside and out, modeled all through high school, had no imperfections, and, in my mind, was the most beautiful girl I had ever seen or met.

I knew coming home late and lying about why I was late was wrong, but I felt at the time the bigger problem was that when I did make a mistake, there was no forgiveness or a showing of love or encouragement to do better. There was only ridicule and criticism. After years of that, I just gave up because I felt I could never please him. So there was no incentive to admit mistakes and every reason I could think not to. All I ever wanted was to be loved and trusted. I felt he cared only as long as I did as he suggested. I felt his love, if he ever loved me, was conditional. He would say he cared as long as I did what he wanted. But I felt unloved and unwanted if I ever did something he disagreed with. There was no teaching or forgiveness. This drove my behavior growing up because I could not make mistakes to survive in my home. If you did make mistakes, you did not tell anyone about them.

A short time after my girlfriend and I broke up, I spoke to her mother, and she told me that what he had said to them was not what they had experienced with me. But they felt it was best not to go against his wishes or put me in a difficult situation with him. They knew I was not a liar and I had demonstrated that I was trustworthy in every respect with them. I then explained to her what happened that night and how he reacted by calling them and using that to end the relationship. I needed further to explain the relationship between my Stepfather and me so she would understand. Ultimately, she understood but was disappointed because they had all grown as fond of me as I was of them.

Later that week, my girlfriend dedicated a song to me on the radio. It was Whitney Houston's song, "I Will Always Love You." Still, I cannot hear that song without thinking back to that time and wondering what would have happened if that relationship had continued. She was someone whom I truly loved, and she helped me be the best version of myself that I could be. Her family loved me, and I loved them. They helped me make up for what I lacked in my home, so I lost more than her when we broke up. I felt like I lost part of my family. It had not been easy for me to open up to them. It took me a while to feel safe with them and see their sincere interest and concern for me. But once I opened up, I let them in. I gave my heart to my girlfriend and her family.

After I broke up with this special girl, I stopped dating girls except when there was a dance to go to. Then I would ask girls with whom I was only friends to go with me and my group. I did this because I did not want my Stepfather to ruin another relationship for me, and also because I never really got over my ex-girlfriend in high school. My senior year I spent wishing I were with the girl I still loved and the family I still missed.

The way my Stepfather intervened in my relationship with my girl-friend was reminiscent of how he did the same with my youth leaders, my Dad, and anyone I would get close to or love growing up. I felt like his own insecurity was the reason why he sabotaged relationships. This was the case with one of my youth leaders. He enjoyed playing tennis; and when he found out I played, too, he invited me to play with him. We had fun and decided to go and play on a fairly regular basis. That is when my Stepfather intervened and told my scout leader that he did not want us to play tennis anymore. There was no other reason, besides he did not want us to play. So, being the respectful person that my leader was, he told me it would be best if we did not play anymore. This is how he was with people in my life. If I began to get close to someone or started spending time with them, and seemed to enjoy it, he would end it. This happened with my girlfriend, youth leaders, friends, and neighbors.

One neighbor in particular I felt very sorry for him. His daughter had a crush on me and lived in a basement apartment my Stepfather rented to father and daughter. Once, she left a letter in our mailbox telling me she liked me and thought I was nice and cute. That was all she did; we never dated, and nothing happened to her. She only wrote me a note and put it in the mailbox. She was a very innocent and sweet friend. My Stepfather found out and went over and confronted her father and told him she was to leave me alone and not have any contact with me anymore. I was so embarrassed that he had said that to this poor girl's father. He also threatened him with eviction or calling the police if she ever contacted me again. I am sure this girl and her father were confused and offended by what he said for no good reason. She wrote me a sweet note expressing interest innocently. I was not interested in her but could not help but feel sorry for her after my Stepfather had completely overreacted to her letter.

Another interesting thing about my high school dating life was my reputation for being a gentleman. If you were to read any of the things written in my yearbook by girls who knew me and had been on dates with me, it was nothing but how nice I was and how well I treated them. I was often told how girls who knew me respected me for my values and for being so respectful to them. That was my reputation and who I was. But my Stepfather tried to get people to believe otherwise. He accused me of having a child with a girl in our ward shortly after we graduated high school because he said the child looked like me somehow. I had never been on a date with this girl nor had any interest whatsoever in her, yet he tried to convince others of this terrible lie. My friends and others who knew me knew the truth, but those who did not know me were fooled and influenced by the lies he told. That was why people who knew me did not understand why my Stepfather would say those things. My experience in dealing with him was that he was delusional and paranoid and that is why he would make up things that in reality never happened.

After my senior year, I had one more date with my ex-girlfriend. We decided to go to see a movie at the local theater. We went with some mutual friends. When we broke up, we both regretted that we never had the first kiss we planned to have at some point. So, on this date, the plan was to finally kiss her because we both agreed we wanted our first kiss.

As soon as the movie started, we began to hold hands, and it seemed almost like we had never stopped dating. I soon found myself leaning close to her and had stopped watching the movie and was lost in the moment. I wanted to enjoy every second with her because I did not know if I would ever get another chance to go out with her again. She leaned her head on my shoulder, and I felt at that moment I was as happy as I had ever been growing up. I felt loved and with someone who cared about me—which I rarely felt in my home. I did not want that moment to end.

When I took her home that night, I dreaded saying goodbye. Somehow, I knew this would be the last date I would ever have with her. It felt like we had never stopped dating the way we interacted that night, and I knew she wanted me to kiss her before she went inside. It was a picture-perfect night with the moon casting a light on the porch like a stage. As we walked toward her porch, it felt like it was the closing scene of a play where I was to finally kiss the girl I loved to make for the perfect ending. As we stood looking at one another, I knew that kissing her would only make things harder for us. Though I wanted to, I opted to kiss her on the cheek instead. Then I hugged her and turned and walked back to my car. She waited momentarily on the steps, looking at me, then turned and went inside. I had tears in my eyes as I got into my car that night because I knew that was probably the last time I would go out with her, and it was.

When I had my mission farewell a couple of years later, she and her family came to the church to hear my farewell address. It was good to see her again, but also hard because I still had not gotten over her. I do not know that I ever really did, and that stuck with me for many years afterward.

That was how dating went for me in my teenage years. I could not fall in love, date who I wanted, or make my own decisions. These were all made for me mostly out of fear of making mistakes. Interestingly, I never drank in high school or did anything inappropriate with a girl, nor did I smoke or use any drug. I do not say that to brag or boast but to illustrate that I was not a bad person in high school. But because of the restrictions and the way my Stepfather acted and portrayed me, you would have thought I was involved in all kinds of bad things and needed constant supervision. Also, his reasons for breaking up my relationships were inspired by unrealized fears of things that almost always never happened. I, of course, made mistakes and did things I regret doing, but not the things I was held hostage for by my Stepfather. I avoided most major mistakes in high school, not because of his limitations, as my Stepfather would later take credit for. It was because I chose not to engage in those things.

Despite my restrictions, there were still plenty of opportunities to do things I should not have done, and I just declined to do them. However, the restrictions limited my ability to make mistakes and learn from them before I went out alone. It was a handicap that I took into my college years and life beyond college. Partly because I was sheltered from making decisions and from situations I might have encountered in high school when I went on my own, I made some poor decisions. I was curious and wanted to know what I had been missing. I did not limit myself to coming home at a certain time, I stayed up late and dated girls who were not the type I normally looked for. I did all the things I never could when I lived at home, just because I could. It taught me that when you suffocate your children and do not allow them to learn from their mistakes or make some decisions as they grow up, they will be more likely to make mistakes when they get out on their own. They have yet to learn responsibility because their parents made their decisions.

SCOUTING AND YOUNG MEN'S

Participating in the scouting and young men's programs gave me valuable experience and life lessons. I had dedicated scout and church leaders who spent time helping us learn outdoor survival skills and spiritual lessons to overcome worldly challenges. The things they taught me have benefited me at various times.

When I moved into the ward, I first noticed how the leaders took a genuine interest in each young man. They encouraged us to participate in the programs offered through the church and to live our beliefs through example. These leaders helped many of my friends achieve their Eagle Scout and Duty to God awards. I have some of my best and fondest memories of my teenage years from our scouting trips and the friendships I made through these programs. Our best trips were 50-mile hikes into the mountains or down the Colorado River. These trips brought us together, strengthened our belief in God, and helped us learn vital life lessons. I remember a few trips being particularly influential in strengthening my testimony of God. On these trips, we experienced divine protection and help and recognized the Lord's hand in our lives. These experiences helped to galvanize friendships and strengthened our testimony of God.

The first time we went up into the mountains for a 50-mile backpacking adventure, I should have known by how things started that this trip would be challenging and unique. The night before I caught my leg on a nail jumping over a fence and tore a two-inch gash on the inside of my left

41

leg. I still have the scar from it to this day. It was fairly deep and painful; and if we were not heading out the next morning on our trip, I would have gone to the ER for stitches.

The next day, as we reached the trailhead and began to hike up the trail, I started feeling a pain in my leg where I had gashed it the night before. As the day wore on, the pain increased until I was unable to walk with my backpack on. When we reached our base camp that night, I was in intense pain and had to have the wound drained. Leaders could squeeze and clean a large amount of pus from the wound. The next day, it felt a little better and improved each day afterward.

On our third day, we were scheduled to climb to King's Peak, over 13,000 feet. It was a difficult and slow climb once we reached the peak base because it was like climbing a rock pile. Once we reached the peak, we buried a time capsule, and our leaders shared thoughts about what the climb could represent in our lives. There was always a lesson they wanted to impress upon us; after the difficult climb we made, their message was that we could do that with any mountain we had.

After our talk, we noticed the weather began to worsen. Clouds were rolling in, and we knew we had to get off this peak quickly. We descended to the tree line without further hesitation before the oncoming storm hit. One thing we learned about being in the mountains was that the weather can change instantly! We had enough time to reach the peak base before the clouds rolled in and visibility was almost zero. Then, the lightning and thunder began to hit and shake the ground around us. We were above the tree line so the only hiding places were behind rocks. We all took cover wherever we could find a spot to hide and waited out the storm. I remember being very frightened because of the proximity and intensity of the lightning and the sounds of thunder. Huddling behind a rock, I prayed repeatedly that we would all be okay. I thought someone would be hit by lightning or injured by the storm. It was one of the scariest moments of my life to that point.

Eventually, the storm stopped, and everyone was okay. Returning to camp that night, we were all grateful to be spared injury. Later that night, we had a chip dedication where each of us tossed a wood chip into the fire and expressed our gratitude. Hearing expressions of gratitude, there was not a dry eye at the campfire. Each of us had seen firsthand the Lord's protection on that mountain that day, inspiring us with a greater sense of gratitude for the blessings the Lord had given us. There was a strong spirit there that night, and none of us wanted to leave the campfire. I remember experiences like that often from my trips with our scout group. Those happened because we had leaders who were in tune with the Spirit and led by example.

A few years later, we had a canoe trip that almost ended in tragedy. We were canoeing down the Colorado River for fifty miles. The first few days were in fairly calm waters with few rapids. Then, on the third day, we would encounter rapids most of the way. We said a prayer that morning asking for the Lord's help and protection. We also planned for emergencies in case a canoe overturned in the rapids: we all would stand by to help one another should anyone overturn or have a problem. My goal was to keep our canoe upright at all costs. We managed to do so and then waited for the next canoe. We thought everyone was going to make it okay. That was when it happened. One of the canoes turned sideways and slammed into a giant rock protruding out of the water. The force of the water was so strong that the canoe wrapped around the rock. The contents of the canoe flew out and floated down the river. We quickly worked to retrieve the items.

As we checked on those in the boat, we noticed that one of the scouts from the canoe had not surfaced. We searched the water to see if we could see him, but there was no sign of him. We were all anxious and unsure of what to do. Then all of a sudden he came up out of the water. One of the canoes behind them could get close enough to put their paddle out, and he grabbed on and was pulled out. Relieved, we all said a silent prayer, thanking the Lord that both people in the canoe were safe. He said he had been caught in an undertow and could not reach the surface. He also said that he thought he might not make it, and then something happened he could not explain. He said he could suddenly push himself to the surface as if someone had pushed him up from underneath. He said without the push, there was no way he would have made it to the surface. At that point, we knew he had been protected and helped out of the water.

Another example of where we felt protected and helped by the Lord during this trip happened when my partner and I in the canoe somehow managed not to overturn any of the rapids we faced. Most of the other canoes turned over at some point. But no one was hurt; against all odds, we made it home without any major incidents.

On almost every trip we took, we encountered situations where someone could have been seriously hurt or killed, but miraculously, none of us ever were. What did happen, though, was that we experienced firsthand some incredible blessings of protection and outpourings of the Spirit that helped each of us know that God truly is real. That knowledge strengthened our testimonies of the gospel, and it gave me my first personal witness of God's existence.

SPORTS

At an early age, I actively played various sports: baseball, football, basketball, and soccer. I usually did pretty well in all of them. When I was in ninth grade and had grown to be over six feet tall, my friends encouraged me to try out for the basketball team. At tryouts, because of being overly nervous, I did not perform well and ended up not making the team. I knew I could play better than I had and even outplayed most of the boys who made the team in our gym class. However, when everyone was watching, I choked and did not make the team. At that moment, I decided I would make it the next year because I knew I was good enough.

During the off-season, I practiced and worked on what I needed to improve. That meant a lot of time shooting the basketball and dribbling. I also ordered a jump program called Air Alert Two that increased my vertical jump dramatically. After all my work, I felt ready for basketball tryouts at the beginning of my sophomore year. During tryouts, I was matched against the boys who made the team the year before. This time, I did not get overly nervous and outplayed the other boys who had made the team the previous year. The coaches were impressed enough to put me on the team. It is normally hard to make the team after ninth grade because they usually just cut a few off last year's team to your senior year where they only keep five or six seniors. However, I made the team my sophomore year and each year until my senior year.

Basketball was an important thing for me in high school. It kept me busy, and physically fit and brought me new friends. I enjoyed the games and the competition. Being on the team also brought with it increased popularity in school that I had never had before. We were required to take strength training classes to be on the team, so I became stronger and more confident. Making the team was a great accomplishment, especially considering my lack of support at home to play. My Stepfather did not like sports and was not impressed when I made the basketball team, but my Mom was proud of me.

Even with basketball, my Stepfather made things hard for me. When the cheerleaders came to decorate my room, as was the tradition for one of the home games, my Stepfather would not allow the girls into my room to decorate as the others on the team had allowed. I was the only one who did not get my room decorated. It was just a fun thing that was done each year for players on the team, but not for me. I always seemed to be the one who could not do even the harmless things others could do.

My parents also did not pay for my athletics, so I had to pay my way if I wanted to play. I did so by working at a grocery store as a bag boy for $3.83 per hour. It was demanding work; and when I was not playing basketball, I was working to meet player expenses. As soon as I turned sixteen, my parents made me pay for everything but room and board, including sometimes even milk!

I also joined the track team in my junior year. I competed in the 400-meter run, the high jump, and the long jump. However, I thought I would enjoy it more than I did; after a few meets, I decided not to continue because I did not like it.

My basketball coaches also coached the football team. They tried to get me to play football as a wide receiver. I was fast, had capable hands, and had a good vertical jump. However, to play football and basketball, I could not work because of conditioning and practicing during the summer and winter months. Also, many of my friends injured their knees and shoulders playing football, so I thought it would be better to focus on basketball.

In my sophomore and junior years, everyone but my sister and older brothers went to Maui, Hawaii, for a week because my Stepfather attended a conference there. We spent time in a condominium on the beach and ate fresh pineapple, mango, and papaya. I had a great time playing in the gigantic waves common that time of year and filming the trip on our video camera. I also could not stop eating! One morning, we went to an all-you-can-eat buffet and spent 45 minutes eating some delicious food. Then, on our way home, I asked my parents if we could stop at McDonald's to get more food! For some reason, I could never get full—mostly because of all the daily swimming.

Another crazy thing that happened on the Hawaiian trip was a shark attack on the beach where we stayed. We had just been snorkeling and returned to find police and fire trucks around our condominium complex. We asked a lady standing close by what had happened, and she told us a tiger shark had attacked and killed a woman who was swimming. We were all a little shocked and scared to go out in the water after that, especially because we had been in the water where she had been attacked the day before. We stayed close to the beach for the rest of that trip and did not venture out too far into the water. I was already afraid of sharks, but now I was constantly checking all around me because I was paranoid about them.

I had to clear it through my school coach to go to Hawaii. He allowed me to go but wanted me to run on the beach and maintain my conditioning. When I returned, I was tan, and my hair was bleached blonde. My teammates and the opposing teams' fans gave me a hard time. They called me "90210" about a popular television sitcom. This led to a picture being taken of my girlfriend and me with my tanned face and body. She was a natural blonde with blue eyes, so the picture ended up in the yearbook under the caption "Ken and Barbie." It was a good picture, and we looked really good together.

About halfway through my senior year, I started questioning whether I wanted to continue playing basketball for my high school. Our head coach was frustrated because we had not played well recently. Instead of talking to us individually about his issues, he pulled me out of the lineup one day in practice. Instead, he inserted a junior at my position and made me stand on the sidelines to watch. This was embarrassing, and I used my body language from the sideline to tell the coach I was unhappy. He never took me aside to talk to me about if he was unhappy with my play or if I did something wrong. Instead, I sat on the bench the next game and somehow became the odd one out of the rotation. After it happened the second game in a row, and my coach had yet to explain to me why he was not playing me, I decided I would have more fun playing church basketball. I went into my coach's office the next day and told him I quit. I threw my bag with everything on the floor before him, turned, and walked out. Later on, he asked me to come into his office to talk and asked me why I had decided to quit the team. I explained that I thought I would have more fun playing church basketball instead of sitting on the bench because he had benched me and had not even told me why. He told me he wanted to see if changing things up would help the team play better and wanted me on the team. He said if I wanted to return, I had to apologize to the team and ask for permission. At this point, I felt what was done was done, and I declined to do that and again left his office. Later that night I told my parents I had quit the team. They were upset with me and set up a meeting with the principal and coach, but I had decided. I wanted to play where I could have fun, and I was not having fun watching the games instead of playing in them.

Looking back now, quitting the team was wrong, and I wish I would have stayed on the team. Giving up was a product of my low self-esteem; and when I felt singled out and embarrassed by my coach, I quit rather than continue to feel that way. It was the easy way out, which was what I was getting accustomed to doing when life seemed hard and complicated. So when I could avoid hurt or pain, I did. Being humiliated by sitting on the bench and watching games just seemed like too much to deal with at the time. But life sometimes is hard, and my quitting the team led to me quitting other things. Looking for the easier way is not the best solution to life's problems. Going through challenges and difficulties and not giving up leads to greater success in all aspects of life, as I would learn the hard way later.

I went on to play with my friends on our church basketball team and had fun, but later on in life, I wished I had not quit on my friends, coaches, and team. It was a selfish thing to quit. I spent three years practicing and playing with them; the minute I had to sacrifice for the team's best interests, I left because it was not what I wanted. The team was always bigger than one person, and I realized that years later as I reflected on things I wished I had done differently. I was proud of my accomplishments in making the team for three years and lettering in basketball. My only regret about my high school career was not finishing the year with my team.

FRIENDS

My group of friends I had as a teenager were instrumental in avoiding drugs, alcohol, and other problems that were happening in high school. I was blessed to have friends in many diverse groups. This enabled me to choose which group I wanted to hang out with. I had friends from my basketball team and other sports, the school band, various clubs, and girls and boys with whom I went to church. If I knew a group of friends would be doing something I did not want to do, I would do something with another group of friends. Much of my time in high school was spent with friends. I did not pair off with girls or spend a lot of time alone with girls. This helped me avoid bad situations and temptations I knew I needed to avoid. My closest friends were the ones I went to church with and those I lived closest to. We had a lot of fun playing all kinds of games. We played basketball, football, baseball, trampoline, and board games. We also would get together at night and play games—murder in the dark being the one we played the most. Like hide and seek, one person would hide, and the rest would try to find him. But if he were able to get you before you saw him, you were dead and would have to sit out until either he was caught or he was able to catch the rest before they caught him. Our neighborhood was perfect for the game because of only one streetlight by our house, leaving most of the neighborhood dark and hard to see.

Another favorite game was playing basketball together. We would play for hours, and the games were very competitive and hard-fought. We even videotaped our games on occasion so we could go and watch them later in the house.

The best thing about the friends I had growing up with was that they were true friends. They did not try to influence me to do things I knew were wrong. They did not use drugs, alcohol, or tobacco. They also did not curse or tell dirty jokes and were strong in their faith and beliefs. Most served missions, married in the temple, and had good families. Many of them also earned their Eagle Scout award. It was their friendship and positive influences that helped keep me on the right path up until the time I graduated from high school.

I now realize how much I kept even my friends at arm's length. I never really confided to even my closest friends much of what was happening in my life. From an early age, I learned it was usually not wise to talk about those things to others. As a result, I rarely, if ever, opened up and shared what was in my heart. Consequently, I did not let any of them get close to me—it was just easier that way. I never had someone I could confide in because I seldom felt I could trust people. It went badly when I told my Mom what I had seen with my Dad. When I told my Stepfather things, he ended up using them against me as excuses as to why I could or could not do things or have certain people in my life. If I did something wrong, it was brought up for years afterward and used as ammunition to punish me. So, admitting mistakes was the last thing I wanted to do.

Regarding friends, I found myself doing the same things I had learned to survive my childhood and teenage years: I kept things to myself, and my relationships were very superficial. It was a coping mechanism I used to make it through my life. Though I missed my friends when I graduated, I did not keep up with them because I was never very close to most of them. Only the ones with whom I went to church or lived close by did I really keep and stay close to. I was closed off to people because I feared being hurt and lacked trust in people. This proved to be my undoing later in life.

After high school, most of my friends decided to serve missions and went to various places worldwide to share the gospel. I also intended to do the same but had a bit of a struggle after I graduated and before I turned in my mission papers.

The summer and fall after I graduated was a very important time for me when Satan helped me to realize several areas in which I was very weak—self-esteem and girls. Once I was left to myself and without seminary and friends who supported me and reminded me what I needed to do, I forgot to pray and stopped regularly reading my scriptures. I knew what I had been taught to believe was true, but my testimony was weak, and I was not fully converted. This left me vulnerable to temptations I had been able to resist thus far in my life. During this time, I was left to myself and realized how unprepared I was to make my own choices.

SEMINARY AND GRADUATION

During high school, I also enrolled in the seminary program provided by the church. This allowed me to read the scriptures and have instructions not given in my home. My teacher was a very humble and kind man, and I remember him being a very good teacher. Seminary provided a needed boost of spirituality that I lacked in my home life. This helped me to remain free from drinking, drugs, smoking, and immoral behavior that was going on among some of my friends. It reminded me of what I needed to do and what I should avoid. It also gave me a base knowledge of the *Book of Mormon* and *Doctrine and Covenants* that I otherwise would not have had. I still remember many of the scriptures we were encouraged to memorize to this day. Though I had only a basic understanding of the scriptures then, seminary reminded me of what was most important and gave me a spiritual boost each day.

The seminary program also helped me get into the habit of scripture reading in high school. We had a program called ACAD (A Chapter A Day), where we were encouraged to read at least one scripture chapter daily. During my high school years, I habitually read my scriptures before bed, which also helped me remember to have personal prayers at night.

Looking back now, I can see how important these things were to keep me on the right path and away from things that would lead to problems. Scripture reading and prayer are fundamental aspects of inviting the Spirit into our lives and keeping God's laws and commandments in our minds and hearts daily. Without it, we tend to forget those things and are vulnerable to temptations. We are also more likely to make mistakes. This was evident when I stopped doing these two vital things later in life.

When it was time to graduate from high school and seminary, I thought I was ready for what would come next. I had done well in school and was excited about the next chapter. I received a set of luggage from my parents for graduation, and I was okay with that. I was ready to move out soon on my own. The week of graduation, the seniors had an all-night party at the school, and we played basketball, had music and food, and stayed up all night having fun and enjoying our last bit of time together before we went our separate ways.

That morning after I came home and was lying in bed, I realized for the first time that many of those I saw at school every day for the past six years I probably would not see again. That was the case, as I rarely saw or spoke to those I went to school with after graduating. When I moved out of state several years later, I lost contact with most of my friends from that period of my life. But I still remember how much they impacted my life for the better, and I learned just how important having good friends is to your success in life and living your beliefs. These experiences directly impact the things you do and how you think and act. Choosing good friends is one of the most important things you do as a teenager and throughout your life.

MY FIRST MISTAKE

After graduation, I had the summer and fall to work before turning in my mission papers. I needed to save as much as possible, so I went to work for a department store. They paid more than anyone else at $10 per hour. My first job at a grocery store paid me $3.83 per hour, which was a massive jump. The department store had a call center overseeing calls for people needing appliance repairs. I planned to work there until I turned in my papers and saved the money I needed for my mission.

Up to this point, I had managed to avoid issues with girls and other problems because I had good friends, church leaders, and seminary teachers to help me stay focused on the right things. After I graduated, I no longer had most of those influences in my daily life and found myself less inclined to read my scriptures and pray as I should have. That combined with my relative inexperience with girls, and especially very aggressive girls, left me vulnerable to what I would experience once I started this job at the department store.

On my first day on the job, when I met my female supervisor, I noticed that she was very friendly toward me and seemed to enjoy talking with me more than most. Since I was new, I figured that was the reason for all the attention. Being a bit naive, I was missing the flirty nature of her demeanor toward me. But as the days wore on, I noticed that she continued to give me a lot of attention and always wanted to talk to me whenever she had opportunities.

Finally, one night, as we were leaving work, she asked me for a ride home. She said her car was getting fixed and she lived near me. Because she was my boss, I almost had to say yes. On the way home, she asked me if I could go through a drive-through so she could get something to eat. While we were waiting, she put on some flavored lip gloss. It smelled good, and I asked what flavor it was to make conversation. She told me and then asked if I wanted to taste it. I thought she would just put some on my finger, so I said yes. But instead of putting it on my finger she leaned over and kissed me. Surprised and confused about what was going on, I kissed her back. After kissing her for a minute, she leaned back and said I was a really good kisser. This was a shocking surprise because I had kissed only one girl in my life so far; however, it was also a big confidence boost because she was eight years older and more experienced than me.

I could tell she wanted to kiss some more once we arrived at her house; consequently, we kissed again instead of getting out of the car. I decided then that I was a big fan of flavored lip gloss. But I was also afraid that because she was my boss, I would get in trouble if people found out she liked me or I saw her outside of work. But I figured it was just a fluke thing and that she would act like nothing happened tomorrow. However, that was not at all what took place.

The next day, she was even more flirtatious and aggressive in her pursuit of me. She would follow me into the break room and try to kiss me. She had me come into the room where my calls were evaluated and try to flirt and kiss me. I was uncomfortable with this and was afraid someone would figure it out, and I would get fired. So I told her we needed to stop doing things at work, and she suggested we meet after work.

My self-esteem was very poor and being flattered that a woman much older than me was even interested in me, I did not think it would hurt to see her over the summer. Seeing me after work consisted of going somewhere to kiss. We never went on a traditional date; it was always just to make out somewhere. Knowing I was going to leave on a mission and that I was not looking for a girlfriend at the time, she was okay with that. It was fun to kiss her; she and I knew that was all it was.

Then, after several months, the kissing progressed to things that were beyond what was appropriate, as often happens, and before long, I had crossed lines I never had before and knew were wrong. Feeling guilty for doing so, I decided I needed to talk to someone. Talking to my Stepfather was not an option because doing so would only make things worse. So I decided to talk to a priesthood leader in our ward I felt I could confide in.

After speaking to this priesthood leader, we went together to see the bishop. I confessed what I had done, and the bishop suggested that I needed to end the relationship before it went too far. I knew I would not marry this girl and wanted to serve a mission. I knew what the bishop told me to do was the right thing. So I went to work to break it off with her. I told her we needed to stop seeing each other but that only made her even more determined. She tried to seduce me after that. It was almost like a fatal attraction; the harder I pushed her away, the harder she tried. This went on for a while until I finally gave in to her and continued to see her. Right after I agreed to continue seeing her, it happened. We went too far and were immoral, and I felt guilty for giving in and not doing as the bishop had told me to do. I felt trapped and ashamed and did not want to face the bishop and admit my actions. Admitting things never worked out well for me was a big mistake I feared sharing because of my past experiences. So, after that, I figured it did not matter if I kept messing up for a bit since I had already messed up. As a result, it happened several more times. Then, one day, on my way to work after leaving her house, something changed my life. I was in an accident that I never should have walked away from but miraculously did so because the Lord loved me enough to wake me up.

THE ACCIDENT

It was difficult to stop seeing the girl after spending so much time together. There had not been many times in my life thus far where I had felt wanted and liked. She complimented me, made me attractive, and told me I was a "good catch." Though I am sure it probably seems strange or foolish to those who have not suffered from low self-esteem, for me it filled a desperate need I had to be loved and wanted. So, abandoning that affection was harder than I thought it would be. Walking away from that would leave me lonely and alone again, and I hated that feeling.

Like when I was forced to stop seeing my high school girlfriend, not seeing this girl left a void that had not been filled until she met me at work. Though the relationship had progressed to something it should not have, it filled an emotional void that I had in my life and made it hard for me to walk away entirely. I tried several times only to be drawn back by the physical and emotional desires I had and not to feel lonely, desperate, and alone. Knowing my difficulties leaving the relationship and desire to do what was right, I felt like the Lord intervened miraculously.

One afternoon, after going to see my girlfriend and not keeping track of time, I quickly left to get to work. I was driving a 1982 Ford Thunderbird, which I affectionately nicknamed "The Tank" because it was a big car and felt like it could drive through a wall and be just fine. I joked that if I were ever in an accident, I would be fine because my car would destroy anything it hit. Little did I know that the car would save my life one day.

As I pulled up to a stop sign and prepared to cross a divided highway to merge into traffic heading the opposite direction, I looked and saw only one diesel truck pulling a trailer getting ready to turn right off the highway. I saw no other cars coming behind him or in the other lane. I did not realize until it was too late that there was a truck behind the diesel; however, when he saw the truck ahead of him turning right, he changed to the left inside lane and accelerated to pass him. Because of the angle of the highway and the truck blocking my view of the inside lane, I thought I was clear to cross the highway and merge into the traffic on the opposite side. But as I pulled past the truck onto the highway and turned to the left to look for oncoming cars, I saw a flash of red and blacked out. The truck that had moved to the inside lane to pass the turning truck had struck the front end of my car just in front of the driver's side door hinge and rolled over the top of my car and down the road six or seven times. Directly behind me was an off-duty EMT, who watched the entire incident and immediately came to my car to render aid. The EMT said when he looked in, my eyes rolled into the back of my head; and he thought I was gone. As a result, he went to help the man who hit me. While this was going on, I regained consciousness, not knowing what had happened. I began to panic and became anxious. Then, I heard a voice as clearly as he was sitting next to me say, "Don't worry, help is on the way." At the time, no one was in the car but me, yet I heard the voice as though someone were sitting next to me. At hearing this, I relaxed and passed out again.

The next thing I remember was the EMT in my car holding my neck and asking me what my name was, what my Dad's name was, and how he could contact him. At this point, others were around my car, and he was telling them the extent of my injuries that he could see or determine from talking to me. He said he thought my ankles were broken and that I had possible head and chest injuries. He also indicated they would have to cut me out of my car because of the extent of the damage. Once they could remove the top of my vehicle, they placed me on a flatboard and started toward the ambulance. It was then that my Stepfather arrived and asked if I was okay. He seemed genuinely concerned, and hearing him, I told him I was okay. He said he would follow us to the hospital.

That evening, there was a potluck dinner at the church; my Stepfather called my little brother, who was at the house, and told him I had been in an accident and to let my Mom know when she arrived home. He also told my little brother to go with the neighbors to the church for the potluck dinner and to stay with them until he came home. So needless to say, the entire ward was made aware of my accident, and prayers were offered on my behalf. Meanwhile, at the hospital, upon visual exam, they noted some cuts and bruises and even a large piece of glass that was in my mouth, yet my mouth had no cuts in it. Even more remarkable was the fact that after getting x-rays, they found I had no broken bones or any other physical injuries from the accident. No one could believe it based on the wreckage and assessment of the first responders who called the accident to the hospital. They were prepared for much worse, but it appeared that I was fine. So they released me to go home a brief time later with the caution that if I had any sudden nose bleeds, I needed to come back immediately because that could indicate some head trauma.

On the way home, I finally felt like the shock of the accident had finally passed, but I still was trying to figure out exactly what had happened and also who it was telling me to relax and that help was on the way. For some reason, the words I heard seemed to be impressed upon my mind, and I kept thinking about what happened over and over.

When I arrived home, my Mom made me some soup and I tried to eat. However, as soon as I did so, my nose began to bleed into my soup, and immediately, I was rushed out to the car to head back to the hospital. On the way, we stopped at the church for a Priesthood blessing in the bishop's office.

THE BLESSING

I cannot recall most of what was said in the blessing, but I do recall that I was told I would be okay and that the Lord had protected me from grave harm that night. After the blessing, we went to the hospital where they did additional tests and determined I was okay after all. I was then released to go home. However, I do believe I had some head trauma that night, which caused my nose to bleed. But I also believe through the power of the Priesthood, by the time I arrived the second time at the hospital, the injuries I had sustained had already been healed.

After coming home the second time, the EMT who had been behind me when the accident happened, called to see how I was doing. I was then able to thank him for helping me, and I also inquired about the voice I heard when I first awakened. He said he was the first person who got into my car, and he immediately secured my neck and began to ask me my name. I asked if he said anything else before that, and he indicated he did not. Then, I realized that the voice might have been heavenly and not earthly. It was the first time in my life that I heard such a voice, and so distinctly in my mind, it was as though a person were speaking to me.

I did not fully comprehend the meaning of this until the following day when I went to the junkyard to retrieve my personal belongings from my car. As I walked up to the wreckage, I realized that my walking away from the accident or even being alive was more than just luck. Looking at where my body had been in the driver's side of the car, it looked as though some force field had protected me or that I was inside of a protective sleeve because everything around my body had collapsed or been destroyed except around my immediate person.

As I sat there and stared at where I had been in the car, there was no doubt anymore that God had spared my life and protected me. Even more, I heard a voice from above letting me know I would be okay, and that help was coming. I did not imagine it or hallucinate. I heard a voice speak to me as though he were sitting beside me. Upon further inspection of the car, the truck hit my car just inches in front of where my feet were. If he had hit me any closer to my feet than he did, my feet would have been gone. If I had pulled out one second earlier than I had, he would have hit me directly in the driver's side door, and I would have been killed for sure. But he did not hit my feet, and I did not pull out one second later, and a heavenly power had intervened to protect and save my life. It was obvious to those who were familiar with the circumstances of my accident that God had a hand in my preservation and that experience changed everything for me.

The week of my accident, my brother was having his missionary farewell that Sunday. When my Mother got up to speak that day, she referenced the miracle of my being there that day and that God had some purpose in sparing my life. It had a very big impact on me because I knew it, too. I have always believed God existed, but now I had a firsthand experience where that reality was made clear to me. At the time, the Lord intervened to change the direction of my life. It would not be the only time He intervened in a very personal way to redirect my course in life to bring me back to Him.

As a result of that life-changing experience, I resolved to make the necessary changes in my life. After the sacrament meeting that day, I spoke to the bishop, told him I needed to repent, confessed my mistakes, and told him of my willingness to do whatever I needed to do to serve a mission. This time I felt more determined than ever to make it happen. The timing of the accident also was no mistake. That evening, the girl I had been dating purchased a ticket for me to visit her family's home in Seattle. If the accident had never happened, I am convinced I would have been on that plane and my life would have turned out very differently. Because of the accident, I never went on that plane, I never saw the girl I was dating again. Instead, I stayed home and called her to say I would not be coming to see her. I never saw or spoke to her again after that.

That accident experience changed the direction of my life for the better. It was a blessing that the accident happened. Though I was stuck paying for a demolished car for several years after, it also woke me up to the direction I was going and helped me get my life back on the right track. It was hard to go through the repentance process and wait for a year to turn in my mission papers, but it also gave me a chance to get a dog, spend time training her, and get myself ready to leave when the time came.

Looking back, the Lord often humbled me or compelled me to be humble by my circumstances and experiences. Unfortunately, I often did not learn to listen to those who were wiser than me and avoid the sorrow and misery that I ended up experiencing. I just thought my situation would be different, or that I somehow knew better than everyone else who had told me otherwise. But now looking back, I see the wisdom of those who told me to avoid the mistakes I made and wish I had listened. Because I did not, and for reasons I do not yet fully understand, the Lord intervened and helped me redirect my life. This is why I stress so much to my children and anyone who will listen to me that each decision we make can and will drastically affect our future. Only upon reflection and after many years can one fully appreciate how much the choices can and do affect life's outcomes.

When I took the time to reflect on my choices years later, it was then I could see just how much every choice I made had a direct impact on other choices and on the path I ended up taking. All of my choices mattered, and everything I did had a consequence either when I made poor choices or later in my life.

MY DOG BRITTANY

After the accident and the meeting with my bishop, I told my parents what happened with the girl I had been dating and that my mission was going to be delayed for at least a year. It was then that they agreed to let me get a dog. They wanted me to have something else to focus on and devote my time to. It was a good idea. I went to the animal shelter and came across a yellow Labrador Retriever and immediately knew she was the one I wanted. I named her Brittany. She was a very sweet-natured dog, and I fell in love with her from the start. I chose a hunting dog because I envisioned training her to go hunting with my brothers and me. Growing up, my brothers and I had often talked about having a dog to take hunting, and I was excited to begin training her. After purchasing several books on how to train a dog, I began training her immediately. From the start, Brittany was easy to train. The first few days, she had already mastered sit and stay; I was working on her extending her paw to shake and come to me. One thing that aided in her training was a dog biscuit she loved! She would do anything for these treats. She even did things without me asking her to get a treat if she knew I had one in my hand.

As she continued to grow, I spent hours with her in the yard training her to find things. I bought a pigeon cage and pigeons to train her to hold birds carefully in her mouth and bring them back to me without crushing them. I also bought pheasant scent, put it on a shirt, and would drag it around the yard while she was in our garage. then, I let her out and watched her retrace my steps until she found the shirt and brought it to me. I was always amazed at how good she was at everything! I often would show my brothers how good she was when they came over and even took them to the park where I trained her with the live pigeons and practiced with her. Everyone loved Brittany and was so impressed with how well she performed.

As fall approached and the time to turn in my mission papers drew near, I could not wait to take Brittany out hunting with us at least once before I left on my mission. We found a place to go, and I could hardly sleep that morning. I was excited to see how Brittany would do her first time out. It was overcast, cold, and threatening rain that day, but we were all anxious to cut Brittany loose to see what she would do.

Once we were all ready and started walking into the field, I told Brittany to go and start working the field. She froze not far into the field and looked straight into a bush ahead of us. We waited, but nothing happened. Then we approached her, and as we walked up to where she was pointing, we could not see how a bird could be hidden in such a small bush. We were so close I thought maybe she had seen a mouse or a squirrel or something when suddenly, Brittany stomped her foot, and the pheasant flew right out of the bush she had been pointing to. We shot, and the pheasant came down, and Brittany went to retrieve it. She brought it back and carefully put it in my hands as she had been trained. I was so proud I could not stop bragging about her! Everyone else did, too, and now we knew we all needed to be ready when she froze like that.

The rest of the day she could scare up any birds in the field and even swam across a creek to retrieve a bird that fell into the water. We were all so impressed at the end of the day that we decided to go hunting with Brittany again before the end of the season. This was one of the few times I had seen my Dad since he had given us up for adoption. Now that I was eighteen, I could see him if I chose to do so. However, after we returned from hunting and we told how well Brittany had done, it came out that my Dad had gone with us. My Stepfather became very upset when he found out my Dad went with us and said that if he went hunting with us again, we could not take my dog.

The next time we tried to go hunting, my Stepfather would not allow us to take my dog. He did not trust that we were not meeting my Dad to go hunting with him. Feeling frustrated because I felt my Stepfather was using my dog as a way to punish us and keep us from hunting with my Dad, we ended up getting into a physical altercation and a war of words that resulted in my being compared again to being "just like my Father," and my Stepfather lying on his backside after I shoved him away from me when he attempted to throw me out of the house physically. He never tried again to physically harm me after that because I made it clear that day that if he ever tried again, I would make sure it was the last time he ever put his hands on me.

This was pretty typical of how things went at home for me. If I did what my Stepfather wanted me to do, he would claim he loved me and would support me in his way. If I did anything he disagreed with or did not like for whatever reason, I was kicked out, disowned, or abandoned to take care of myself. It was his way of forcing me to do what he wanted, or I would suffer the consequences. He did that in every aspect of my life. There was no reproving me sharply at times and then showing an increase of love afterward so that I did not think he hated me. I believe he did. I felt he rarely showed any real love toward me, so I have felt he hated me pretty much my entire life.

But when it came to the dog, she was mine. I raised her, took care of her, and spent hours and hours training her only to be told I could not take her and use her for what she was trained. It was very frustrating, and my anger and resentment toward my Stepfather only grew and deepened as I got older and he became ever more vindictive and mean. But we did not take my dog with us and only had one outing before I turned in my papers and left on my mission.

PATRIARCHAL BLESSING

As the time approached for me to turn in my mission papers, I was preparing also to get my patriarchal blessing. A patriarchal blessing is a personal communication from the Lord. In it, He declares your lineage, guides you and sometimes warns of things to look out for in your life. The Lord also sometimes reveals different blessings that He has given you, things about your life, and His mission for you. The most amazing part of it is that it is truly from God. I know this because He told me things in my blessing that only He could know or tell me, confirming that God truly inspired it.

Knowing this, there were several things that I asked the Lord to know about my life going forward. I wanted to know if He had forgiven my mistakes and accepted my repentance. Next, I prayed to know about my mission, and finally about my future wife and family and what direction the Lord wanted me to go to fulfill my life mission. I fasted and prayed for the Lord to give me the answers to the questions I had and that he would grant the desires of my heart. Most of my siblings, Mom, and Stepfather were present when I went to the patriarch's home for my blessing. I was anxious to know what the Lord would reveal to me.

When the Patriarch put his hands upon my head and began to speak, I felt at once a very peaceful feeling come over me and it helped me to focus on every word that was said. The first thing he spoke about was my family's love for me. This brought tears to my eyes because I often wondered if they truly loved me or if anyone did. The Lord, knowing this, reassured me of that. Next, I was informed that the Lord had accepted my repentance and remembered my previous sins no more. The joy I felt at hearing that overwhelmed me, and I broke into tears. How happy I felt to be forgiven for my mistakes and know that the Lord had forgiven me and knew my heart. Then, I was informed I would serve a foreign mission and be able to speak the language with all the sincerity of my heart. Because I had yet to receive my mission call, this was very exciting news and I had wanted to know in my heart—to go overseas to serve.

Throughout the rest of my blessing, the Lord guided me through the various aspects of my life, from when I came home to when I had children and later in life to teaching and raising them to know what was important. It also told me of gifts the Lord had given me and what He wanted and expected of me. It was a road map through the different paths of my life. It was a very real answer to my prayers and answered all I had requested of my Father in Heaven.

When the Patriarch was through with the blessing and removed his hands from my head, I was overjoyed with happiness, gratitude, and relief. The Lord had forgiven me and provided many great insights into who I am, what I needed to do, and what He expected of me. In it, He also admonished me of things I needed to remember and avoid, which I ended up struggling with because I forgot the Lord's counsel. It was a very sacred and amazing experience. If I had done all the Lord told me, my life would be different today.

Patriarchal blessings are personal scripture from the Lord to us. I remember reading mine several times when I received a copy shortly after my blessing, but then tucked it away and did not read it much after that for many years. It was a grave mistake on my part. Because I did not read it, I missed so many opportunities to be guided by the Lord at various crossroads. In fact, over time I forgot much of what my blessing said. As a result, I went contrary to the counsel it provided me. I always had my blessing close by in a top drawer or my scriptures, but I did not use it as I should have. I regret that now and make it a point to read it regularly to remember what the Lord revealed. I want to be sure not to forget my mission and purpose He revealed.

Most importantly, I have learned the value and sacred blessing of receiving a patriarchal blessing. I have learned the truthfulness of my blessing about my life, and the warnings and counsel the Lord gave me. The Lord knows me personally, revealed quite clearly in my blessing as I read it now and recognize what the Lord was trying to help me avoid. Like all parents, the Lord knows us like we know our children, even better than that. As such, a patriarchal blessing can and is one of the greatest helps for us in life because it is from our Father who has our best interests in mind when given to us. If we are receptive and willing to listen to the Lord, He will help us choose the right path and avoid the pain and misery of wrong paths and choices.

One concern I had later in my life after I had made many mistakes and had been estranged from the church for many years was if the blessings I had been promised in this patriarchal blessing were still in force, or if I had forfeited them because of sins and choices. When I sought repentance, and in seeking a blessing from my bishop, he was inspired to tell me that all of my blessings were still in force and would all be fulfilled if I were faithful and sincere in my repentance. I know the Lord inspired the bishop to say that to me simply because I had never told him my concerns about my blessing when I saw him. In my heart, I had been very concerned, and the Lord, in his mercy and love toward me, reassured me of my standing with Him. My blessing reminded me often of the Lord knowing the desires of my heart; this was further proof that the Lord knew mine.

Chapter 7

Mission

The time was now fast approaching when I would receive my mission call. Already having received my patriarchal blessing, which told me I would be serving a mission in a foreign land, I was anxious and excited to know in what area of the world I would serve.

THE CALL AND THE MTC

Finally, the day arrived, and my call came. I remember sitting around the kitchen table with family members as I opened the envelope. As I read the first page announcing the call, I had never even considered the location I was now reading—Portugal! I had to get a map to be reminded of its location. I was shocked and excited. I had waited and anticipated my call that entire year, and now, in a few short months, I would be entering the MTC, or Missionary Training Center, and would begin learning the Portuguese language.

Before entering the MTC, I went to the temple and received my endowment (a religious ordinance). There, I spent the day with those in my family who could be with me. That was a wonderful experience and helped me see just how much I had yet to learn about the gospel and the covenants we make with the Lord in the temple.

On the day of my church mission farewell, many friends and family were able to attend. My old high school girlfriend and her family also came in a show of support. They were always so good to me, and seeing them was bittersweet. I struggled with a topic to speak about, so I decided instead to share the story of how I finally made it to the pulpit that day and what I learned.

The day I went into the MTC was difficult. It was my first time leaving home; the challenge of learning a new language, sharing the gospel in a foreign country, and going overseas was a little bit daunting. It hit home as I said my goodbyes to family members. Yet, I was excited to be a missionary, and it had come through sacrifice and sore repentance to have the opportunity to serve. So, after many tears, I left my family and walked through the doors to begin this next chapter in my life.

After leaving my family, my first day in the MTC was a blur. I met my companion and the rest of the missionaries who were heading to Portuguese-speaking missions. Some were heading to Brazil, others to different cities in Portugal, and some to the Azores. That first night we met our Branch Presidency and were admonished that they would meet with us that evening if we had any outstanding sins or issues to take care of. After their talk, many of us went to speak to the Branch President to be sure we were free from any sins that would prevent us from having the Spirit with us. One thing I learned quickly at the MTC was how powerfully the Spirit is present in that environment. If you had any sins you had not repented of, your conscience would overwhelm you. After talking with the Branch President, my conscience was clear, and I was ready to go to work.

All the missionaries were easy to work with, and we got along well. In our classes, we would spend time reading the scriptures and then learning the basics of Portuguese. We were fed well and could eat as much as we wanted. I gained about fifteen pounds in my time there and loved the food. But I had one persistent problem in the MTC—my ankles.

ANKLES IN TROUBLE

In high school, I used to sprain my ankles on a routine basis. I never thought much about it until my senior year when I rolled my right ankle and ended up breaking off a large piece of bone. When I went to the doctor, he said I could play with the injury, but it would be very painful. It was painful, especially with an ankle brace that pressed the broken piece against the bone it broke away from, creating an odd debilitating sensation that sent shooting pain up my leg. Nevertheless, I played through the pain, and eventually, it subsided. By the time I entered the MTC, I had forgotten about it.

Once I started playing basketball in the MTC, I was quickly reminded of my ankle issues. Shortly after I arrived on our once-a-week P-day (preparation day), I was playing basketball when I rolled my ankle, which hurt badly this time. I went to the medical center and the medical staff wrapped it and gave me crutches. After a few weeks, it got better, and I was off the crutches and ready to try again playing basketball. But once again I sprained my ankle and again needed crutches.

By this time, the elders and sisters in my Portuguese class were starting to think I was the unluckiest man they knew. Things just seemed to happen to me that did not happen to others. Admittedly, I felt the same way. Frustrated that I kept getting injured and had to limp around on crutches all the time, I wondered why I seemed to be more injury-prone than others. In high school, I played through ankle sprains all the time, but for some reason, now, every time I turned my ankles, I could not walk, and they were more painful. Whatever the reason, life in the MTC was hard for me and my companion, who had to wait for me as I was often on crutches and behind the group.

After recovering from another sprain, desperate for exercise and to play basketball, which I loved to do, I played again. This time, the injury was the worst yet. When I fell, I knew something was wrong as I felt and heard a pop in my ankle. Not only that, but my ankle swelled to the size of a football, and the pain was excruciating. I could not deal with the pain and was sent to the emergency room at the nearby hospital for treatment. It was a Sunday night when I arrived; and while lying on a gurney waiting to be seen, a doctor peeked in to see how I was doing. He noticed I was a missionary and inquired about my injury. I did not realize then that he was an orthopedic surgeon and one of the best in the state.

After reviewing my information, he said he would help me and gave me an examination. He determined that I had reinjured the ankle injured in high school, and the bone fragment that had reattached had broken off in my latest injury. He said I needed surgery to remove the bone fragment and scheduled me to have surgery in a few days. He would be the doctor performing the surgery. I was extremely blessed and fortunate to have one of the best orthopedic surgeons in the state to do the procedure. He told me he normally was not there on Sundays, but it was the night I came in. I do not think it was a coincidence. He would later be instrumental in helping me in future months—but that is something to discuss later. A few days later, my parents came to the MTC to take me to have surgery. It was a local procedure where the doctor numbed the area, but I remained awake and could watch the removal of the bone piece. During the procedure, the doctor and his staff gave me additional medication because I could feel the cutting and that made me sick to my stomach. They removed the fragment, and I was allowed to return to the MTC. However, I had to use a wheelchair until I departed for Portugal. My ankle issues were a big challenge in the MTC, which was very frustrating. However, the problems with my ankles would persist once I arrived in Portugal, and more surgery would need to be done to correct the problems.

The classwork, scripture study, and firesides at the MTC lit a fire within me for the work. I loved the Spirit that was there and met several General Authorities. Their words prepared us to enter the mission field. One of my favorite songs was "Called to Serve;" to this day, it gives me goosebumps to sing because of the memories of the strong Spirit that was always present in the MTC when we sang that song.

We also had excellent teachers who had served in Portugal and Brazil and taught with the Spirit. They encouraged and supported us as we worked hard to learn the language. I grew to love the missionaries I was within the MTC and was sad that several of them were going to Brazil.

Another thing that happened at the MTC, I ran into my best friend with whom I grew up until my parents divorced. It was great to see and talk with him for a few minutes. He looked the same but had been diagnosed with diabetes and struggled with that from a young age. But overall, he was good, and I was happy to see him.

Another thing worth mentioning about my time in the MTC was that one of the sisters going to a Spanish-speaking mission made it a point to speak to me when we were in the cafeteria or anywhere else she saw me.

At first, I thought it was because she felt bad that I was always on crutches and would be sweating from the exertion of having to crutch around everywhere. But as time passed, I noticed some of the same things from her that I used to see from my former boss. My companion also noticed her behavior and told me he thought she liked me. She was nice, and I saw no harm in giving her my address so she could write to me in Portugal. For whatever reason, it seems at this point in my life, girls seemed to take notice of me, and it took me a while to figure that out and not dismiss it as just being friendly or nice. It is also my humble opinion that Satan also understood what my weaknesses were and worked hard to exploit them going forward in my life. I struggled to feel wanted and loved my entire life, and my self-esteem reflected that. So, all this new attention was flattering and hard to ignore or turn away from.

PORTUGAL MISSION

After three months of learning Portuguese in the MTC, the time came for us to head to Portugal. This was before 9-11, so parents and family could come to the departure gate to see us off. Many of the families of the missionaries I served with in the MTC were there to see their children leave for New York, then on to Lisbon, Portugal, and then finally to destination cities.

Again, it was hard to say goodbye to loved ones, but we were also ready to leave, buoyed by the spiritual environment we experienced over the past three-plus months in the MTC. There, I did not have distractions like television, radio, or movies. That dedication to serving the Lord each day for the past three months helped us feel a level of spirituality I had never experienced before. Thinking that what I had just experienced would be the same in the mission field and that the missionaries in Portugal would be like those I had served with in the MTC, left me confident that this experience would be the best yet.

We got on the plane, flew to New York, and then flew overnight to Lisbon. The next morning, as I looked out the window at the red-topped roofs in Lisbon, I realized that I was in a vastly different country than I was used to and had no idea what to expect. Regardless of the unknowns,

I was anxious to meet my mission president and new companion and get to work.

Since I arrived in Portugal, my ankles have been okay. However, the cobblestone roads were challenging, as my ankles were very weak. I often caught myself before turning an ankle and falling to the ground. But my luck did not last for long.

After a few months, I was playing basketball when my legs were taken out from underneath me, and my head hit the pavement. I do not entirely remember what happened after that. I do recall being taken in an ambulance to a hospital and being placed in a dark room that had only a small window in the door. Other than that, the room was pitch dark. My Portuguese was not exceptionally good, and I struggled to understand what they were saying. I had no idea where my companion was or what had happened. I was completely confused and disoriented and began to panic. They left me isolated in this dark room for hours until the assistants to the Mission President came to get me. I do not recall ever seeing a doctor or being examined; it was a strange experience. I am pretty sure I had a concussion. Still, not experiencing any lingering issues, I decided I was okay—just another accident and injury to add to the list I had sustained so far on my mission.

Before entering the MTC, I never really got hurt or had any issues with my ankles that caused me much of a problem. Even when I broke a piece of bone in my right ankle, I played through the pain. Suddenly, I felt like I was getting hurt all the time and could not figure out why. But as I would soon find out, the worst was yet to come.

My companion and I had been together for several months by this time. He was a good man but also what people in my mission would call "trunky,"—meaning he was close to going home. He was not as focused on missionary work as he was on his girlfriend back home and other things. We worked, but not as hard as we should have. Also, there were things that my companion and the zone leaders started to do that were against mission rules. For one thing, they planned to see a R-rated movie in the theater. I was still new to the country and should have said "No," but I did not. I was afraid of being the odd one out. I was not strong enough to stand up for what was right. I did not enjoy the movie and felt bad about going. I was also surprised and disappointed with our zone leaders for setting a bad example.

As I came to find out later, we had a noticeably big problem with elders in the mission habitually breaking mission rules. It was no excuse for me to do it; but as I said before, I had low self-esteem and wanted the other elders to like me. I felt vulnerable in a country where I did not speak the language well and needed my companions to help me. I felt trapped and compelled to go along with what they were doing, even though I did not like it. I started to wonder if anyone in our mission was doing missionary work because of the stories I heard about things that were happening in our mission. There were many good missionaries; however, more were not I was surprised to learn, and I became discouraged after figuring it out.

Between missionaries' behavior and what I saw in this new culture, I remember writing home and saying how people in this country were doing so blatantly against God's laws and feared the end was near. They would openly be immoral in public, display pornography, and watch pornographic programs on television in the evenings. Also, once a year during Carnival, they would celebrate for days by randomly hitting each other in the streets with plastic hammers, playing loud music, drinking, and indiscriminately acting immorally all along the beach and other places. Coming from a conservative culture, I experienced a huge shock and became aware of how degraded the world was quickly becoming. On top of that, having already witnessed many in my mission who were breaking the rules, I, along with them, had me depressed, and I began to struggle with the work.

The next transfer day, when I became a companion to an elder working and doing as he should, I was relieved to be with a good elder. We started to study together and began to work hard each day like we were supposed to be doing. Then, I had more setbacks: walking down the cobblestone streets several times my ankles rolled into road potholes. The old injuries reappeared; and since ice was not readily available to take down the swelling, we were forced to go to the market and buy frozen vegetables and put them in the bathtub to soak my ankles. They were swollen and painful, so I saw a doctor but quickly learned they could not help me. After voicing my concerns about the doctor's ability to help me, I was able to see a specialist. Thankfully, the doctor could speak some English, and I could explain to her the problems I was having. After my explanation, she claimed she needed to have me remove my pants, shoes, and socks to examine my ankles. Confused about why I needed to remove my pants, I again reiterated that my ankle was injured, and she still insisted that I remove my pants. The fact that the doctor was female made it even more uncomfortable, but reluctantly, I agreed, and my companion tried not to laugh as I removed my clothing and sat on the exam table.

After carefully examining and probing my foot and ankle area, the doctor claimed she knew exactly the problem. To prove it, she wanted me to go over to a wall that had wooden handles up the wall and put all my weight on my bad ankle while holding onto the handles for balance. She claimed that it was all in my mind and that I had imagined these injuries. When she said this, my companion looked at her as if she had lost her mind. I was also surprised and just looked at her in disbelief. She then repeated what she said, and at that point, my companion spoke up, pointed to my football-sized ankle, and asked how I could imagine these injuries. They went back and forth for a minute or two until finally I said I would do as she asked to prove this was not a joke or a figure of my imagination. With the help of my companion, I limped over to the wall, took a deep breath, and then tried to stand only on my injured foot. The result was predictable: my ankle looked like it crumbled under the weight of my body, and I went to the floor screaming in pain. The doctor looked shocked and alarmed and said perhaps she was wrong. A few minutes later she came in and put my ankle in a cast to stabilize it. I was desperate for relief then, so I agreed to have her do it.

One thing I learned quickly about healthcare in Portugal is that it is behind the rest of the world. This was evident when they put me in a plaster cast that felt like it weighed fifteen pounds and had a rubber peg in the middle of the underside of my foot. Later, my stateside doctor informed me that they used those twenty years ago but not any longer. It was so heavy that I almost had to drag my foot along the ground beside me. Then, to make matters worse, they brought me crutches that would do well for someone of typical height in their country. However, with my six-foot-4-inch frame, the crutches were a good eight to ten inches too short for me. But it is all they had, so I had to use them.

After this medical experience, my companion and I had to use taxis, buses and trains a lot more. This stretched our finances, and we had to get creative to eat and have money for transportation. During this time, I lost a lot of weight and developed sores under my arms because of the crutches rubbing the skin raw. While this was going on in Portugal, my doctor, who had operated on me while I was in the MTC, was consulted about my problem. Everyone was trying to decide if I needed to come home to have surgery or if I should have the surgery there. There was no question now surgery was necessary, but how well it could be performed in Portugal was the issue. After experiencing the healthcare to the extent I had, I was convinced surgery here would be a mistake.

So, while this decision was being made, my companion began going out with other missionaries. At the same time, I stayed back in the apartment resting because I had so much trouble getting around and my underarms needed a break. But I was also frustrated because the doctors in Portugal did not seem to know what to do to help me, and I was getting impatient with the back and forth about where and who would do the surgery. This left me, for extended periods by myself, feeling depressed and deflated. Fed up with waiting, I decided I might help everyone decide if I did one last bad sprain on my already weak ankles. With this in mind, while alone in my apartment, I tried several times to jump off a chair and roll my ankle to be done with it all. Ironically, I could not purposely hurt it when I tried to! It seemed that something always happened to derail my success whenever things started to look up or go well for me.

Feeling sorry for myself, I contacted the sister who had been writing to me since the MTC. She was aware of my ankle issues and had given me her phone number in Chile. And at this point, I felt desperate to talk to anyone, so I called her. We talked several times over several weeks until I was informed that the Mission President wanted to see me at the mission home. I was told to bring all my belongings with me and anticipated that I was leaving to have surgery. The Mission President confirmed that as he informed me I was going home to have the surgery. Afterward, I spoke to my parents, and they said they would be there to pick me up the next day and were incredibly supportive. They were worried about me and were anxious to see me. I had very mixed feelings at that time. Part of me was relieved to get my ankles fixed and excited to see my family. But then there was a part of me that felt sad that I was leaving my mission and had not accomplished much up to that point. I figured once the surgery and rehabilitation were over, I would be reassigned to a stateside mission and would not be returning to Portugal. But once again, the Lord had other plans for me.

HOME FOR SURGERY

The following afternoon, my Mission President said goodbye to me and expressed his disappointment I had to go. I thanked him for all he had done for me and set off with the assistants to the airport. I had two pieces of luggage, a shoulder bag to carry around, crutches, and a giant plaster cast on my right ankle. Then, having lost so much weight by the time I went home, my clothes were hanging off my body, and no doubt I looked pathetic. I had a little Portuguese money, but finding a place to exchange with me on crutches was not feasible, so I decided not to worry about it. Once the assistants dropped me off and helped me get to the counter, they wished me luck and left. It was a struggle to get anywhere, and I had to take frequent breaks while also working up a good sweat to get from one plane and terminal to the next.

The first leg of my journey was a short flight to Lisbon, less than an hour in the air. The next leg was just over eight hours and overnight, so I hoped to be able to sleep most of the way. My Portuguese had improved by this time, and I was able to assist some American tourists who were asking for help. However, I was embarrassed by how they behaved. They were very obnoxious and rude.

Once on the plane from Lisbon to New York, I passed out and slept most of the time. After arriving at Kennedy Airport, things were a complete nightmare! Upon landing, I had to go to a completely different terminal to catch my flight home. I had eaten hardly anything, was tired, and my ankle hurt. It took me forever to get through customs, figure out where I needed to go to board my plane and crutch my way there. People could not help but stop and stare at me as I was hunched over crutches that looked better suited to fit a child, was drenched in sweat, and had on a missionary name tag.

After reaching my plane, my underarms were so raw that moving was hard. I dropped into a chair and was relieved I had reached that point. While waiting to board the plane, a man sitting nearby began talking to me. I found out he was a church member and was curious about my injury and where I had been serving. We had an enjoyable conversation and talked until it was time to board.

I was relieved that the worst was now behind me and my family would be at the next stop. But that was short-lived because as so often had been the case on my mission, something would go wrong as soon as things seemed to go right. As I boarded the plane, made my way slowly down the aisle to my seat, and managed to put my crutches up and sit down, I began to relax. But no sooner had I done so than someone approached me and told me I was in her seat. I pulled out my ticket and showed her that I was assigned to the seat, and she replied, "Oh well, then we have a problem." She then turned around and stomped up to the flight attendant who paged me to the front of the plane. When I heard her call me to the front, I almost broke down into tears right there. I was exhausted and had just put away my crutches, relieved that I was finally settled.

I had to get up and walk around all the people in the aisles to return to the front of the plane. I did so trying to hold back the tears. I took out my crutches and apologized to everyone who had to move out of the way to let me through. At about this time, I was worried that something was wrong and I would not have a seat on the flight. That would leave me stuck in New York with little money, no food, or a place to stay. Once up front, the flight attendant looked at my ticket and showed me the problem. I had the right flight, but the wrong day. I was scheduled to be on this flight, but not until the following day. My worst fears were realized. I went back to my seat to get my shoulder bag and get off the plane, not knowing what I would do.

As I returned to my seat, the man with whom I had spoken briefly before boarding inquired about what was happening. I told him my ticket was the next day and I had to get off the plane. Then, as I was preparing to leave, and he watched me grab my bag and struggle to go back up the aisle to leave the plane, he suddenly stood up, grabbed my bag, put it in the overhead bin, and said to me, "Elder, you need to get home more than I do; take my seat and tell my wife I will be home tomorrow." I was stunned and did not know what to say. I broke down in tears and thanked him with all my heart. He smiled warmly, shook my hand, wished me luck, and left the plane.

As I sat there thinking about the kindness of that man who barely knew me, I thanked the Lord for this small miracle. I had no business being on that plane, yet I was heading home there—even though my ticket was for the following day. I had no idea that I was not to be sent from Portugal until the following day when I landed and spoke to my family, and they explained what had happened. After the assistants dropped me off and were on the way back, they received a call from the mission office telling them not to send me on the plane. They could not get me a flight home from New York until the following day. So, if they sent me, I would be stuck in New York for a full day before I could fly home. But I was already on my way to Lisbon by the time they figured it out. So, they contacted my parents and told them the situation. They kept calling the airlines to see if I had made the flights to arrive in New York, and I had. Then, once I was on the plane from New York, they again called to see if I had somehow managed to get on the plane. When they realized I had, they called the mission office to let them know I made the flight. The Lord helped me get home, and I was grateful to have made it.

The flight was long, and I had only eaten what we were given on the plane since leaving Portugal. By this time I was tired, physically exhausted, and ready to collapse into my family's arms. But first I had to make sure and thank the wife of the man who gave up his seat to me. When I arrived home, the flight was behind schedule, so they asked those who did not have a connecting flight to wait until those who did exit the plane. I waited until I was the last one on the plane, then put my bag over my shoulders and crutched my way up the ramp toward my family who were relieved to see me and awaiting my arrival. I fell into their arms and was relieved to be home. Tears of joy and relief washed down my face, and then I looked for the wife of the man who gave me his seat.

A woman was waiting near my family, and because I was the last one on the plane to get off assumed she was the one I was looking for. I crutched over and asked if she was the wife of the man who had given me his seat. When she said she was, I was overcome with emotion as I shared the great kindness her husband had extended to me. Upon seeing me and the hardship I endured, she, too, was teary-eyed and grateful her husband had been willing to help me get home. I informed her he would be on the same flight the next day and thanked her again before we left. Then as we waited for my luggage at the baggage claim, my family told me of their concern after learning my flight was not until the following day. I had no idea I would not be sent from Portugal until the following day when I landed and spoke to my family. I made it home that day only because I had help. The Lord helped me to get home, and I knew it and felt very blessed that I made it without a valid ticket.

When I arrived home, I immediately called my dog, Brittany. She went crazy trying to get to me. I had missed her so much, and she was so happy to see me. Sleeping in my bed that first night back was the best night's sleep in the past six months. It felt weird to be home as a missionary, and it was also hard to stay focused at home.

The next day, I ate a huge breakfast that consisted of all the food I had not eaten since I left for Portugal: pancakes, eggs, bacon, orange juice, and cold milk. The previous two months, because of my ankle problem, we had cut back on food to compensate for the money spent on transportation. I would eat flour and water pancakes in the mornings, followed by cheap deli rolls for lunch, and then some pasta for dinner. Therefore, I was overjoyed when I saw all the food that morning! I had not been full for months, so it was good to eat again.

That afternoon I had an appointment to see the doctor who had performed my same-day procedure while at the MTC. He said he had not seen a cast like the one I had on my right foot in 20 years. He was amazed at how far behind they were in the medical field. Then, after removing my cast, he examined my ankles. He did some tests and took some X-rays of both feet. What he said after he finished his examination of my feet shocked me. He said my left ankle was worse than the right one, which had not been in the cast. He told me the ligaments and tendons had been stretched so they no longer supported my ankle. He said he was unsure how I had been walking on it. But somehow, I had walked on the ankle, which had not given me nearly as much trouble as the right one. Again, the only explanation that makes sense is that the Lord had been helping me. There was no way physically that I could have been walking otherwise. But that was not the only evidence of the Lord's help.

When I went in for surgery shortly thereafter, they found numerous bone spurs and growths in my joints and ankles that should have made it difficult to walk in normal conditions, let alone walking on uneven cobblestone roads like the ones in Portugal. In addition to those things, my ligaments and tendons were stretched so they no longer supported my ankles. My doctor said I had a natural curvature in my ankles, making me more susceptible to sprains. That explained why I had sprained my ankles so often in high school and sports. It was also a big reason I struggled so much in Portugal. To fix the ankles, he cut the tendons and ligaments and crisscrossed them to help restabilize my ankles. He also removed the bone spurs that made it painful to walk. When I awakened, I had two large casts on my feet and had them elevated. I tried to eat breakfast but could not keep it down. Instead, I was released shortly and told to try food again once I got home.

It was June when I had my surgery, so it was hot and uncomfortable. My room being upstairs made it that much worse. I had my ankles elevated and had to sleep on my back. My Mom gave me a sponge bath the day after I came home. She seemed intent on bathing all of me until I told her I could manage it and she let me finish the bath.

The next day, not wanting to get another sponge bath from my Mom, I managed to crawl out of bed and drag myself along the floor into the bathtub to bathe myself. I repeated this process for the next two months. Whenever I was not crawling on the floor, I was in my bed lying on my back. After two months I could make my way downstairs by sliding down the stairs on my stomach while keeping my feet elevated.

I also had several visitors, including one of my MTC teachers. This upset my Stepfather, who assumed there was some love interest and let her and I know he was not pleased she came over. Embarrassed, I apologized to her and thanked her for coming to see me and told her my Stepfather had always been overprotective and assumed the worst. She understood, but I could tell my Stepfather's insinuations hurt her. There was no love interest; she was just someone who had seen my struggles in the MTC and wanted to come and encourage me. Having friends around my stepfather, even as a missionary, was a struggle.

While I was home, my parents received a call from my Mission President. He first asked how I was doing and then inquired about some long-distance calls from my apartment phone bill. I explained what had happened and was told I needed to pay the bill. I learned the hard way that long-distance calling from Portugal is expensive.

After another month of basically being confined to my bed, I had my casts removed and was able to start using a wheelchair to get around. I would go outside, sit with my dog, and enjoy fresh air. I still had another month before I could start rehab on my feet, and the time seemed to drag.

After three long months, it was finally time to start my rehabilitation. After not walking for three months, I was excited to use my feet again. Initially, once they removed the soft casts and I stood up, my feet felt like bricks, and I could not walk. My legs had shrunk to practically nothing, and I had to learn to walk again. I started going to rehab twice daily and quickly regained my strength and mobility. I recovered so quickly that the therapists said they had not seen many people recover as quickly as I had from the same surgery. Normally people do not have both feet operated on at the same time; but being on my mission, I did not have the luxury to do one at a time. It would have taken a full year had I done that, and my mission would have been mostly over. Doing both at the same time saved me six months.

While rehabbing my ankles, I met a girl who was rehabbing at the same time each day from a knee injury she sustained while playing volleyball. We casually talked as we had to sit in a room together to receive electrotherapy for our injuries. When I finished my rehabilitation and knew I would return to the field, she asked if she could write to me. She seemed nice, and we got along well, so I agreed and gave her my information, and she gave me hers.

As I awaited my new mission call, I was nervous and did not know where they would send me. Everyone said it would probably be somewhere stateside because of my surgery. However, when I received my new call, I was again called to serve in Portugal. I could not believe it and was blindsided. I was sure I was going stateside and had not been studying Portuguese. I had not spoken a word of Portuguese in close to four months. I felt unprepared to return and afraid I would be behind in the language. I did not tell anyone how I felt, but was afraid to return to Portugal. After missing my time, I did not think I would be effective. I know my parents sensed it at the airport because the look on my face said it all. Going back was hard. I was so excited to go when I first left. I was excited to see a new place, to learn a new language, and to teach people the gospel. But when I arrived, it was not what I thought it would be: missionaries were breaking the rules, the culture was a huge shock and hard to adjust to, and most people did not want to talk with us. Consequently, my first impressions negatively affected my wanting to return. Also, I was not strong enough in my testimony and convictions to stand alone and do the right thing myself. All these things combined made it hard to get on the plane to return—but I did! This, to me, was the pivotal moment of my life. The things that happened to me later in life were largely set in motion by my decisions while on my mission.

When I was called back to Portugal, selfishly I did not want to go because I knew how hard it would be for all the reasons mentioned. The question was about being willing to submit to what the Lord wanted me to do, rather than what I selfishly thought was right for me. Being willing to submit to what the Lord asked of me has been the greatest struggle of my entire life. When I returned to Portugal, my heart was not in it. I did it simply because that was what was expected of me. Though I had a few great experiences, eventually, I gave in to selfish desires that led me down a road ending in the destruction of my beautiful family and where I am today—incarcerated and alone.

I want those who read this to understand that in life certain decisions can sometimes affect our entire lives. Those decisions can set in motion a chain of events that can lead to painful outcomes and consequences if choices are contrary to what we know is right, happy, or joyful in following the path the Lord has set for us. I can speak from my own experiences that there is no happiness in doing things contrary to the Lord. There is only temporary happiness and then long-term misery. If you do not believe me, the following chapters may help you to change your mind.

BACK AGAIN TO PORTUGAL

When I first arrived back in Portugal, I met the Mission President and his wife at the airport with a group of missionaries I had come with from the MTC. After heading to the mission home, my companion and I left for my new area. This elder was from Arizona, and we got along well. However, I struggled and called the Mission President because my heart was not in it. He assured me it was normal to struggle at first but encouraged me to get back to work and give it time and things would be okay.

So, I tried to do that, and my companion and I came across a family of five who had been taught the gospel before but had not been baptized. We decided to visit the family to find out what held them back. We learned the father had a problem with drinking and smoking. The family included three daughters, who were very receptive to the doctrines we taught them. The father had tried to quit several times but had not succeeded. We asked them if we could teach them again and they said yes. We worked with them for several months teaching and encouraging them until the father managed to stop smoking and drinking.

Once these things happened, we invited the family to be baptized. They agreed, and we baptized them—it was a wonderful experience. It was extremely rare to have an entire family baptized at one time, so we felt very blessed to have been a part of their joining the church. It was amazing to see the changes in the father as he gave up his habits and became active in the church. He was much happier and brighter than when we first met him. They were a sweet family who stayed connected with me after I came home. I will always remember that going back to Portugal allowed me to help that family come into the church, and that is something for which I will always be grateful I was there to be a part of this family's happiness.

STRUGGLES SURFACE AGAIN

After that wonderful experience of baptizing a family, my companion and I struggled. He was going home soon and did not want to work much after we baptized the family of five. So, I began exercising in our apartment and tried to find other things to do while he slept. One day, I went downstairs to grab a croissant from the bakery below us when the thought came to me: I needed to get a piece of paper from the newsstand just down the street. This was another wrong decision; I never should have gone to the newsstand. That choice led to me making other bad choices that led to my downfall in Portugal.

When I got to the newsstand, however, I saw a magazine I should not have been looking at with pornographic pictures and bought that instead. Right after I bought it, I knew I should have tossed it in the trash, but I did not. Instead, I returned it to my apartment and looked at it while my companion slept. This was the beginning of a very precipitous fall for me on my mission. Looking at the magazine dulled my spiritual senses, and I lost my desire to work. Those pictures made me think about going home, dating, and having a relationship, not focusing on missionary work. The more I looked at the pictures, the more selfishly I wanted to go home, have a girlfriend or wife, and start the next phase of my life. Somehow, I convinced myself I had helped baptize a family and had been through a lot, and everybody would understand if I came home. Things just kept going downhill from there. After a brief time, my companion and I started thinking about doing things that would have been out of the question only a few months before. Now, they seemed like good ideas. One was inviting a couple of sisters to our apartment to see a movie. Sadly, they agreed to come over and watch it with us. We made food and nothing inappropriate happened between us and the sisters; however, having them over to our apartment was out of bounds and wrong.

Then, I had a problem getting my residency card back from the Portuguese Consulate. I had to surrender my residency card to customs when I went home. So, when I returned, I was again required to have that with me to be in the country legally. My unusual circumstances of leaving to go home made it difficult to get it back; and after being stopped by law enforcement, I contacted the mission office to see what I needed to do. This happened for several weeks, and then I made another terrible mistake.

Because I was having trouble getting my card back, I saw an opportunity to use that as an excuse to return home. I would tell my family I had to leave the country because I could not get my card back. Law enforcement warned me I would be put in jail if they stopped me again and I did not have it. This was my chance to leave, I thought. Determined in purpose, I contacted the Mission President and told him what the police said. He told me to come into the mission office to get it taken care of. When I did, I told him I had just decided to go home because they were having trouble getting it back. He said that was not necessary, but I was determined now in my mind to go.

The police stopping me and threatening me was all the excuse I needed to go ahead and push to leave. The Mission President suggested I call my family before I decided, but I had already decided. I wanted to go home, start dating, and start the next chapter in my life. I was determined to do it no matter what. My parents tried to get me to stay, as did my Mission President, stake president, and even the area president, but I was not listening. I was selfishly focused on what I wanted, so they relented and allowed me to leave. I have regretted that decision every day since.

Chapter 8

Life After Mission

Coming home early from my mission was harder than I thought. Having served about 15 months when I decided to leave, I did not stop to consider what it would be like to come home and how that would affect me or how others would receive me. I quickly learned that most people did not know what to say, so they did not say anything. My Stepfather, whose love I had always felt was conditional, told me when I came home I had to move out. Not feeling loved or accepted was nothing new, and coming home and being kicked out was expected. What a difference it would have made to have someone caring enough to ask me what had happened lovingly and kindly, not accusatory. Instead, nobody spoke to me about it, so I did not talk about it either.

When people asked me why I came home, I was defensive and blamed it on the residency card issue, which was a real issue but one that would have been resolved at some point. The real reason I came home I kept from everyone. I had violated the law of personal chastity, viewed inappropriate material, and had not kept the mission rules. My disappointment with the mission challenges led me to feel sorry for myself. I wondered why I had to have so many health problems and why my life just seemed to be so much harder than everyone else's. These selfish thoughts led to a lack of the Spirit and a lack of desire to do missionary work. Instead, I focused on pursuing worldly things and my interests back home.

CONSEQUENCES OF CHOICES

The consequences of my choice to come home were very costly and affected my life negatively for years afterward. I had no idea at the time that decision would be as costly as it was. Leaving Portugal was a fork in the road for me and changed the course of my entire life. Looking back, I see how that decision affected every other aspect of my life. My patriarchal blessing laid out the roadmap of my life if I had remained faithful to God. But instead of reading that regularly as I should have, I forgot what it said and allowed myself to give into selfish temptations and desires. If I had stayed in Portugal, though I had made mistakes, I could have repented and refocused on serving the Lord. That would have kept me on the path the Lord set for me. The Lord warned me in my blessing to wait until the appropriate times for me to do certain things. I was unwilling to wait and be patient for what I wanted.

By coming home early and giving in to what I wanted, I ended up dating people who were in a similar place as I was and were spiritually sick like me. They were not bad people, just those who, like me, were struggling with living as they should. Like in other aspects of life, we are drawn to people who are like us and have similar morals, beliefs, and standards. So, whatever level we are on—spiritually, morally, or any other—we tend to gravitate toward those who are also on our same level. Conversely, if we are spiritually, morally, and ethically strong and have lofty standards, we will seek those who have like standards. Who we are has everything to do with whom we associate or marry. I have never questioned whether the church was true. I knew it was. I had many experiences that helped me to know it was true. But at this point in my life, I was selfishly more interested in what I wanted than living as the Lord expected. I rationalized that one day, I would make things right with God, just not right then. Experience taught me that when selfish desires rule our world, we do not stop to think about the consequences or the people our selfish actions might hurt or how their lives might be destroyed.

LIFE ON MY OWN

After being told to leave by my Stepfather, my Mom helped me find an apartment and paid the first month's rent. She also gave me a little money for expenses and then it was up to me to fail or succeed entirely. Once in my new apartment, I immediately began searching for a job. My Mom helped drive me to places I needed to go and offered to help me get to work initially. Eventually, I found a job that had me working overnight at a food packaging plant. It paid well but overnight work was hard. My brother also hired me at his company and would pick me up from my overnight job in the morning and take me to work. I worked the two jobs for several weeks before the lack of sleep caught up with me, and I stopped working for my brother and kept the overnight job instead.

In the meantime, I lived in an apartment complex where most residents were students at the nearby university. I had three other roommates who were all good men who got along well. That first Sunday after I moved in, I went to the student ward and met many more from my apartment complex. When new people moved in, residents held an open house at the apartment of the new people to introduce them to the ward and to meet the members. So, we had a meet-and-greet for my roommate and me on Monday night. During this meet-and-greet, I met a girl whom I would later date. She and her roommates learned it was my birthday the next day and brought me breakfast the next morning. Her roommates were not shy about their interest in me, but she was not enthusiastic, and I was intrigued as to why. Perhaps it was the challenge that drove me to want to date her, or just the thrill of the hunt; but whatever it was, I decided to get her interested in me one way or the other.

In the meantime, the girl I met while rehabbing my ankles learned of my being home and wanted to meet up for a date. When I arrived at her house, her parents invited me in and talked with me while she finished getting ready. Minutes turned into a half hour, and before long her entire family was sitting in the living room talking with me. I then realized that we would not be leaving the house that night. It was strange that her entire family was there, almost like it had been planned that way.

However, initially, I did not think about it much and thought it was a coincidence. After this girl assured me it had all been a coincidence, I set up a second date with her. However, when I picked her up this time, she asked if we could stop by her grandma's house to drop something off. Once again we were brought into the house and had a conversation with her grandparents, and then were joined a brief time later by her parents, who also brought cheesecake with them. Knowing these two incidents were not coincidental, I decided not to pursue anything further after I left the second time.

The next time she called, I told my roommates I was busy. This kept happening until one day as I was leaving my apartment, she randomly appeared and began to accuse me of seeing someone else. She was convinced that was why I was suddenly busy. Then, I told her it was not another girl, but I was uncomfortable with what had happened the first two times we tried to date. I then informed her I was not interested in pursuing things any further. She apologized and wanted to try again, but I declined.

About a week later I received a letter from her. She had decided to follow me and documented with whom I had been for the entire week! Then she mailed me the list, proving in her mind that I was seeing other girls. I was dating other girls, but that was not why I declined to go out with her. The more I refused her advances, the more she seemed obsessed. I began to get nervous about what she would do next.

Then, my fears were realized when I received a call from my Stepfather. He had a letter put on his windshield from this girl who claimed I was the best lover she had ever had and that I was a liar and a cheater. None of those things were true, but it was the worst thing she could have done to me. My Stepfather, already convinced I had fathered a child out of wedlock with a girl from my home ward, was now convinced I was having an immoral relationship with this girl. Frustrated, I explained to my Stepfather the story of what had happened with this girl who left the letter, and he contacted the police to warn her not to contact me or my family again. After the police contacted her, I did not hear from her again. However, the damage was done by my Stepfather, who was already convinced I was guilty of many things. In reality, most of those things he thought about me were figments of his imagination.

After that experience, I had some other dates with girls I met from the complex or had worked with at a restaurant before my mission. Though I was not guilty of any major sins or standard violations of the church while dating after my mission, I was not doing all I should have done to live the gospel upon my return. Once home, I took the scriptures and prayer for granted, stayed out later than I should have, and did not maintain the exacting standards that the Lord expects from those who belong to the church. Work and dating became the focus of what I was doing in my life, and everything else took a back seat.

After a few months, I started working for a man from my home ward who owned a construction company. My sister's new husband worked for him also, and I was ready to have a job that allowed me to work during the day instead of at night. After working for him, I had more time to see the girl from my complex whom I had met at my open house. We began spending more time together, and I thought it might lead to something. The other girls I had been dating I slowly stopped seeing because I was spending more time with this girl. After a few months, we finally decided not to see anyone else and instead focus on each other and get more serious. At that point, I thought it might be time to bring her home to meet my family, so I invited her to come with me for a Sunday dinner.

NEW GIRLFRIEND PUSHES TRUST

My girlfriend's family had a prominent history in the church, making her very popular with my Stepfather. But others in the family saw things I did not and were surprised I was dating her. However, they never voiced their concerns at that time. Only years after the divorce to this person did they voice their concerns and doubts. I was blinded by the desire to be married, have a family, and start a life with someone. I wanted to be loved and have someone to love in return. This led me to overlook many things that should have given me pause; however, they did not because of where I was at the time. To be fair, I was not the man I needed to be and did not set the proper example by living my beliefs. It was my responsibility to live what I believed; and by not doing so, I made poor decisions in my relationships and my life at that time.

As the relationship with my girlfriend progressed, I got excited about surprising her and doing unexpected things for her. One weekend, I surprised her with a trip to Vegas. Then, when the semester ended, I planned a romantic dinner for her in her apartment after her last final. At this point, we were serious. We had agreed not to date anyone else and to see where our relationship was going. So, that was my expectation. However, when I went over to surprise her with dinner on the last day of the semester, I found out that she had been seeing another man the whole time we had been dating and telling me and her roommates something entirely different.

As I was preparing the romantic dinner, she came home in between classes unexpectedly. Before she came in, her roommates hid me in the kitchen pantry. Upon entering they told her she had a message from a man she had been seeing for a while, unbeknownst to me. By this time we had been exclusive for several months, or so I thought. After hearing that he called, she seemed excited and called him back. The phone was next to the pantry, so I could hear the entire conversation. He asked her if she could come to his apartment, and she agreed to go over briefly later. After she left, I came out of the pantry and her roommates apologized for not telling me about this other man. They said he had been coming over periodically to watch movies with her and that she had been seeing him for longer than we had been dating. They felt bad because they thought I knew about him, but I told them I had not. When I asked where he lived, they said he was in the apartment directly across from mine.

After hearing that he had been coming over for a while, I got upset and returned to my apartment, unsure what to do. From my room, I could see into his apartment, and as I peeked through the blinds, I saw this man and my girlfriend kissing in his living room. I was shocked that she would do that to me. She had told me she was not seeing anyone else, but she was kissing him here. I had begun feeling for this girl and thought we were serious. Now, I realized I was the only one who felt that way. It hurt because I had begun to trust her and did not think she would do something like that. Like many other times, those I opened up to and trusted would lie to or leave me. This is what I had come to expect, but not from her. I thought she might be different, but she was not.

I debated whether to cook dinner for her, but decided I would so I could ask her about this man. I wanted to see if she would tell me the truth or lie to me as she had to her friends. Her roommates had already shared a lot, so I had a pretty good idea of what was happening. They also tried to warn me that she had done this to other men, but I did not heed their warning and returned later to make the meal. Later that night when she arrived home, I had dinner ready for her. I bought flowers and tried to make it nice, even though I was angry and hurt inside. As we ate, I casually started to ask her questions. I asked her if she had come home that afternoon. She said she had not. I asked her if she had talked with any other men that day and she said she had not. Then I asked if she saw anybody besides me, and she again said no. At that point, I told her I knew those things were not true.

After explaining that I had been there earlier and had heard her talk to the man she went to see and saw her kissing him, she finally admitted she had been seeing him behind my back. Her excuse was that her mom told her she was not married yet and should have fun. If she wanted to kiss other men, she should. It was not what I expected her to say, which was another red flag I disregarded. After a lengthy conversation and her promising not to see or kiss other men, I agreed to continue to see her; however, the trust was gone. I never truly trusted her from that point forward. My self-defense mechanisms learned while growing up kicked in, and I kept her at arm's length because I worried she would do something else to hurt me again. I did not trust that she would not try to see the other man again without telling me. At this point, I decided if she could see other men, I could see other women. Furthermore, I did not tell her I started seeing other people because she had purposely lied and hid the fact that she was dating and kissing another man, so I decided to do the same. The trust had already been eroded before I asked her to marry me. But naïve and young, and thinking that love could conquer all, I continued to date her but never again gave her my whole heart.

Many other things happened that should have given me pause about whether she was the right girl to marry. Some of the biggest ones were that she questioned many of the basic tenets of our faith and she had not been truthful about various things. Often her mom encouraged her to hide things from me or to do things and not tell me. Her mom also made me agree to put her through school first before me, going against my better instincts. Looking back, if I had been in the right place spiritually, I would never have married her because she lacked spirituality. But I was with her because I was in a similar place then and wanted to be married, have intimacy, and have what I thought was love. Later, I learned the hard way that what I thought was love was more about the desire to fulfill physical urges and less about real love and commitment to each other. We later revealed we had doubts about whether we should have married but did not act on those, so we ended up getting married anyway.

ENGAGEMENT TO SOLVE PROBLEMS

After dating seriously for about a year, I asked my girlfriend to marry me. I thought marriage would solve all our problems and give me what I needed physically and emotionally. I thought I was in love and truly knew what love looked like. But in reality, what we had was not love but rather an imitation of it. Growing up, I never really saw what true love looked like at home. My parents were already struggling when I was born, and I did not see true love and genuine affection from them. To be fair, I did not know that my parents ever learned what true love looked like from their parents, so the cycle continued.

When my Mom married my Stepfather, there was anything but real love in their relationship. Instead, theirs was one of mistrust, contention, abuse, neglect, and lack of physical affection. Similarly, what I had with my girlfriend was not unlike what I saw growing up, I thought that was just how relationships were supposed to be. I had never seen a healthy, loving relationship and had no idea what it would be like. Thinking back to the first girl I ever really had feelings for, I should have known that what my girlfriend and I had was not real love because it felt nothing like what I had with my first one. My girlfriend and I had fun together, and we were friends but lacked the openness and honesty essential to genuine feelings of love and affection. We did not have the most important aspect of a relationship—trust. Physical urges and desires took the focus away from developing true love and friendship.

The girl I dated back in high school was the first girl I had genuine feelings for; without knowing it at the time, I handled things right in that relationship. Because I had yet to experience physical intimacy with a girl, the focus was on who she was as a person, our friendship, and not on the outer appearance or physical things. We did not engage in inappropriate behaviors; we were best friends. Because of that, I had the highest respect for her and never wanted to do anything to ruin that. Unfortunately, after I graduated high school, the next girl I dated was focused entirely on physical desires and not on me or who I was. That relationship led to the only thing it could have: me making a major transgression. It introduced me to a level of intimacy that should be reserved for marriage. Then as a result of that experience, it was much harder to focus on getting to know the other person and becoming best friends instead of focusing on the physical desires and urges.

My fiancée and I were not guilty of major mistakes, but we did do things that were not appropriate and crossed boundaries. As a result, the relationship predictably focused more on the physical than on getting to know each other. I liked her; but looking back now, I never really loved her, at least not at the beginning. Years later when we divorced, my sister told me that during a wedding shower for my fiancée, she told my sister that she was not sure she wanted to marry me. But it was passed off as wedding jitters; however, it simply shows that neither she nor I were in love when we married. Lack of trust and respect left us anxious and unsure about things. Our parents seemingly struggled with intimacy and true love in their relationships, and what we saw from them manifested itself in our relationship. We had to learn to love each other in healthy and appropriate ways, something we never fully could do while married. More on that later.

Concerns notwithstanding, I asked my girlfriend to marry me by going to our favorite sandwich shop and enlisting the staff to bring her the ring with her food. The entire staff watched as the food with the ring was given to her and I proposed. It was a happy moment, yet not what I thought it would be. For me in particular, I could not help but feel a little empty inside because I did not feel that she was the girl of my dreams or the girl who had everything I wanted in a wife and companion. But I still forged ahead because I thought things would improve once we married. Interestingly, my patriarchal blessing spoke about finding a girl who would fulfill my dreams when I was ready to get married. Still, I had forgotten that admonition and never once asked the Lord if she was the right one to marry.

Now that we were engaged, we started planning the wedding. My fiancée and her mom got into full gear and began looking at dates, venues, wedding dresses, and the like. I was not too concerned about where we were married or the venue; I just wanted to get married. We decided to marry where she grew up and flew there a few days before the date. My parents were delayed because their plane had mechanical issues; consequently, they arrived on the wedding day. The morning of the wedding, my fiancée's mother gave me the birds and the bees talk because she said my Stepfather would have done so if he had been there. It was an uncomfortable conversation that I thought my fiancée's father should be giving me—not the mother.

Later that morning, we married in the temple, and my fiancée's grand-father, a temple sealer, performed the ceremony. My grandmother, Step-father, and Mother were on hand for the ceremony. It should have been a joyous experience to be in the temple with my spouse and be sealed for time and all eternity, but that was not the case for me. I smiled and was excited to be married, but I was not in love and knew I was not worthy to be in the temple that day. So, the experience was one of sadness and disappointment on my part. Ironically, the rest of the day was not particularly great either.

MARRIAGE CHALLENGES

After we were married and had pictures taken, we had a nice luncheon at a fancy venue. It allowed us to eat and visit with family and friends. Then, that evening, as we arrived for the reception, we had drenching rain that knocked the power out not long after the event began. We were rushed to change our clothes and get out before the backup power ran out. We missed many traditional rituals and fun events that normally happen at a reception and instead had to call it a night early and head out to where we had planned to stay for the evening. Having looked forward to our wedding and night together for so long, it was not turning out like I thought it would. But it was a fitting end to a day I regretted the next morning.

I still remember sitting on our bed the morning after we were married while my wife was in the shower, thinking I had made a terrible mistake. It was not my wife's fault—it was mine. We had not been worthy to go through the temple, and the experience was not a happy one for me. I never asked my wife how she felt about it, but I imagine we both had similar feelings. Even more troubling was that I knew I was not in love with my wife, which was the one thing that hurt me the most. I genuinely cared for and liked many things about her, but I did not love her then. I had kept my heart closed off to her ever since she lied to me and kissed the other man. Then I had reservations about what she said to me and what her mom told her was okay to do that I did not agree with or feel was right. I did not consciously keep from giving her my whole heart; it was a self-defense mechanism that I had learned growing up to keep me from getting my heart broken. I had no idea at the time I had a habit of doing this; I only realized it years after having to stop and think about why I kept people at arms' length, and why I did not let people get close to me. But I had asked her to marry me, which was my fault and mine alone.

Because I struggled with knowing what true love was and was not, and I struggled spiritually, worldly cares ruled the day, and selfish desires drove my desire to marry. So, this left me feeling very empty the day after we were married. To add to this disappointment, I felt trapped now that we were married and did not want to turn around and admit it was a mistake. Instead, I determined in my mind I would try to make it work, even with the doubts and uncertainty I felt in my heart. I did care for my wife, and I thought that might be enough to make it work.

Our first home together was in an elderly woman's basement apartment. I had furnished a small apartment with furniture purchased at a garage sale. Money was tight, so we had a budget. True to my word, I worked while my wife was finishing school to fulfill the promise I made to my mother-in-law before we married. I had two jobs for a while to help support us. Once my wife finished school, I started taking classes again and continued to work.

We moved into another less expensive apartment to save money to buy a house. The house had a dirt driveway, and it was an odd-looking apartment with a toilet raised like a throne in the guest bathroom. During our time at this apartment, a new thing was starting to become popular on the internet—chatrooms. I started hearing people at school talk about these online chatrooms and logged in to see what they were all about. I first thought seeing what people said in their conversations was funny. There were many different rooms you could go into to talk, all with different subjects and topics being discussed. My wife would often listen to me as I told her what people were saying, and she would also watch as the responses came on the screen. Chatrooms were pretty innocent at first; but as with all things, as time passed, people began to use them for other purposes. With the advent of webcams and other technology, new and even more tempting options became available for people to use; and that is where I found myself before too long.

I did not get online to meet people and never intended to do so when I got into the chatrooms. However, as chatrooms became more popular and people started posting pictures of themselves when chatting, the sites became more like dating sites than chatrooms. People were starting to look for people in their area and trying to meet up with them. I did not do that, but I did find myself talking to a woman who was funny and from another state. We would laugh at other people and make comments about them to each other, and it became friendly. Over time, I began to look for her and looked forward to talking with her. Being married, I did not tell her about my wife. I avoided talking about it. It all seemed harmless at first, and I had no intention of meeting this person nor did we talk about inappropriate things. In my mind, I did not think it was all that bad.

When my wife completed school, she considered taking a job that would move us across the country. I was excited to move to a new place and purchase a new home. After going out to see the area, and looking at new houses, she agreed to take the job. We found a house just being built and decided the final changes and options we wanted. After several months, we drove to our new home and began living in a new place without family or friends.

CONTINUING MARRIAGE CHALLENGES

Once we moved in, I began looking for a job and had already been accepted at a local university. I found a job as a veterinary technician, mostly because I loved working with animals; but the schedule also worked for me to go to school. We also located the meetinghouse to attend church and began attending there weekly.

When we moved, I thought our marital relationship would improve because we had to rely more on each other than ever. We did not have a family where we moved; the closest relative was a thirteen-hour drive away. Being young and far from home, I assumed it would be good for us to be away to figure things out. But the distance only seemed to accentuate existing problems. It is not that we did not get along well because for the most part, we did, but we still had our struggles that were there from the beginning.

All marriages have their issues, for one reason or another. In reading a book on relationships, I came across some things that helped me understand the natural evolutions relationships go through, although mine did not follow the pattern. Most couples go through the "in-love" phase of a relationship, feeling the other partner is perfect and can do no wrong. This phase lasts almost two years, then the relationship changes into the "loving" phase. This is the phase where you now realize all your partner's faults and imperfections, but you choose to love them despite their imperfections. By loving them as is, you choose to trust, sacrifice, and put the other person's interests ahead of your own. Doing so helps to keep the love and commitment between a couple strong because the needs of each partner are being met. Should either partner choose not to "love" the other after the "in love" phase wears off, issues begin to surface, and the person who feels neglected or unloved begins to seek other means to have needs met.

My relationship with my wife never really had the "in love" phase at the beginning where we felt the other was a perfect partner. We both questioned whether getting married was the right thing to do. We also had trust issues. I came into the relationship with difficulty trusting, and my wife violated that trust early on. Subsequently, I felt distant from her most of the time. Her hiding things from me, like money her mom would give her, things she would buy, and the feelings she had only made it harder to trust her. Being young and lacking trust and communication skills, talking about our problems and issues was difficult; consequently, we did not talk about our problems. Often, we were more like roommates than spouses. This lack of intimacy was related to our unwillingness to "love" each other, to trust each other, and to sacrifice and put the other person first. That led to major problems later in the relationship.

Something else happened as a result of the move. My wife suddenly felt a need to control things. She had been that way to a certain extent before we moved, but she tried to control most things after we moved. Before moving, we would go each holiday to visit her family because we lived close to mine and saw them year-round. After our move, when neither of us saw our families, we still ended up going to visit her family each holiday when we would go out of town. I never had the chance to visit my family for a holiday after we moved. She also wanted to control the finances, where we went to eat, and where we went on vacation. It became hard for me to have much of a say in anything. She had a better-paying job and seemed to feel that it gave her the right to make most of the decisions, even though I sacrificed my schooling to put her through school. That was a sacrifice she never acknowledged or seemingly appreciated. This was how her mother was in her relationship with her husband, so it did not surprise me to see her do the same things in ours. My personality being pretty laid-back, I let that go on for a time, thinking that at some point she would let me have a say; but that never happened, and we began to fight more as a result.

She also became anxious about me being in school and around other women. Once I started taking classes at the university nearby, some of the classes required that I work on group projects with other students. I had a cell phone; instead of giving people in my class my cell phone number, I gave them our home phone number to call me about school projects and group work. I thought this would be the best way for people from school to contact me if needed. However, when a woman from one of my classes called about a project we were working on, my wife got extremely upset and began questioning me about what she looked like and if I thought she was attractive. To this point, I had not taken notice of this woman and was more annoyed than upset. Even after I explained that I gave my home number so they did not have my cell number to alleviate concerns, she still was unhappy. I assumed my wife reacted the way she did because she found out I had looked at pornography on our computer. Having done so several times, I assumed she was reacting to that. With that in mind, I always thought it was my fault my wife reacted the way she did. The reasons I sought for an outlet, like looking at porn, were varied. Our sex life had taken a dramatic nosedive after a couple of years of marriage, and I felt my wife was not interested in sex, or me, or both. The lack of intimacy left me feeling empty and unloved. Consequently, I rationalized that if we were not having sex, pornography was the next best thing since I was not physical with another woman—just looking at pictures. However, that began a problem plaguing me for the next twenty years.

MARRIAGE PROBLEMS ESCALATE

After about a year of getting settled into our new house and our routines with work and school, I went by my wife's office one afternoon to surprise her for lunch. She had been traveling quite a bit the previous six months, so I took opportunities to see her whenever possible. Her company designed educational programs for the classroom and provided and installed the equipment needed to use their products. Her job was to go to various locations to train people to use the programs once the equipment was installed.

One of her friends, whom I also knew, was sitting at her desk when I came in to see my wife for lunch. According to my wife, they had been going together on these trips for the past six months and she had mentioned they had another trip planned for later in the week. When I asked this woman if they were still planning to leave Thursday, as my wife indicated, she said she had not gone out of town with her for a while. Then she told me it was just my wife and the installer who had been going for six months. She seemed surprised that I did not know that. But my wife had never mentioned that her girlfriend had not been the one going with her; on the contrary, she would tell me stories about her trips, including this woman being with her. She never once mentioned an installer being on the trip or that the installer was a man. Knowing she had been dishonest only confirmed my lack of trust in her, but it still hurt me to think that something might be happening with someone else. I went to lunch with her and decided to wait until that night to ask her about it. I also needed time to gather my thoughts and not blow up in her office.

So, that night after she came home, I casually asked her about her upcoming trip on Thursday. She confirmed it was still on and that she was going with her friend, the woman I had spoken to earlier that day. Confirming all the details as she had many times before, and this time knowing they were lies, I let her know that I had spoken to her friend earlier that day and knew she was lying to me about the whole thing. The look on her face said it all. She immediately got defensive and said she did not tell me because she knew I would be upset. I would not have been if she had been honest from the start. All the lies she willingly told me for the past six months helped me to know there was much more to the story than her being worried about me getting upset. I knew she was hiding a relationship with this man; based on her reaction, it was not a professional relationship.

Though she never admitted it, I was convinced she was having an affair. Hearing her excuses only infuriated me even more, and the cup of water I had in my hand I threw to the floor as I yelled back that I did not believe a word of what she said. When the cup hit the floor, it bounced toward my wife and hit her on the leg. She then used that as an excuse to accuse me of throwing the cup at her, which I did not. The argument escalated as she retreated down the hallway and into our bedroom. A war of words and accusations followed. Finally, she made a very sarcastic remark that I took great offense to, and I snapped and slapped her across the face. I was shaking and angry and hurt all at the same time. I knew I never should have slapped her, but the anger and hurt feelings I was being cheated on and lied to overwhelmed me. The little trust and respect I had with her was now gone.

I knew she was having an affair. All the signs were there, and how she reacted to my questions and how defensive she became told me all I needed to know. She had been going alone with this man for six months. She stayed in the same hotel, collaborated with him at the schools, ate dinner, and drove alone for hours in the car. And she kept him a secret, lying about him for six months and telling me it was a woman with whom she was working. Why would anyone lie that much if there was not something to hide? I told myself she must be cheating on me because there would be no reason to go to those lengths for anything less than an affair. Ironically, six months later at a Christmas dinner for her company, a man approached our table and shook hands with all but my wife, whom he bear-hugged rather comfortably until I stood and introduced myself. He seemed rather shocked because he had no idea she was married. When I inquired who this man was, I discovered he was the installer with whom my wife had been going out of town. Everyone at the table looked extremely uncomfortable and I knew why. They all knew what was happening, and I was just figuring it out.

After our confrontation about her apparent affair with her co-worker, we did not speak to each other the rest of the night or the next day. A couple of days later when I returned home from work, I found a note telling me she had left to go to her parents' house and not to contact her. She left and emptied our bank accounts, canceled all our credit cards, and left me with no money or access to our accounts. Then, to top it off, that night, two sheriff's deputies pulled up to the house and issued me a restraining order taken out by my wife. Shaken, I returned to the house, feeling like my entire world was suddenly coming down all around me. Feeling alone and unsure of what to do, I called my best friend, and he came to be with me while I tried to figure out what to do next. Over the next several days, checks bounced and were sent back because of insufficient funds, and I had no money because the paycheck that I had just received and put into the bank my wife took along with everything else. I had no money to put gas in my car, pay bills, or even buy food.

MARRIAGE RELATIONSHIPS STRAINED

After my wife left, I started to think maybe it was my fault she cheated on me. My tendency to blame myself because of poor self-esteem kicked in and I felt responsible somehow for her being with another man. Being abandoned by my Father when I was very young, those same feelings came rushing back when my wife left. Not wanting to be alone, I forgot all about her infidelity and became desperate to apologize to her and make things right so she would come back to me. Feeling bad for what had happened, I went to see the bishop. I told him about the argument and that I slapped my wife and that I had viewed porn on our computer. Feeling remorseful for my mistakes, I was willing to do whatever the bishop asked of me. He counseled me on what I needed to do to repent and then told me he would assist in any way he could.

When my wife returned from her parents, she would not allow me to talk to or call her. She stayed in an undisclosed place and would mail me letters from a post office box address. She later said she was with a female coworker, but I never did find out exactly where she stayed for the six months we were apart. She also met with our bishop and told him she needed time apart to decide what she would do. During this time, I told the bishop I could not cover my electric bill or pay for groceries because she had taken all our money. The bishop helped me with the bills and sent me to the bishop's storehouse to get food for the next month until I could get another paycheck and put money in my account.

After she spoke with the bishop, my wife sent me a letter outlining what expenses I would be responsible for with the house and her terms for communication going forward. I could only communicate through letters, so I wrote her letters and apologized for all my mistakes. I was sorry for hurting her and for all that had happened. In her letters, she focused on all she felt I had done wrong and the things I needed to fix about myself. There was no apology for her affair, for lying to me, for taking all our money, or for the hurt she caused. Instead, she outlined things she needed to see from me before considering even going to counseling. She needed me to prove myself to her. Feeling responsible for what had happened, I did not question her or her demands. Instead, I tried my best to do all she asked of me, but it never seemed to be enough. She made it clear in all her letters that any mistakes by me, and the marriage was over. She also told me her parents did not want her to be with me anymore, so again I felt rejected and felt she was going to leave me like everyone else did eventually.

Once I had begun the repentance process, the Lord began to open doors for me at work. I was asked to take another position that paid me more so I could cover the bills I was now responsible for at home. Then, after a few months, I moved into a managerial position and received another pay increase. I stopped viewing pornography, went to church each week, and was doing all I could to show my wife I was sincere about working things out.

As time passed, people at my job heard about what my wife was doing and felt sorry for me. Many times, I came to work in tears from letters I would receive and felt alone, abandoned, and vulnerable. Needing someone to talk with, I began to share with some of them what had happened. Thinking they would all be on her side after hearing about me slapping her and the porn viewing, I was surprised to hear they thought she was manipulating me because of the affair that I presumed she was having. My habit of feeling responsible for everything was a product of my self-esteem. After speaking to others, including my best friend, I thought maybe I was not totally at fault for all that had happened. I had made mistakes, but they did not justify what she had done in return. Talking to other people made me think about things in a different light, and I began to think that my wife was using what happened to take the focus off her affair.

Almost five months had passed since my wife left, and I was beginning to be okay with her being gone. She was still writing letters and demanding that I do certain things, but I was beginning to feel like it was a waste of time. So, I stopped responding to her letters. Then she called me and said she was ready to go to counseling. She lost control of me, and she panicked. Once I agreed to go, she told me it would be good for us to work on my issues together. She just assumed she had no issues and that all our problems were because of me. Interestingly, after she picked the therapist and had a few sessions with him, she decided she did not like him. He seemed to focus too much on her, and she said it was because he was a man. She then picked out a female and the same thing happened. I learned from the sessions we had that there were many issues on both sides; however, I was the only one willing to admit my mistakes and express a willingness to work on them.

My wife also revealed a few other revelations that I did not know about that made it hard for me to be intimate with her or even stay in the relationship. One of those revelations was that she had been fantasizing about my best friend and other celebrities during intimacy, making it hard for me to engage in intimacy moving forward. Through the counseling sessions, I found out she had been hiding much more from me than I even realized. Almost the entire time we were apart, I had done all in my power to convince her I wanted to change and fix things; however, after going to counseling, I realized she was not going to change. Instead, she insisted the problems were all mine. Both therapists made it clear she must make changes to have a healthy relationship moving forward; however, she would not admit her faults and instead maintained I was to blame for our problems.

COUNSELING UNSUCCESSFUL

While we were in marriage counseling, a woman at work asked me to spend time with her. I declined her advances and wanted to give my marriage and counseling a chance. But after going to counseling and hearing what my wife had to say, I found myself wondering why I was even trying anymore. She denied any role in anything that happened between us. She would not acknowledge her affair, not acknowledge that it even happened, and would not take any blame for her behavior and all that went wrong with us.

After going to several sessions and opening up and accepting responsibility for my mistakes and her denying she made any mistakes, I mentally checked out. It was clear to me that she did not appreciate or acknowledge all I had done over the past six months. She was not willing to open up or work on the issues. I wondered how someone could love or care for someone and treat them like she treated me. I concluded that she did not care about me enough to work on fixing our problems. She instead continued to blame me for our problems and continued her efforts to control and manipulate me by declaring I was the reason for all that was wrong between us. My Stepfather also liked to blame me for the issues my wife and I had. Whenever that happened, I shut down. This is when the self-defense mechanisms I learned in my youth kicked in, and I did not care anymore because that way it did not hurt as much. No one cared about me, so why should I care about them or how they felt? Counseling had not helped, and now I did not care anymore.

In this angry and resentful state, I went to work, and again, the woman from work asked me if I wanted to see a movie. This time I said "Yes." Going out with her, I knew, would not lead to good outcomes, but I did not care. It was not right for me to do, and I knew that, but at the time, I felt I had tried to do all the right things, and where did that get me? I was vulnerable and alone, and I was also angry and hurt and decided I was tired of not getting what I needed. This other woman gave me what my wife would not—affection and reassurance that I was a good person and that I was wanted. I desperately needed this, which I had not had in a long time.

That same week, my wife decided to return to the house, and I agreed to have her back. It was not because I was happy to have her there; I could not explain why she could not come home. But I had already checked out of the relationship mentally and decided that I did not need to tell her I was seeing this other woman because she had done the same thing to me. Divorce was not an option at that time because of my financial situation and the stigma of being divorced. Also, I did not want to leave like my Father did to my family. My Stepfather always told me I would be like my Father in that respect, and I would not give him the satisfaction of being right.

This began a very dark time that would last many years. Seeing this other woman I worked with required me to do everything my wife and others had done to me, and now I was doing it to her. This led to lying about where I was going and what I was doing, to spend time with this other woman. Also, I stopped going to church and lost my desire to fix my relationship with my wife. I started viewing porn again and watching inappropriate movies. Nothing seemed off limits anymore as I completely lost control of my life and any standards I previously had. I never should have agreed to see my coworker or have a relationship with her, but I did because she gave me all the things I did not get at home and did not try to manipulate or control me.

This stalemate continued until my wife suddenly suggested we have a baby. In our situation, I told her I did not think it would be a good idea. She had an appointment coming up to see her doctor and she agreed she would renew her birth control because I would not agree to having a child at that time. However, three months later she informed me that she was pregnant. Because we very rarely, if ever, were intimate, I knew exactly when it happened because she had initiated the encounter while I was half asleep. It was the only time we had been intimate in that time frame. Confused, I asked her how the one time we had been intimate in the last three months might have resulted in her getting pregnant while still on birth control. Then she told me what I had suspected from the start. She had decided on her own to stop taking birth control after seeing the doctor three months previously. Then, the only time we had been intimate in the past three months, she initiated intimacy because she wanted to get pregnant and knew exactly when to make that happen. It was a mixed bag of emotions I felt as she admitted what she had done.

I was angry that she lied and then used me to get pregnant knowing how I felt about it at the time and because our relationship was not good. But then I became excited about being a Father. Having a child was always something I had wanted, but not under the current circumstances. In my mind, I knew our relationship would never last, especially when I told her I had been seeing someone for a while now.

Frustrated at the reality that we would be parents to a child together, I embraced it because there was no turning back now. Once I found out my wife was pregnant, I told the woman I worked with that we needed to stop seeing one another. I did not want to have a relationship like my parents and wanted to try to improve our relationship by not being with another person. I wanted our focus to be on getting ready for the new baby. My coworker was upset, but she agreed to stop seeing me and my focus changed toward being there for my wife and child.

NEW DAUGHTER BORN

I tried hard to try to make things work after I found out my wife was pregnant. I went with her to doctors' appointments and a birthing class and tried to focus on being a good Father in every way. The past hurts and problems, however, were still there; and my wife focused more on having the baby and becoming a Mom than working on those issues with me.

As the time for the baby arrived, we went to the hospital because the contractions were getting more painful and frequent. As she was getting checked out by the doctor, her water broke and she was admitted to the labor and delivery floor. After getting an epidural and a heart rate monitor on to track the heart rate of the baby, we relaxed in the room to watch a movie until she was ready to deliver. I will never forget when the nurse came to check on her and discovered the baby was already coming out! She once called for the doctor, who told her not to push anymore until she arrived. From there it was only a few minutes before our child was born. She was beautiful and healthy. I was so happy to be a Father and called the family to share the news. Though my relationship with my wife was not good, being a Father was something I always wanted to be, and I was so glad to have our daughter.

After arriving home, my wife made plans to take the baby to visit her parents. Knowing how her parents felt about me, I decided it would be best to stay home and not try to go with her. That was another dividing issue in our relationship because I no longer felt welcome at their home. Of course, my wife never told them why our argument led to our separation, or what her role was in that situation. She told them her side of the story and that I slapped her, and they suggested we get divorced.

While she was gone, my friend came in from out of town to spend time with me. We were in failing relationships and felt the same about the future. I knew my relationship with my wife was not going to last. I knew what I had done would become known eventually because I would tell her when I was ready. But with the baby coming, I did not want to make things more complicated until things settled down after the baby was born. I felt like my wife ambushed me by not telling me she was getting off birth control, I felt like this was her way of trapping me into staying in the relationship. She knew after going to counseling how I felt about how she treated me, and her refusal to accept responsibility for what the counselors told her she needed to work on only solidified my feelings that things would not work out with her. She had cheated on me, denied it, and refused to talk about it. She lied about it for six months, and only when confronted did she admit her lies. Then she took all of our money, canceled all our credit cards, filed a restraining order against me, and controlled every aspect of my life for the next six months through manipulation and fear. She knew of my abandonment issues because of my childhood trauma and used that against me to control me and get me to do what she wanted. Also, she lived in an undisclosed location and did not let me know where or with whom she was staying. I was not even allowed to call her to talk.

Looking back I am embarrassed that I allowed her to control me the way she did. She completely turned everything that happened into my fault and focused entirely on what she felt I needed to fix, ignoring entirely her infidelity and lies that she had been caught in that started the entire fight that night. It was amazing how quickly she agreed to try to work things out when I stopped doing as she wanted me to do. But I had already made up my mind after counseling that the relationship was not salvageable. I was willing and ready to work on our problems and the things I needed to change. But she refused to see a need to change anything she did and instead blamed the counselors, saying they were wrong, too. She was in denial, and I could see that now that I had time away from her.

One of the issues that came up during counseling was my wife's attraction to my best friend. She admitted during counseling that she fantasized about him and other celebrity men during intimacy. This hurt me more than I led on at the time, but I felt deeply hurt and betrayed at hearing this. My best friend and I had known one another since I had been married. We had trips together and had him and his wife visit our house often. From day one, my wife had secretly been thinking about him and others during our intimate times together, so when he came to visit, I shared that with him and asked him if anything ever happened between them. He said no and was repulsed by the suggestion. But this angered him also, and we both decided we did not care anymore and would do what we wanted to do that weekend. After we talked, we invited some girls over to the house and they spent the night with us. I did not even try to hide my disdain anymore and left the evidence in the bedroom where I knew my wife would find it when she arrived home. It was a terrible thing to do, and I regret doing it now. At the time, I was angry and hurt and wanted to send her a message that if she could cheat on me, I could cheat on her, too. The message was received, and she found what had been left of that weekend. She called me at work to tell me my bags were packed and waiting for me when I got home that night.

When I arrived, I could not enter the house except to get my bags and leave. I had no place to go and could not afford a hotel, so I called the woman I had become friends with from work and asked to stay with her. During this time, I began to feel guilty for leaving my daughter and not being there for her. I did not want her to grow up without her Dad, and I did not want to have what my Stepfather said about me be true. Despite not wanting to be with my wife, I did want to be with my daughter, so I decided to try to go home. However, all my attempts to talk or work with my wife failed. She was determined to keep me away. As a result, I became desperate and did something that I will always regret doing—lying to my family about having a terminal medical issue. I cannot explain why I was willing to go to the extent I did to get back home. The only thing I can say is that it took me going to that extreme to get my wife to agree to have me back. But once my family insisted on speaking to my doctor, who did not exist, the game was over, and I had to admit I made the whole thing up. The disappointment and hurt my family felt was all too real, and the shame and embarrassment I felt was, too. After that, I pulled away from everyone and began to rely on those I worked with to talk to and to spend time with. I was going to be divorced and now needed to figure out where I would live and what I needed to do moving forward to ensure I was a part of my daughter's life.

SINGLE AGAIN

The transition to being single again was not an easy one. After failing in my marriage and leaving my daughter without her Father, I felt overwhelmed with sorrow and remorse for my mistakes that contributed to the breakup. I never wanted to be like my Father in that respect, but now I was just like him. This took a huge toll on my self-esteem, which was already poor because of past experiences. That left me vulnerable to whatever I could do to alleviate the pain, and I did so at that time in ways that were not healthy or appropriate.

There were also new challenges with my now ex-wife when it came to visiting my daughter, finalizing our divorce, and dealing with the manipulative and deceptive behaviors that she engaged in following our separation. Unfortunately, she also took advantage of my parents during this time as they offered to help us. Being taken advantage of by my ex-wife surprised my parents because they had yet to experience that with her. When I explained to my parents why we were divorcing, I told them I made some big mistakes but decided not to share many of the things that my wife had done. I feared that by sharing some of the things she did, my family would choose not to associate with her or at least distance themselves from her, as often happens in a divorce. When my parents told their respective families what had happened between them, my Dad's family stopped speaking to us. Not wanting to alienate my family from my daughter and ex-wife, I refrained from sharing the details of our breakup. To me, it was not worth sharing what my ex-wife had done and risk hurting her and my daughter's relationship with my family members. For many years after, I let people think it was mainly my fault for how our relationship ended, but I was only telling my part of the story. What my wife did remained mostly a secret until now.

Because of my hesitancy to paint a negative picture of my former spouse, once we were divorced, my family was surprised to see the things she was doing, not knowing these were the things she had been doing all along. Some were aware that my ex-wife tended to be dishonest, manipulative, and controlling; but these behaviors had progressively gotten worse after we separated.

DIVORCE CHALLENGES

My Mother witnessed this manipulation as we settled a financial matter that had been agreed to in our divorce papers. She was in town after our house sold and was with me at my ex-wife's apartment to pick up my portion of the money already agreed to from the sale. However, when it came time to write the check to me, my ex-wife decided that because I no longer needed certain household items at my new place, she was changing what we had already agreed to in the divorce decree. She wrote me a check for hundreds of dollars less than I was owed. When I disagreed and reminded her of our previous agreement, she told me I either took what she gave me or nothing. My wife knew she had the upper hand because the money was in her account. Rather than fight a losing battle, I relented and took the amount she would give me. My Mother was shocked to see her act so dishonestly, but this was not unusual to me—just more of the same behavior I had dealt with since I had met her. Sadly, this was how things would go for us for many years to come—my ex-wife trying to take advantage of me or manipulating me to get the things she wanted. I accepted it to keep the peace so my daughter did not constantly have to fight and squabble over money and other issues. My parents did that to one another, and I swore I would not do that to my daughter. I wanted to spare her the hurt and pain it would cause to see us fighting and talking badly about one another.

Not long after that experience with my Mom, my ex-wife was also dishonest with my Stepfather to get money from him. This happened when my daughter was just a couple of years old and needed tubes put in her ears to help them drain an infection. According to our divorce decree, we were each to pay half of the medical expenses, which I did as soon as the invoice was received. However, when my Stepfather called my ex-wife to see how she was doing, she told him I had not paid my part of the medical expenses and that she had to pay the entire amount on her own. However, the amount she told him I owed was double the actual bill. My Stepfather, rather than confirming this with me, paid her the entire amount that she claimed was owed. Then he called me upset that I had not paid my part of the bill. After explaining what my ex-wife had told him, I was frustrated and upset! She not only lied about me not paying my part of the bill but also told him the bill was twice the amount it was and allowed him to pay the entire bill! Not only had I paid all I had to pay the previous month, but I also had checks and bank statements as proof.

Angry at the lies and stories being told by her, I took matters into my own hands bought a small tape recorder, and went over to my ex-wife's apartment to confront her about the lies she told my Step-father. While there, she admitted that she had lied to my Stepfather when she claimed I had not paid my portion of the medical expenses and lied when she claimed the bill was twice what it was. When I asked her why she would do that, she said he would pay her whatever the bill was, so why not?

Disappointed and angry, I left having all the evidence I needed and called my Stepfather and Mother and played the tape for them over the phone. Then I sent copies of bank statements detailing my payments to my ex-wife that refuted her claims I had not paid my part. My Stepfather did not say anything when I played the tapes and never apologized for accusing me of being delinquent. But he always assumed I was the only one in the wrong in my marriage, so that was not surprising. After these experiences, however, I realized I had to protect myself going forward with my former spouse, never knowing when she would lie and put me in situations where I had to prove that what she was saying was false. This was nothing new, growing up with a Stepfather who never believed in me. It would also prove a wise strategy with her because she continued to manipulate and lie going forward.

Despite all that happened and would happen between my ex-wife and me, my goal was always to try to have the best relationship I could with her for my daughter's sake. Over the years since, I have often had to make compromises that were not fair or right to make the relationship work;

however, by doing so, my daughter had both parents in her life, which was worth it to me.

After settling into my townhouse and making new friends, I began to spend more time with people from work. Knowing I had recently been divorced, they invited me to eat and socialize after work. While married, I had not spent much time with people I worked with outside of the office, but now I felt I needed to get out of the house, so I agreed to go out with them. Up to this time in my life, I had never had alcohol and had not seen anything good come from drinking, so I stayed away from it. But I quickly learned that drinking was a very normal thing to all my coworkers. One of the first evenings, I decided to go out with my coworkers, our boss took us out to a sports bar and he ordered a pitcher of beer for the table. Everyone poured a glass, including me because I did not want to be the odd one out. I was also curious about what was so great about drinking. After I drank the beer, I just felt silly and lightheaded. I was fortunate that I did not enjoy drinking like many of my coworkers did. Several of them drank excessively and got into trouble at work outings, trouble in their relationships, and trouble with their health by getting addicted to the habit. I drank to fit in socially and never kept any alcohol in my house to drink on my own.

Being single again and not actively going to church, I realized quickly that the people I was choosing to be around loved to drink. In fact when I decided to get online and meet someone from a dating website, which at that time was the new way to meet people, most suggested meeting first for drinks. You were weird if you did not drink, so I obliged but never really enjoyed it. But by not going to church at that time and knowing no self-respecting woman who belonged to the church would date me in my current state, I resorted to dating those who would accept me as I was at that time, and that left me with lower standards to meet those of this new world.

SHORT REMARRIAGE

Lonely and wanting someone to talk to and spend time with, I found a woman with whom I connected. She had two small children, which

I was not sure about, but she seemed nice. I was drawn to her because I felt sorry for her. After hearing her sad story, I thought I could help her, and we started spending time together. After a brief period, I started coming over after the kids went to bed because our time was limited with her having two young children. Eventually, I started spending the night on occasion and crossing that line is where the problems began. Her ex-husband found out I had stayed the night and got upset because of the poor example she and I were setting for the children. Though we were discreet, one morning, the kids still saw me leaving, and that is how her ex-husband found out. Our poor judgment led to threats for custody and eventually a court hearing about her ex-husband seeking full custody of the children.

Feeling partially responsible for her situation and getting pressure from her family to fix it, we decided to get married to alleviate the problem. So, we went to the county courthouse and were married. It was not for love but out of a sense of duty because I cared for her and did not want her to lose her children. Our marriage was short-lived and only lasted about six months before she approached me and said she was leaving. It had given her time to look for a house, and I had helped her get out of debt. She was ready to move on and I did not stop her, knowing it was for the best. Embarrassed and ashamed of the choices I was making, I never told anyone in my family that I had married her, and it was over so quickly I never had to. After she left, I never spoke to her again except to receive money payments I had given her and that she was required to pay back as a condition of the divorce.

SINGLE YET AGAIN

After that relationship ended, I joined a gym nearby and began hanging out with men I worked with because I needed time before I dated again. Many men would go out almost every night during the week to dance, drink, and carouse with random women. This was out of my comfort zone because I had never been one to go to clubs or places to dance. However, they kept asking me, so I finally agreed. One convinced me to come and meet girls and have fun and dance because, unlike dating, no expectations were met this way. After getting hurt over and over, I just wanted fun without the pressure of a relationship and started going with them to these clubs and bars.

Then, after making many bad decisions, even worse decisions followed. One of the bad choices was to go to the Super Bowl in Detroit. The company I worked for provided the equipment and furniture used by the teams and the NFL during Super Bowl week. My company flew a handful of us to Detroit to help set up and take down when the game ended. While there, we stayed in a rented house and had a suburban to drive around town. Going with the other men, I was at their mercy to do what they wanted. So naturally on the first night, while driving for a place to eat, we stopped at what appeared to be a sports bar. However, when we walked in, we were asked to pay a ten-dollar cover fee for what we thought was live music. Once we paid the fee, we realized we had found a strip club instead—and not just any strip club. It was an all-black strip club, and being in Detroit and all of us being White, it caused some major tension when we walked in. Afraid to turn around and leave, we quickly sat down and ordered some drinks. After gulping them down and leaving hefty tips, we hurried out while people stared at us.

Feeling lucky to get out of the strip club without getting killed, we decided to try our luck at another place that the door attendant at the strip club suggested. Of course, it was another strip club, but a mixed crowd this time. This was the first time I had ever been to a strip club in my life. The rest of the week went pretty much the same way. After we returned, I went to another strip club with a few coworkers. However, I decided that was not the lifestyle I wanted and stopped going with them. This was one of those moments where I realized if I were meeting and dating people with low standards and morals, I would never find a woman I could trust or with whom I could fall in love. Sadly, that was what I wanted more than anything else—someone I could love, trust, and be best friends with. After growing up around girls who went to church and knowing that was where I would find the kind of woman I was looking for, I knew I needed to return to church to find a woman with exacting standards. But I hesitated because I would have to admit my faults and repent. I was ashamed and embarrassed to do so. So I told myself I would, but just not yet.

Instead of attending church, I went back to online dating to meet someone. In time, I ended up meeting a woman I liked. We got along well and started dating. Before long, I was spending more time at her house than mine, and because it was closer to where I worked, I started sleeping there to make my morning commute easier. After a while, she told me to move some things to her house because I was always there. Then she approached me about renting my townhouse to her mom and her boyfriend. Because I was rarely there anyway, I agreed to let them stay there and pay me what was owed on the mortgage. This arrangement worked well for a few months and then the mom and boyfriend started having problems paying the rent.

Around the same time, I discovered some things about the woman with whom I shared the house. What I found did not make sense. She said she had no children, but I found out she had one in Florida whom she was not allowed to see. I did not know the reason for her being denied visitation, but I was uncomfortable finding out that she lied about having a child. She also hid from me that she had recently filed for bankruptcy. She had favored my staying there from the beginning and now I knew why. She wanted me to help her pay for things and now I was trapped. When I asked her about the things I had stumbled upon, she was not honest, which immediately alerted me. Being hesitant to get too close to anyone already, I distanced myself from her once the lies started and started looking for a way out of the relationship. I informed her mom that she and her boyfriend needed to look for another place, and I told the woman I was staying with that I was uncomfortable with what she told me. In the meantime, I began to get online again to talk to other women and date.

Though I was still living with this other woman, the relationship was over as far as I was concerned. But as I began to date and see other people, the woman I was living with became upset after she saw another woman's text on my phone. Though things were over, she still went into a rage and started throwing my belongings onto the front lawn. There was no talking to her at that point, so I just started packing my car and prepared to leave. But as I tried to go upstairs to get the last few things I needed, she confronted me on the stairs and would not let me pass. She yelled at me, then started hitting me and flailing her arms. I blocked her arms and moved past her. But she did not stop hitting me as I got my things and tried to leave. She then called the police and told them I had assaulted her, which I had not. The police arrived, spoke to us separately, and checked her out to see if she had been hurt or had any injuries. She did not, and the police allowed me to leave after getting the rest of my things.

I thought after I left that would be the end of it, but sadly I received a summons to court not long after I moved out claiming I assaulted the woman with whom I was living. I found out she had contacted my ex-wife who told her I had slapped her, and so both she and my ex-wife were at the hearing when I arrived. I did not have an attorney because I thought it was ridiculous that she would claim I did anything to her as we stood before the judge. When the judge asked the woman what happened, she claimed I somehow assaulted her and had pictures to prove it. The judge asked me if I objected to allowing her to show the pictures; with nothing to hide, I agreed. The pictures showed someone with bruises, but there was no way to determine when the pictures were taken and who the person was in many of the pictures. I knew I had not done anything to her and had not put my hands on her at all, other than to protect myself and to stop her from hitting me. The judge also questioned their legitimacy and ultimately threw out the case because her story did not match what I told her or the police report of the incident. My ex-wife and her new husband were never called to testify about anything but were behind us watching the spectacle. Without saying a word to my ex-wife after the proceedings ended, I left and went home. The most surprising part of that experience of going to court to resolve the frivolous case was that my ex-wife was involved. I was disappointed and frustrated that she would side with this woman whom she knew nothing about and do so at the threat of my going to jail. It is one thing to be upset about a breakup, but it is quite another to back up another's claim that I did someone harm, especially at the threat of my going to jail and ruining my life with no evidence. I did not do anything wrong. Though I made mistakes with my first wife, she knew me better than that. But whatever her reasons were, she would continue to side with whomever it was who would level a claim against me. This would not be the only time she appeared in court on the opposite side to oppose me and ultimately see me put in prison for crimes I did not commit.

PIVOTAL TIME IN LIFE

Describing this pivotal time in my life, it is important to understand where I came from before moving into this next chapter. I had been married twice—once because I just wanted to be married, and the other time because I felt it was the right thing to do. Neither time was for love. Not since high school had I been able to trust someone completely about their past, or situations involving other men. There were always things that came out contrary to what they told me. So, when it came to dating, I was skeptical of what people told me and did not trust that anyone would be honest with me. I was hesitant to share things about myself. This led to most of my relationships with women being superficial—not in a physical way but emotionally. This allowed me to avoid talking about or sharing personal things that required me to trust them. This enabled me to avoid talking about myself or sharing personal things about myself. I could keep people at arm's length and avoid getting too emotionally involved.

After my initial divorce, I remained inactive in the church. However, throughout this very challenging time, I never wavered in my testimony of the church's truthfulness. Nevertheless, I was not strong enough to admit I was a member because the people I associated with mocked those who did. Instead, I denied I was a member to those who would ask, being tired of the comments and questions that would follow. In my heart, I knew what was right, even though I was struggling to live as I knew I should.

After the experiences I had been through, I was skeptical of ever having a real relationship. Dating and meeting people were now happening mostly through internet dating but having so many options online made it hard to find someone who was not seeing multiple people simultaneously. With the ease of having hundreds of options at the touch of a button, many people struggled to settle on just one person. This led to dating multiple people, who then lied to those they saw because no one wanted to date someone dating five other people simultaneously. This was the case for me, too. I found it hard not to talk to many people simultaneously and focus on just one person. My experience was that internet dating was a tool to meet and have fun with people but not to find someone with whom to settle down. At least that was until I met someone who was not like all the other people I met online. She was different from the rest; for the first time, I was genuinely interested in her and drawn to her. I thought this was a woman I could see myself being with permanently.

DATING A PROMISING WOMAN

We met on a dating site I tried for a month, and I did not find her until the last day before my membership expired. She was the last person I sent a message to because something about her caught my eye and my interest right away. She was beautiful, smart, and focused on other people. A comment she made on her profile caught my eye. She said, "Life is better shared." I felt the same way and decided I needed to get to know this woman.

We messaged back and forth and then spoke on the phone several times. The conversations were easy and fun, and I was increasingly excited to meet her. When we started talking on the phone, she said she was out of town visiting family, so we decided to meet as soon as she arrived home—literally at the airport! I still remember the first moment I saw her coming up the escalator when she turned and looked at me and smiled. I could not take my eyes off her while waiting for her luggage. Then on our date, it seemed we had been together already for years. We got along so well, and it was easy to like her.

We talked for hours on the first few dates because I wanted to know everything about her. When she spoke about her parents and family, she described a life I had never experienced but always envied in others—parents who loved each other and were still in love after years of marriage. They were not religious but did not drink or smoke were faithful to each other, and taught their children to work hard, manage their money, and take pride in what they did. These were all things I admired and respected. She was the first woman since my high school girlfriend with whom I was intrigued. I had never felt that way about anyone I had been with before. This led to my wanting to be with her whenever I could. With her, nothing was lacking, and she seemed like the woman I had always been waiting for and finally found. Not being one to fall quickly because of my hesitancy to give my heart to another, I was surprised at how quickly I lowered my defenses and allowed myself to start falling for this amazing woman.

But just as I fell hard and fast for this woman, something backed up my defenses. She received an expensive bouquet from someone shortly after returning from her trip. Curious, I asked her who had sent the flowers, and she told me her mom had sent them. When she told me that, I sensed she was not being honest with me and got a sinking feeling in my stomach. Eventually, I learned she had a boyfriend back home and had been to see him while talking to me on the phone. I did not see that one coming at all, and it sent my heart and head reeling when I realized she had hidden that from me and then lied about it. The flowers, it turned out, were from this man and not her mother. She had told me she was not seeing anyone when we talked; and I had stopped seeing the people I had been dating, except her. After she misled me about this other man, I felt myself retreat from her emotionally and again put up the defenses around my heart. Though I was infatuated with this amazing woman, this triggered my self-defense mechanisms learned in my youth.

The saddest part for me was that I had opened up to this woman unlike any other woman I had ever dated since high school, and she hurt me deeply with this lie. Although she had been different from the rest, and I felt drawn to her in ways I had never experienced, I fell back into my old ways once that trust was broken. I held things back and protected myself because I feared getting my heart broken again. Finding out about another man when first dating someone might not have been so devastating for someone else. But all my life, the people who were supposed to protect and love me were the ones who lied or broke their promises to me. My dating experiences were not any better. My ex-wife lied while we were dating and then later in our marriage, she cheated on me. In the age of internet dating, most of the women who had told me I was the only man they were seeing or talking to were dating multiple people. So, to find out this new woman for whom I was falling fast had another man she was seeing was devastating to me. The part that hurt the most was that she was not truthful about him when I asked her, and that hurt me more than I ever admitted at that time.

This course reversal caused issues for us from this point forward. Early on I told her everything and was completely honest with her. I ended all other relationships or associations with other women and showed her the texts and the women's responses to my texts—ending associations to build complete trust. I desperately wanted that in a relationship because I had never had it before. She told me she wanted the same things I wanted and I believed her. So, I opened up to her and shared things with her; then when I realized she was not sharing everything with me, I felt cheated and stupid. Without consciously doing it, I became fearful of her wanting the other man, or deciding she did not want to date me anymore. It had happened to me many times before, so it was my natural reaction to her telling me things that were not true.

After this initial loss of trust, I began questioning other things she told me. She revealed things about other men whom she knew that intensified my distrust. These men were doctors and lawyers—successful in their careers and friendly with her and her friends. I had not finished college, had a mediocre job, and began to question why she would ever want to be with me in the first place. Not having high self-esteem, I was always worried that this beautiful woman would wake up one day and realize I was not worth the effort and leave me like everyone else had. I considered her way out of my league, and deep down, I worried she felt that way, too. I feared it was just a matter of time before she would tell me it would not work out for us and I would be alone again.

Another factor in all of this was the conditional love I experienced from my Stepfather throughout my teenage years. If I did as he wanted or expected, he supported me and showed forth some affection. However, if I did anything he did not approve of, or behaved in a way that he disagreed with, I was kicked out of the house, abandoned, and disowned.

This led to fears of conditional love in my dating relationships. The most distressing fear I had throughout my life was losing those I loved, or them abandoning me. And all my life the things I did and said seemed to directly affect and correspond to whether people stayed in my life or left. So, naturally, I was very scared that anything I did or said might make or break things with those I loved. When I made mistakes, the last thing I wanted to do was make them known to people I cared about for fear they would leave me, too.

Now that I questioned whether I could trust my new girlfriend, I began to hold back anything that made me look bad. To show my best side, I only shared those things that painted me in the most favorable light and left out things I did wrong or thought she might not like. This was not something I had done with other people I dated, mostly because I did not care what they thought of me. This woman was different; how she felt about me was everything to me. So, not feeling I could trust her and wondering what other secrets she might have, I kept most of my thoughts to myself.

Also, other things made me more hesitant to open up to her. She drank much more than I did; I was not always comfortable with that. Her friends did also, and some of her friends were promiscuous and dishonest in many ways. This made me wonder if my girlfriend was like them as well. After the past several years of dating people who drank, went to bars, and were like those of her friends I had met, I wondered if she was hiding that side of her from me—like I was hiding the bad things from her. None of the people I had met who lived that lifestyle were people I could see myself with long-term. That was not the lifestyle I wanted for me or any children I still wanted to have. Though I was not active in the church then, a part of me always knew that one day I would go back because I knew in my heart it was true. So, finding someone who did not drink, smoke, or want to live a lifestyle that would be opposite to my beliefs was important to me.

This new woman did like to drink but was not like her friends in most respects. She came from a family where her parents loved and were committed to each other. They were not part of any religious affiliation and did not have a set standard to live by. Those without a religious background tended to do whatever they wanted to do. Morals and integrity tend to come from religious teachings; without that foundation, often, anything goes wrong. But my girlfriend's family, they were part of that small group who were not religious but still taught their children to have high standards and not to indulge in things that would be harmful to them or interfere in their relationships. Although there were some things I was not comfortable with, there was so much more I loved about her that I decided the other things I could accept.

We continued to date; and after a visit to her family, the topic of getting married came up. Her parents suggested we not wait long if we wanted to be together. Though I had doubts and fears, I wanted to be with her. She was the best thing ever to happen to me, and I did not want to lose her. So, I decided to get a ring while on vacation with my family. I called her parents and asked her father for her hand in marriage. They were happy for us, and I was excited to get home to ask her to marry me. Being anxious and lacking the patience to set up any elaborate setup, I asked her to marry me in her apartment one evening shortly after I returned home from vacation. She said "Yes," and we immediately began planning our wedding.

When I called my Mom to tell her about my fiancé, she seemed happy that I found someone I truly wanted to be with. Mom and my sister were very supportive of the marriage. My Stepfather claimed he had a conference to attend and could not come to the wedding, but I knew the real reason he did not come. He would not support me marrying someone outside of our faith. Without ever meeting her or her family, he opposed it and then lied about having a conference to attend. His conditional love and non-acceptance were to be expected.

When our wedding day came, I was excited to marry a woman I truly cared for and wanted to be with. She truly was a woman I thought was amazing. I was proud to be her husband and hoped she would be proud to be my wife. We had a backyard wedding with close friends and family at her parents' house. My sweet three-year-old daughter was our flower girl. My sister fixed her hair that day, and I will never forget her walking toward me tossing flowers and looking like a little angel. It was one of the best days of my life to that point. My beautiful bride and I danced and had a wonderful time at our wedding, and for that day, there was nowhere I would rather be and nobody else I would rather be with.

Chapter 9

Marriage and Addiction

BABY ON THE WAY

Despite the challenges and problems we experienced meeting our needs as spouses, we were overjoyed at the news my wife was pregnant with our first child. Being a father has been the greatest joy I have experienced. I made it a point to go to as many doctors' appointments with my wife as possible, started preparing the baby room, and helped my wife as her needs changed. I put in new crown molding for the baby's room, painted it various purple colors, and put together the crib and other furniture. I was proud of how it looked and often thought as I worked about what our little girl would look like and what she would grow up to be. It was a happy time and one for which we were both excited.

RELATIONSHIP CHANGING

During this time, I noticed other changes in my relationship with my wife. Most of these would be temporary, so I did not think much of them then. In hindsight, I realized things never were the same again. My wife's personality is one of being a perfectionist. She does everything well, with her whole heart, especially with work and children. She is very enthusiastic about these two things, and I admire and respect her. Our children are lucky to have a mother who is very attentive to their needs and loves them with her whole heart and soul.

To give her whole heart and soul to the children and to her work, our time and intimacy suffered by default. We would no longer sit down to talk and find out how the other person was doing. Our physical and emotional intimacy began to diminish. We spent less time going on dates and spending time together. My wife was entirely focused on our baby and her job, leaving her exhausted and unable to give much to me. In many ways it is understandable and to be expected. Our relationship had to change because our circumstances changed, and we had to adapt. Being a parent and navigating work and parental responsibilities required much effort and teamwork. We were good at helping each other and making it work in those areas; however, we struggled to care for each other's emotional and physical needs.

I often sat down and talked with my wife about how I felt and what I needed from her and invited her to share her needs and feelings with me. That was what I had been good at in marriage, being the communicator, at least to the extent of expressing basic wants and needs. I was not good about sharing my fears, insecurities, and mistakes; however, wants and needs I could share. Each time we had these talks, we would agree to help each other with the things we expressed and said we needed. Being a people pleaser, I would try hard to do exactly as she asked. That was one way to express my love and affection for her and vice versa. I also needed to follow through on things, so I did so for her. But this often was not reciprocated. She would agree to try, and then not follow through. This left me with feelings of hurt, anger, and disappointment—which translated into feeling unloved and unappreciated. I have always interpreted love by what a person does, not by what they say. So, empty promises and words are very hurtful to me.

NOT MEETING NEEDS

When I would express my feelings about the lack of follow-through, she became defensive and frustrated. She would say she was tired, had too much work to do, or just forgot. Whatever it was, I was left feeling like I was not a priority and that nothing I said was going to change that. Things that were important to me just were not that important to her. Her needs were different from mine. Rather than compromise and help one another to get our individual needs met, she neglected mine while I fulfilled hers. My requests were reasonable and considered our circumstances, yet she rarely made the effort. This left me frustrated and lonely.

When I met my wife, I stopped some of the bad habits I had picked up over the years because I wanted my relationship with her to be different than what I had in the past. I wanted to be faithful and true to her. In my heart and mind, I started that way; then after I found out my wife had not been honest with me about people she was seeing after we started dating, I felt betrayed and stupid for thinking it would be any different with her. In my life thus far, people just never seemed to be true to each other. Despite what I was trying to do, I felt like it just was not appreciated or given to me in return.

PAST SINS RESURFACE

Feeling frustrated and like circumstances would not change, I began to indulge again in past sins that were increasingly more difficult to ignore. With my wife getting up early to go to work, and up at night with the baby, I was left alone to watch movies, play games, or surf the computer. It was during this time I began to look at pornography again. I rationalized this to meet my needs, but it was selfish and wrong. It left me feeling bad about myself and feeling different toward my wife. I resented her more after I viewed it. I was angry with her indifference toward my needs and her lack of initiative to fulfill them. I was putting forth the effort, but she was not. So I continued to view it at night, and for a while, that pacified me. But as time passed, I craved physical touch and the attention I was no longer getting. Therefore, I began to visit dating websites to look at the profiles and pictures of the women. Initially, I had no intentions of speaking to or meeting them; but after a while, I decided to make a fake profile and begin talking to them. Again, I told myself I would message them and would not meet in person. But it was only a matter of time until that changed, too.

One thing I learned early on in life is that if you allow yourself to do things you should not, even innocently, it leads to worse things down the road. This was exactly how things progressed for me with my addiction to pornography. Returning to dating websites progressed into meeting people and violating my marital vows and commitments. I never intended to do the things I eventually did when I started; but once I allowed myself to do things I knew were dangerous or wrong, it led to worse and worse outcomes. That is the nature of addictions and mistakes, and it was true for me.

By this time, my wife was pregnant with our second child, and I was engaged in many things I should not have been. When the baby arrived and my wife was completely preoccupied with our girls, I was meeting people and spending time away from home. When I was home, I was the best Father I could be, but when it came to me personally, I was meeting my needs through other means outside of my relationship with my wife.

NEEDS CONTINUE

By lying and misrepresenting myself to those I met, I painted the picture of myself that I wished was my reality. I was honest about my hobbies, interests, and desires in my profile. But I was dishonest about my age, marital status, and education. For obvious reasons, I also had to choose a different name. This false persona allowed me to get some of the things I felt were lacking at home. The people I met found me attractive, flirted with me, and complimented me. Because of poor self-esteem that had been an issue for me most of my life, this filled a need I knew I had.

It is hard to admit these things even now. If I had been doing what I was supposed to be doing in my life during this period, I would not have felt a need or desire to have someone else tell me I was special or wanted. I was not going to church, not doing what I knew in my heart I should be doing, and allowing my past to be my excuse for making mistakes. I blamed others for my behavior and let past hurts justify not trying to fix things. Ultimately, this left me feeling worse than ever before and completely lost and unsure of how to get out of the mess I had created for myself.

As time passed, my wife came across things on the computer and my phone that confirmed her fears about what I was doing. She confronted me several times with what she found. I only admitted to viewing things on the computer because I could not deny them, but I denied having affairs. We had terrible arguments about these things, but I insisted that it was not the case and would stop doing those things for a while. To this day, I deeply regret my dishonesty and infidelity to my wife and for not seeking help for us to fix our relationship problems. We did go to counseling, but it came after I had already begun living a double life. I feared admitting these things would only lead to divorce. I loved many things about my wife and cared deeply for her, so I did not want our relationship to end. I also felt trapped by what I had done and could not see a way out. My children were also an important consideration. I did not want to leave my children because I loved them too much to be away from them. My choices had put me into a box I felt I could not get out of without destroying my life and the lives of those I loved. Times and opportunities I had to tell my wife the truth were never used; instead, I would eventually go back to the double life once things settled down.

The fundamental needs that all people have to feel loved, wanted, and needed are hard to ignore. When my wife was not filling those basic needs, I was tempted to fill those needs in unhealthy and destructive ways. My lack of a moral compass and disregard for others and their feelings were a result of many years of selfish decisions that took me away from the church and its standards. I became what I detested in others and hurt those I truly loved to be with people for whom I had no emotional attachment.

Having already been on dating websites, I was aware that people on those sites were notorious for misleading their profiles, putting up old pictures on their pages, and looking for people only to have fun or other immoral behavior. That had been the vast majority of people I met on those sites. So, when I felt lonely and unhappy in certain ways in my marriage, I used the site for things I knew others were looking for, too. I just wanted attention, physical gratification, and fulfilled desires. This also helped me avoid getting attached to or seriously involved with the people I met. I would see them only briefly and then move on to someone else to avoid personal attachments and feelings. Also, on the first few dates, people were fine to meet for drinks or food; after a few dates, they would want to come to your house or see where you lived. That was when I would end things. So this is how I managed to keep myself from any emotional attachment, and for several years that worked.

Then, I had an experience that should have made me stop my extra-marital affairs. I met a woman one evening for drinks, and afterward, it was late, and she asked to come with me back to my house. She was persistent about coming back with me, so I felt uncomfortable. I told her that was not an option, but she kept persisting. So I told her to follow me; I sped off when she got out of my car and into hers to follow me. I was not sure what else I could do and needed to get home. She got upset and claimed I had used her because we had fooled around. Consequently, she made a complaint to the police.

Not sure what to do, I contacted a lawyer the next day after receiving a call from the police. After meeting with the lawyer, I took a lie-detector test and passed. The results were given to the police. They decided not to pursue charges because my story and hers were almost identical. The entire situation was consensual and mutual, but I suspected my speeding off made her angry and resulted in her accusation. But the truth was I was married and could not let her come with me, so I put myself in a situation to be accused of something worse.

DIVINE INTERVENTION

I heard a divine voice intervene in my life for the second time. It happened just after my attorney informed me that the case against me had been dropped with no charges filed. I was relieved and was in my bathroom already thinking that next time I would be more careful when suddenly I heard a voice in my mind as clearly as if someone were standing right next to me speaking. The voice said, "If you don't stop, you will go to prison." At the time, even though I distinctly heard the voice, I ignored it. The Lord warned me that this kind of situation would happen again if I did not stop, but I ignored the voice and instead decided to take a break and wait a while before trying again. This should have awakened me to all the potential problems my behavior exposed me to; instead, I resolved to be more careful in the future. The Lord warned me, and I did not listen. I have only myself to blame for what would happen in the future.

Sadly, it only took a short time before that warning I had been given would come to fruition. By this time my wife had taken a new job and was traveling several days a week. With my wife being out of town for work, I had to drop off and pick up the children by six each day from daycare. My job at the time did not allow me to do that. So we decided I would quit my job and find something that would allow me to drop off and pick up the children from daycare. I did not get a job right away and instead kept our youngest at home with me while the oldest was in kindergarten. This was a horrible mistake as it left me with substantial free time that I filled up with talking to people online and on my phone. I also began going to the gym more often to work out and bought a new sports car.

SECOND THOUGHTS

During this time, I got off of online dating because I had second thoughts about what I was doing. I often wanted to tell my wife everything, and several times, I almost did. I was tired of the lies and the way I felt about myself. It was hard to look in the mirror sometimes because I knew what I was doing was wrong. Often, when I was by myself and my girls were in bed, I would cry on the couch because I knew I was not the Father I should be or the husband I needed to be. It scared me to think of the consequences of my choices. Somehow, I convinced myself God would not even forgive me for what I had done. It was a fearful feeling. But instead of facing my fears, I looked for someone to make me feel better. That is when I met a woman who made it convenient for me to see her.

This new woman worked a lot and did not like to communicate during the day—all things that were good for me. After seeing her for several months, I found out she had been lying to me about people she was seeing while also seeing me. It did not bother me because I was married and was not honest about my situation either. But I used that excuse to keep her at arms' length and keep things where I wanted them. Once the woman I saw began to push to get more serious, I began to back off and decided to spend less time with her. I made up reasons not to see her and even got back online to find someone else to spend time with because I had no desire to get emotionally involved.

That is when I started talking to another woman, and we set up a date for drinks. Later that night after we scheduled a date, she called me from a bar and asked me to come out and meet her and some friends. I could tell she was drunk and I declined. However, she continued to text me and even called and woke me up at 1:30 a.m. The next morning I texted her that I was having second thoughts about meeting because of what happened the night before. She claimed she did not remember what happened nor that she had called and texted me. Though I had proof on my phone, she still denied it, blaming her friends. I should have known better not to meet up with her after that early indication of who she was; but after she insisted that we still meet, I agreed to an afternoon date. I figured this would not go anywhere, so leaving after a few drinks would be easy.

WARNING COMES TRUE

When we met, she was better than I anticipated, so we talked all afternoon into the evening. She was supposed to go and watch her nephew that night but decided to change her plans and stay with me instead. I, too, had plans, so I texted the other woman I had plans with that I would be later than I thought and blamed it on work.

When we left the restaurant, I would follow this woman I met to her apartment to meet with her sister. However, after I got to my car and she had not texted me where to go, I thought maybe she had changed her mind. Then, as I was pulling out to leave, I saw her walking toward me. She asked if I could drive instead. I agreed and she gave me directions to a place where a family member was that she wanted me to meet.

Once we arrived at the place, we stayed in the car instead of going inside, and one thing led to another. A brief time later, we were intimate in the car. Not being in a condition to see her family members after that, we decided to go back to the restaurant so she could pick up her car and call it a night. She kissed me before she got out of the car, and I turned around and left as she went to get her car. Up to that point, everything had been good, and I thought it had been a good date.

She emailed me the next morning. I had a bad feeling about the questions she was asking me; therefore, I was careful not to say anything about the date that she could use to accuse me of something that did not happen or twist something that did happen into something bad or criminal. After being falsely accused once, I was afraid that this woman was also up to something based on the questions she was asking me. I suspected at that time that she had her friend look up my phone number, discovered my actual name, and learned that I was married. I used my cell number, so if someone simply googled my number, my actual name popped up. I am surprised that others did not do that, too. In this case, she had to because she did not have her phone. Then, I thought she was trying to set me up afterward to share the emails with my wife. That was my fear at the time. This led to me lying about what happened on the date, not because I did anything wrong as far as a crime, but because I feared her exposing me to my wife. Of course, those lies were then twisted and used against me later on to show I was hiding what happened because I had committed some heinous crime. That just was not true and not why I did it. The truth was I was afraid of her revealing my behavior to my wife and thought she was trying to set me up after discovering I was married. Satan is an expert at twisting the truth into something else entirely to destroy us, and he did, in this instance, destroy my life and marriage. Sadly, I allowed him to do so by being there with her and allowing things that never should have happened from the start.

LORD HUMBLES AND INTERVENES

Later that day, she went to the hospital and claimed she could not remember what happened on our date and that she had been assaulted. This initiated a sequence of events that, looking back, helped prepare me for a heavenly intervention that would change the course of my life. The Lord had to humble me and soften my heart, and he did so through extraordinary means.

The first means was a letter from the IRS indicating we owed back taxes from several years back. The initial amount was fairly small, and I ignored it because I thought it was not legitimate. I had never received something like that and thought it was a scam. But the letters kept coming. Before long, the amount had ballooned significantly, and I started to panic. We did not have the money to pay it, and they threatened to put a lien on our home and bank accounts. It was at this point I called my Father-in-law for advice and help. This man was one I respected, and I felt he would know what to do. When I spoke to him, he was reassuring and offered to help us pay the debt. Humbled by his willingness to help and generous offer, I was relieved, and his love and acceptance enormously impacted me. He did not get upset and instead offered help instead of criticizing. Being unaccustomed to that type of response affected me deeply. That softened my heart because he showed genuine love and concern.

The next means was an incident that had a significant impact on me. My former spouse decided to pursue additional child support she claimed I owed. Without talking to me first, she contacted the child services division and claimed I owed her thousands in back child support. She also told me I was to send my checks to them going forward, and they would send the money to her. She claimed to have the documentation to back up her claims, and that if I had any questions, contact them. When I asked how she produced the numbers she did, she said I had incorrectly been paying child support from the start. I was originally ordered to pay $500 per month based on my income then. That was to be the amount unless we went back to court to have it increased or decreased. However,

I had always paid twenty percent of my income, which was incorrect and excessive. So, in that respect, she was right. But because my income had increased, I had been overpaying for years. Even though there were times when I was unemployed or not working, I had always paid child support. In the end, after going through my records, I found I had overpaid by thousands of dollars and had the documentation to prove it.

When I contacted my ex-wife and explained that I had overpaid and had the documentation to prove it, she still insisted she had her records and would not drop the case. I hired a lawyer, and we ended up in arbitration. In our arbitration hearing, I discovered my ex-wife had no documents and presented no evidence of her claims. Instead, I provided bank records and check stubs substantiating all my overpayment claims in the thousands. My ex-wife was forced to lower the monthly payments I owed her to repay me for the money she had been overpaid for years. The amount would have been even higher had I gotten my bank records from the beginning. Again, it was another attempt by my ex-wife to dishonestly defraud me for more funds that she did not deserve and then lied about having records to prove her case.

I was made to spend money on hiring an attorney and was attacked for no reason by her. I had always paid child support and did all I could to help take care of the daughter we had together. Her attack was hurtful and unfair. Even more frustrating was that my wife and I would pick up my daughter from my ex-wife's home, and our daughter would not have a jacket when it was cold outside. Her clothing would not fit properly, being too tight and short. We often would have to go and purchase clothing that fits to ensure she had what she needed when she visited.

Though my ex-wife continued to attack and, in some cases, did not provide for our daughter's needs, I made it a point not to say derogatory things about her and tried to maintain civil relations with her. But this experience also was another that humbled me in the sense that even with all I tried to do to help our daughter and provide for her, I was still falsely accused of not doing so—even though it was proven to be a complete pretense for getting more money from me.

After getting the child support issue resolved, I felt as though things were piling up and that led to feelings that it was happening because of what I was doing. Feeling remorseful and trapped, I decided to stop doing some of these things. I did not feel a desire to do them anymore. Being a good Father was something I strove to be. I was in some ways, and in others, I was not. I wanted to do the right things and decided I needed to improve in ways I was not. So, I began to distance myself from the woman I was seeing. I started to go weeks without seeing her; when I did, we were no longer intimately involved. I did not want to do that anymore. I wanted to get out of the relationship and then came the final straw to help me end it.

Four months before I was arrested, I was contacted by a detective about the woman I had been out on a date with five months earlier. He claimed that she had made an assault claim and needed to speak to me. Again, confused and unsure of exactly who or what this was about, I contacted an attorney to represent me again. As it turns out, it was about the woman I had met and had emailed me the next day that she could not remember what had happened on our date. She claimed that I had assaulted her and given her something to make her forget about the incident. That was false and completely untrue. As my attorney told me what they were saying, I felt sick to my stomach as I was once again faced with false accusations. This time, the claims were so outlandish that I was at a loss for words about how they came to such a conclusion. They wanted a DNA sample, and I agreed to provide one. I told them we had a consensual encounter and I would cooperate. I was told that once the results came back, there was a chance I could be arrested based on what my attorney told me. I could not believe what was happening. It was all I could do to remain calm at home; and with every car that drove down our street, I would worry it might be someone coming to arrest me on these false accusations.

RETURN TO FAMILY VALUES

Over the next two weeks, I deleted my dating profiles and emails and tried to eliminate all the things I had been doing that I should not have done. Again, I did these things not because I had things to hide but because I wanted to stop doing those things altogether. This last experience was it for me. I was done with online dating and preparing to tell my wife what had happened. I was done with the double life and needed to tell someone what was happening. This last incident had finally prepared me for the experience I would have in the next few weeks.

Leading up to this experience, I stopped the behaviors I had been engaged in and agreed to go back to church with my wife and children. The night before a very sacred and life-changing experience would take place, I approached my wife and told her I would like to start going to church again. We hugged, and she cried as I apologized for not attending church anymore and promised to change. Little by little, I was changing and was compelled to do so because of the circumstances I had been through over the previous six months. During this time, I also contacted the woman I had been seeing and ended the relationship. It was a relief, and I felt so much better when it was over.

PATRIARCHAL BLESSING INFLUENCE

Once these things were done, I was ready for what would happen next. It was a Saturday late in December 2014. I was preparing to go to the gym that morning and was drinking a protein shake in the kitchen when I felt impressed to go and read my patriarchal blessing. I had not read my blessing in years, though I knew exactly where to find it. Feeling compelled to read it, I returned to our bedroom and sat down to read my blessing. During this time, I was feeling very alone and afraid. I had not shared all of what had happened to me because I would have to tell people what precipitated it, which I was ashamed and afraid to do. I feared my family and wife would reject me.

What I read in the first paragraph of my blessing brought me to tears. I read of the love my Father in Heaven had for me and also the love of my family and parents. I was reminded of all the Lord had forgiven me for in my early years and felt my Father's love for me, even in my lost and broken state. Tears rolled down my cheeks as it spoke of talents and gifts I had been given and the realization of other blessings if I lived worthy to receive them. I longed to realize those blessings, and an incredible feeling of love and peace enveloped me. For the first time in many years, I felt the Spirit of God so strongly that fear and anxiety left me, and I resolved to do what the Lord would have me do, regardless of the consequences.

When I finished my blessing, I fell to my knees and thanked the Lord with all my heart for the love I felt from Him. I then promised to do all I needed to do to change, to repent, and to make restitution for all the wrongs I had committed. I am also determined to confess all my unresolved sins and turn completely to the Lord going forward. It was the first time in my heart I had been determined to confess every sin I had committed; and when I had resolved to do so, a peace and a strength not my own lifted me to what I then did next. I immediately called my parents and sincerely apologized for all I had done and for all I had put them through. I thanked them for their prayers and promised to repent and change fully. The Spirit was so strong at that moment that I decided not to go to the gym; rather, I picked up a few things from the store and went home because my wife was the next person I needed to speak to.

TELLING ALL TO WIFE

When I arrived home, I was in the kitchen, and my wife came in. I told her I needed to talk and that what I was about to say might make her not want to be with me, but it was the right thing to do. I was willing to face whatever the consequences were. I then told her everything I could think I had done wrong. Her reaction, much like that of my parents, surprised me. Instead of anger, there was relief. Instead of leaving, she and I just held each other and cried. For years I had dreaded this moment, always knowing at some point I would have to admit all I had done, but I never expected her to respond in love and kindness. Certainly, I was undeserving of that response, but I will always and forever be grateful for the time she stood by me when I needed her the most.

The next day was fast Sunday. I had not been to church in a long time. But I got up that Sunday to bear my testimony. I had always known the gospel's truthfulness, but selfishly, I had gone my own way and had been lost for many years. There were times when I went to church in the past. I even went to the bishop a few times to repent for some things, but I held back the hardest and worst things I had done, fearing the outcome and what I would have to do to repent fully. This left me spiritually dead and to wander and lose my way. But that fast Sunday, the Spirit was still strong within me; and I let the ward know that though I had made many mistakes and sought forgiveness, I was ready and willing to do all that was required to come back and ask for their forgiveness.

After church, I met with the bishop, confessed to him all I could think of, and shed many tears for the burden lifted off my shoulders after so many years. Afterward, the bishop gave me a blessing and a tremendous thing happened. In my heart, I worried that after reading about the wonderful blessings that I was promised in my patriarchal blessing through faithfulness, perhaps after all that had happened, I would no longer qualify for many of those blessings. Secretly, I wondered in my heart if those blessings were still valid. As the bishop placed his hands on my head and gave me a blessing, he told me that the blessings I had read about in my patriarchal blessing were still in force and that no blessings had been lost.

Upon hearing this again, I was overwhelmed with relief and joy and knew my Father in Heaven had blessed me to know these things. I had not mentioned this concern to the bishop and knew that in His mercy, the Lord had given me this reassurance as a blessing for my willingness to repent and to change. I remember being amazed as I drove home that day, relieved of so much guilt and the weight of the sins I had carried for years. I was no longer hiding anything from anyone, including the Lord. I had confessed all that came to my mind that needed to be resolved, and it felt so very peaceful. I felt physically and emotionally drained; but for the first time in years, I felt real happiness and joy.

PERSONAL CHANGES

That weekend changed everything for me. I began to read the scriptures daily and had morning and evening prayers on my knees. I cut out anything in my life contrary to the gospel and began encouraging our girls to learn *Book of Mormon* stories. I would tell them the stories from this book at night before bedtime. When I took the girls to school in the morning, we would sing songs about faith and say a prayer before they left. I even stopped to help a stranded motorist on the road, where days before I never would have paid any attention to that motorist's need.

At church, I began to sit in the front of the class to be able to listen and take part in discussions. I volunteered to help those who were moving and also to help people park for the stake conference. I was on fire spiritually and wanted to do all I could to help and serve others. I also wanted to begin teaching my girls about service, so I texted the bishopric to see if anyone in the ward needed some food or someone to visit them. I was told an elderly lady in the ward could use a warm meal and a visit. We made her a meal and visited her. She was a sweet lady, and our visit made her whole day. The next Sunday, the lady saw our girls, and they both went and hugged her and brought tears to her eyes. We did this again a short time later for a lady who had surgery and her family needed a meal while she recovered. Those experiences were well worth the effort on our part.

But these things were not the only changes that I needed to make. Not only did I need to confess to the bishop, my parents, and my wife. I also felt a need to apologize and confess to my family who had also been victims of my behaviors. So, I wrote an email, sent it to the entire family, and asked for their forgiveness. I also did the same to my ex-wife for the mistakes of the past that I felt needed an apology. For anyone and everyone whom my actions had affected, I sought forgiveness. Their responses were so kind and loving that I was again surprised at their support and love. Each one reached out, expressed support and love, and encouraged me to keep going. That is the kind of family I have, and that support and love continued even after my arrest.

Another change I needed to make was to find a job to help support my family. So that Monday after I had been to church for the first time, I set out to find a good job. But this time I prayed for the Lord's help to lead me to the job I should take. I found a job fairly quickly that I felt was right. It included a week of sales training that helped refresh my skills. Though the job was not what I had expected and only lasted for a week, it gave me what I needed to land the job I found days later. Within a few days after leaving this job, I found a job that seemed right for me.

NEW JOB BLESSINGS

The benefits, pay, and incentives were the best I had received in my career. After approaching the Lord in prayer, I knew it was my right job. During the hiring process, I felt the Spirit very strongly during the interviews and knew the Lord was helping me. I had never sought the Lord's help in searching for a job before, but this time, I invited the Lord to lead and guide me. I felt He did just that. After many interviews and several days, I was offered the position. Before I decided to repent, that job would have seemed out of reach. But now that I had begun the repentance process, I felt confident that I could get that job with the Lord's help, and I did. I will also mention that during that process, doors were opened and everything just worked out. It was not just good luck. The Lord blessed me for trying to do things in His way this time.

During this hiring process, I was also able to go and meet with the stake president and confess my faults to him. My wife accompanied me, and we shared a wonderful moment after our meeting. For the next three months, we had some of the best times of our relationship as a couple and as a family. I was working in a decent job and felt I was doing what I was supposed to do. My wife and I were closer during this time than we had been since the beginning of our relationship. I no longer had anything to hide; my conscience was clear, allowing for a closer and more loving relationship. I felt a desire to serve her and my children in new and exciting ways because the gospel was now the driving force in our lives, instead of being non-existent. We went to church each week and had the missionaries over for dinner at our house. I spent my drives to work listening to conference talks and scriptures to keep my focus on the Lord, and I even listened to them at night before bed. We spent more time together as a family, teaching the girls to serve and asking the Lord for help.

One instance I remember to illustrate what was happening was when a friend of our girls came over to jump with them on the trampoline. The friend was wearing a bracelet she took off before she got on the trampoline. Afterward, she could not find it, and the girls came inside, upset that they had lost it. So before looking for it, we prayed for help to find the bracelet. After just a few minutes, the bracelet was found, and faith was increased. It was a perfect opportunity to teach the girls about having faith in the Lord and that He can help us accomplish anything if we ask in faith.

Another thing we started doing during this time was paying our tithing and fast offerings. I knew that if obedient, we would be blessed temporally and spiritually. This was a test for us, however, because there were times when paying our tithing would leave us short of paying our other bills. I decided to pay a full tithe anyway and trust that the Lord would help us find a solution to have the money we needed. The next day, that blessing was realized. I received a call that Monday that gave us the money we needed and more for that month. We never went without when we paid a full tithe or fast offering. It strengthened my testimony of the true principle of paying a full tithe.

Looking back on that time now, something stands out that had never happened: once I told my wife all that had happened, we never spoke about those things again. She expressed no anger, hurt, or disappointment in me for what I did. I knew those feelings were there, but seemingly, they were somehow left until a later time to be expressed and felt tangibly. Maybe that, too, was a blessing that the Lord gave us because those last three months were so fulfilling and wonderful and needed for the challenges that were about to happen. Almost having forgotten about the investigation and the potential problems that were still ongoing, I had adjusted to my new job and new life and was the happiest I had been in a long time. Then, all that changed in a matter of minutes when we received a knock on the door at 6:00 am that fateful Monday morning.

Chapter 10

County Jail and New Insights

I had just come back from a business trip in Dallas, Texas, and was getting ready for work when the knock on the door came. It had been several months since I had heard anything from my attorney about my case and had almost forgotten about it. My children were with me as I opened the door and saw the two officers there to arrest me. I knew at once what they were there for and just froze as they pulled me out to handcuff me and lead me out the door. When my daughter saw this, she let out a bloodcurdling scream that haunts me whenever I think about it. Her screams and my children's tears are what I remember most about that day. That was the most gut-wrenching, scariest thing I had ever experienced in my life to that point.

As I was put into the vehicle, I pleaded with the Lord not to let this happen and to help me. Surely, He would not let me go to jail for something that did not happen. I remember asking the Lord why He would allow this to happen. He knew I was innocent, and yet here I was being taken away from my family and my life. I kept hoping it was just a dream and I would wake up soon. But as we started to pull away from my house, I realized that my worst nightmares were now being realized and I crumpled into the seat and wept.

BOOKED INTO JAIL

When we arrived at the jail intake, I was searched and led to a large waiting area with many chairs and was told to sit. After a brief time, I was directed to come and sign a sheet with the charges listed on it. This also was a shock to me because both charges were false and outrageous. Not only did they charge me with two heinous crimes that in reality did not take place, but the second charge was even more ridiculous and incredulous than the first. Thinking back to my arrest, I also realized they never read me my Miranda rights as required by law. When I opened the door and they began cuffing me, my daughter began to scream and cry; and they just led me off to the car without reading me my rights.

As soon as I arrived and was searched at the jail, they quickly had me sign the sheet with my charges on it that also stated they read me my rights, which they had not. But being scared and unsure of what to do, I signed the sheet. As I sat in the chair waiting, my life as it was flashed before my eyes. I knew I would lose my job, that everything would be different now, no matter what the outcome of my case was, and that things would never be the same.

I was finally allowed to make a phone call and called my wife. She had called my attorney and was consoling and supportive. We were both in shock at what had happened and were unsure of what to do. I told her how sorry I was that this was all happening and asked her to contact my family. My wife was so supportive and loving during this time, and I believe with all my heart that the Lord softened her heart towards me during this period because of how much I needed her at that moment in my life.

I had been warned about how bad county jail would be, but it was worse than I imagined. My first attorney, who was a very dishonest and unscrupulous man, assured me I would spend only a few days in jail and then I would be out on bond. So, I thought I just needed to get by for a few days. Having never had a problem with the law, nor been arrested before, I was unprepared for what I was about to experience.

After having my fingerprints taken, and a terrible mug shot, I was placed in a holding cell by myself. The cell was filthy and smelled of urine and feces. The walls were covered in graffiti, and there was garbage all over the floor. There was a toilet with no toilet paper and nothing to use to get a drink of water. Feeling overwhelmed and afraid, I laid my head on the bench and tried to close my eyes and forget how I was feeling.

Soon, several others were put into the cell with me, and we were given sandwiches with small cookies to eat. I gave mine away, not having any desire to eat. Later, we were told to follow an officer and ended up in a shower room where we had to strip down completely and shower in front of the officer. It was a very degrading and humiliating experience. We were then given uniforms to wear and had to turn in all our clothing and jewelry.

Next, we were led to an elevator to go to the classification dorm for several days before being placed in a more permanent dorm. Once we were all in the elevator, I had my first taste of racial tension from a Black man who was on the elevator with us. He began to threaten me for no reason other than I was White. He continued to say he would hurt me and that he did not like White people. I did not look at him or say anything in return. However, unexpectedly, the Black man next to me turned to him and told him he would do me no harm, and that if he tried anything, he would protect me. I knew neither man, but I knew that the Lord was protecting me through this man who would not allow the other man to harm or threaten me. This was the first time the Lord intervened on my behalf, but it would not be the last.

When we arrived at the classification dorm, I was put into a cell with another Black man who had been to jail before and helped me to know how things went and what to do. Some things I learned by trial and error, like how to use the bathroom in a two-man cell, what certain words meant that I had never heard before, and what was appropriate prison etiquette. It was not long before I realized I was in a whole different world that I had never experienced before, and I was sure I wanted no part of it.

As soon as I had my things put away in my cell, I wanted only to lie down on my bed and sleep. I was exhausted mentally and wished I could curl up and make myself disappear. But before long, the door to our cell opened, and we were told to stand next to the door. This was the first time I was counted. I soon learned we had to count a handful of times a day and that sleeping was going to be a challenge.

JAIL ETIQUETTE AND PROCEDURES

After being counted, we were allowed to come into what they called the common area for one hour where there were a few tables, phones, a computer kiosk, and a place to shower. My wife had put funds in my account, but I was not sure how to access them or how to use the phone. After getting some help, I called my wife and just broke down. I was not trying to; it just happened. Here I was in jail, and not for any crime I had committed. I felt like a fish out of water, did not speak the prison lingo, and was scared and alone. My wife was loving and consoling. She said she had called my parents and that I should call them.

At that moment all I wanted to do was go home. Why did the Lord allow this to happen? Things in my life had just begun to be the way they were supposed to be, then it was taken away completely by false accusations that now destroyed the life I had. What did I say to my parents? Would anyone believe I was telling the truth? These and many other questions swirled through my head as I got ready to call them. I had told my wife all that had happened, but not my parents. I had apologized for my behavior in the past but did not go into detail about the things I had done. Now, they too would know, and the rest of the family, too. But at that moment I was not concerned about that. I just hoped they would not forsake me and would believe that I did not do the things I had been falsely accused of.

When my Mom answered the phone, it was all I could do to keep my composure. I felt so ashamed to be calling her from jail. But once again she was not angry, just supportive, and loving. She again stood by me and said she would do all she could to support and help me. Relief washed over me, and I was overcome with emotion. Words cannot fully describe the feelings I had at that moment in time. I felt relieved that those I loved were not going to abandon me; yet I also felt a profound sense of disappointment in myself and a deep feeling of shame and embarrassment for being in jail and for the things that I did that led to being falsely accused.

After getting off the phone with my Mom, I was unsure how I would get through what I thought was only going to be a few days. I thought for sure I would get a bond and would be home quickly. That is what my attorney told me when I met with him before I was arrested. He said that if I were to be arrested, I should receive a bond because I had never had a problem with the law, had a job and a family, a house, and children. At the time I was too naive to know better; and with no experience in the legal system, I trusted him and thought I just had to get through a few days. That was my mindset. So, I ordered a Bible and a few snacks off the commissary that were to be delivered the next day; and then our hour was up and we were told to go back to our cells.

Not long after we returned to our cells, we were served a dinner tray. It was my first meal in jail. I do not remember exactly what it was, but it was bland with very small portions. I did not have much of an appetite, so it was fine; but over the next few days when I started to feel the hunger pains, I was grateful to have ordered a few snacks from the commissary. I would have ordered more if I knew that they put no seasoning in the food and the portions were more suited for a child than an adult. It was then that I was told all the seasonings were available through the commissary, and that you had to pay to taste the food.

Jail, I learned, was a way to extort those who were already facing difficult circumstances. The families end up having to pay to speak to their loved ones and to feed and clothe them—and at exorbitant prices. Almost every item was three to four times more expensive in jail than in a grocery store. One example I remember was a five-ounce package of tuna cost $7.95 on the commissary; however, in the store, it was $2. I was shocked at how expensive things were and how they took advantage of people. So, I was careful to order just what I needed to avoid putting undue pressure on my family to provide more than was necessary while I was there.

That first day and night I shed many tears. The profound feeling of being alone haunted me all that day. My stomach was tied in knots, and I had no idea what to do or what to expect. I prayed more and with greater intensity than I had ever done before in my life that first day. The Lord blessed and protected me, and I did feel He was aware of me. However, I could not shake that feeling of loneliness and uncertainty.

That night I also worried about my girls. My attorney assured me that if I were to be arrested, they would contact him and arrange to have me turn myself in. But that did not happen. Instead, they traumatized my children when they came to arrest me, then slowly left the neighborhood with the interior light on in the car so everyone could see whom they arrested. As a result of my arrest, I have always worried about what effect it had on my children and the fear they felt seeing me led away in handcuffs. I have never forgotten it, but I hope that they have. I worried how they would be with me in jail. Would they be treated differently by our neighbors, friends, and teachers? I also worried about my wife and how she would be treated. I felt helpless to do anything and that was gut-wrenching to manage.

I also felt from the start I was treated as if I were guilty until proven innocent. The news media portrayed me as a monster and only gave the prosecution's side of the story. I was amazed that they could say anything they wanted without facts or evidence to substantiate their claims. Then the prosecution manipulated the things that did happen to fit their false narratives, so their story made sense. They even made up things to fill in the gaps and make their story seem more believable.

ADJUSTING TO JAIL

The next morning very early, we were awakened to eat our breakfast—at 2:30 am. It was an adjustment to try to eat so early in the morning, but I learned quickly that you had to try to eat; otherwise, the hunger pains stay with you all day long. The menu at the jail cycled between about five to ten different options for dinner and two for breakfast. One thing you ate every day was a lot of bread. Sandwiches and bread were staple items with every meal. Compared to food from home, the food we had was terrible, tasteless, and overcooked. But it was food; and when you get hungry enough, you eat it.

My first full day in classification was an unpleasant one. First, I was ushered to a holding cell on the first floor to await my initial court appearance. I was put into a cell packed with other inmates also awaiting their initial court appearance. For some, there was standing room only. I waited for hours until my name was called. When I came into the room, my unscrupulous attorney was there and came to speak to me. He told me what the charges were and explained the next steps to me. He then suggested I lie about my charges if other inmates asked me while I was in jail. He said, "They don't like people with my charges in there." I was not comfortable with his advice and decided that honesty was how I was going to approach things. I simply did not need to tell people why I was there, so no need to lie about it. If I lied, that only made matters worse. Thankfully, I did not follow his advice because my case had already been all over the news, and the people in the jail recognized me and knew why I was there from the start.

UNSCRUPULOUS ATTORNEY

Nothing my first attorney told me ended up being accurate or correct. From the start, he manipulated and pressured me into retaining him. Then, once he was paid, I never heard from him unless it was to get more money. He also lied about what the money we paid to him initially covered. He told me that the money we paid at the start would cover his services through my bond hearing. However, once I was arrested, the story changed; and he demanded additional money for the bond hearing, and an exorbitant amount if it went to trial. So, needless to say, I was already regretting my choice of attorney and started asking others about what to expect and also about other more reputable attorneys.

After arriving back at the classification dorm, I got on the phone to call my wife. She told me my employer had been contacted and they had terminated me and had arranged to come and pick up my company car. Just like that, I lost my job and there was nothing I could do about it. That is how these first few days in jail were characterized: by feelings of regret, profound sadness, and loss. Everything I loved and truly cared about was being taken away, and my reputation and name were being systematically destroyed. I worried about how my children were doing and how my wife would manage without me. In the back of my mind, I also wondered if and how long she would stay with me. My prayers at night and in the morning were the sincerest pleadings of my life for my family, wife, and children. I wanted with all my heart to somehow not lose my family. Perhaps that was a selfish desire, considering all that I had put my wife through already, and all she would end up going through before it was all said and done. But the past three months had been the best of our relationship because I was living my life in harmony with the gospel, and that had a profound impact on our relationship and our lives.

SPIRITUAL PREPARATION BEFORE JAIL

Instead of being concerned about what I was not getting or needed, I focused on giving to my wife and children. I enjoyed serving them and found greater happiness in their joy and peace than I ever had seeking my own. That time showed me what we were capable of if we were willing to follow the Savior and live in harmony with His teachings. To this day I consider those few months a tender mercy from God, a gift and blessing that I can look back on and remember as I long for that again one day. I was given a glimpse of what was possible if I were willing to live as God had asked us to live. It was the happiest time in my married life when I did so. Because I experienced that with my wife and children, I long to have that again one day.

Up until that point in my life, I had never been married to someone and living the gospel completely while having also repented fully of all my sins. I had never been worthy of all the blessings because of unrepented sins and not living the gospel in its entirety. Now that I had done both of those things, I was amazed at the difference it made and how much happier I had become. It was liberating and freeing to repent, have a clear conscience, and not worry about things I had done anymore. We still had things to work on, to talk about, and to change; but with the Lord's help, it all seemed possible and doable. These were all the things I realized as I sat on my bed in my cell in the county jail and hoped that I would get a second chance to be a husband and a Father again despite all that had happened. I was beginning to figure things out, I thought and just needed a chance to do things the right way this time.

HEARING FOR BOND

After a few days, I was transferred to the dorm where I would be housed until I was either released on bond or until I went to trial. Up to this point, I was confident I would be released on bond and would fight my charges from home. This was just a temporary thing I thought. Once I arrived at my new dorm and went to my cell, my new cellmate was from Mexico and spoke little to no English. He was quiet and kept to himself; and I did, too, for the first few days. The schedule changed slightly now that I was in the general population. We received 30 to 60 minutes out in the morning, and the same in the afternoon, if they had enough staff. Often, they were shorthanded, and we ended up with 30 minutes for the entire day—if out at all. Violence and gang activity were the reasons that were cited for our lack of free time out of our cells. The county jail I was locked up in had a reputation for gang violence and terrible conditions. It lived up to its reputation. My first few days in my new dorm I spent my time out of my cell either in the shower or on the phone. Talking to family helped to keep me sane and let me know how they were managing. Being in a small cell all day was grueling and hard. My mattress was 30 years old and gave me no support. We had no pillows and one blanket and had cold air blowing on us all day long. The food was terrible, and the nights went on for what seemed like an eternity with the guards coming by every hour waking us up and flashing lights in our faces as they walked by.

Starting at 7 am the guards would turn on the television and allow one of the inmates to select a channel to watch and to turn the volume up to maximum so people could hear it while sitting in their cells. Most of the time we watched reality television shows that were anything but real and were filled with profanity, vulgarity, and immorality. It was torture to have to listen to those shows and be a captive audience unable to block it out because of the volume level and proximity to the television. I wondered how anyone could last for any length of time in a place like this. How do you not go crazy? I figured I just needed to get through a few more days and I was going to be home. I could make it a few more days I thought.

As the day arrived for me to go to the Superior Court for the first time, I was anxious and nervous to go. I had been locked up for what seemed like a year, although it had only been a week, and I thought I would be going home later that day. They called those of us going to court out at 5 am, handcuffed us, and led us down to holding cells to await transport to the court. Once everyone who was going to court arrived, they began the process of shackling our feet and hands together so that we could only move in short steps and had to be extra careful not to fall. Once on the bus, we were taken by police escort through the city to the courthouse. We then were taken through a metal detector and put into holding cells in the basement of the building. The air was frigid and keeping warm was impossible as we waited to be taken to the floor where we would go before the judge. While waiting, we were given a carton of milk, four pieces of bread, two pieces of bologna, and two mustard packs. That was all we received until we arrived back from court that evening.

After I was taken up to the floor where I would be for my hearing in front of the judge, I was placed into a holding cell with others who were there to go before the same judge. My judge was an African American woman who had been on the court for a long time. I later learned she had authored a bill that increased the penalty for the crimes I was accused of. Judges were supposed to be assigned randomly to the cases they were given, but I wondered about that after hearing that she disliked White middle-class men with educations and also those who are accused of crimes against women. All these things applied to my case.

While waiting to see my lawyer and the judge, I heard others telling their stories about how they got away with all kinds of crimes before they were caught this time. They bragged about how they had gotten off on other charges in the past and how they were going to do the same this time. They claimed they knew how to work the system and get away with things, including in one case murder. I sat in stunned silence as I heard these other inmates telling their stories and laughing about how smart they were. I felt uncomfortable listening to these "confessions" and hoped I would be gone after my court hearing.

Finally, I was told my attorney was there to see me and was led to a small desk where my handcuffs were removed, and my attorney was seated across from me. What happened next I did not see coming and to this day not entirely sure why it happened. Instead of my attorney talking to me about what was going to happen next and what he was going to say to the judge, he started smiling and making comments that were completely inappropriate and crude about women, asking how many I had been with and trying to get me to respond. His questions and behavior were so odd that I immediately questioned his motives and did not respond. It seemed like he was trying to goad me into bragging about the girls I had been with and like I had done something worthy of high praise. I felt uncomfortable, confused by his behavior, and told him it was inappropriate.

To this day I believe he had a recording device and was trying to get me to say something that would hurt my case. As a result, I told him I would not pay him any additional funds to represent me for my bond hearing, and he withdrew himself from my case when we went in front of the judge. Later I found out that before my bond hearing, my wife had been to visit my attorney and did not have a pleasant experience with him. His behavior at the jail may well have been a deliberate attempt to hurt my case.

I also noticed my attorney seemed very friendly with the prosecutor assigned to my case. I suspected that he might have been trying to get information for the prosecution because he knew we no longer wanted him to represent me. I have heard that deals are made like that where the prosecution agrees to drop a case for information on another. I have no proof of this, but it would explain the friendliness and questionable behavior. He also had no objection to having the local media come to my bond hearing telling me, " It shouldn't be a big deal if I were innocent." Why would a defense attorney want to draw negative attention to his client's case? All the media attention did was prejudice potential jurors and public opinion against me. In cases I have seen since my trial, I have never seen a defense attorney welcome that kind of negativity towards their client if they are trying to help their case. It seemed clear after all these things took place that he was working against me, not for me.

Despite all that, in the end, I believed that the truth would come forth and I would end up a free man. I knew that I was innocent of the charges and that the facts would not support their claims. It was this faith in the system and also knowing the truth that gave me hope that no matter how terrible things seemed, in the end, it would all work out.

CHANGE OF ATTORNEYS

Because I requested a change in representation, the judge delayed my bond hearing to allow me a chance to retain new counsel. This was frustrating to me because I hoped to get out on bond, not spend another week in jail. But I needed a new attorney who had my best interests at heart, so I had no choice but to have my family find the best option out there for me. This led to my wife asking a close friend of hers from childhood, who had married an attorney, to see if her husband could recommend someone to take my case. He gave us the name of an older gentleman he said could help us. My Mother spoke with him and was impressed with him. He came across in her words as a "Matlock" type of attorney, and she thought he would be a desirable choice for me. None of my family members had ever had legal issues and had not dealt with the judicial system, so we were naive and gullible when it came to legal matters. We believed all that we were told by this new attorney and in the end were lied to and manipulated by him for money.

But before all that happened, he came to visit me so I could make my assessment of him. He also told me all the right things, claiming to have tried many cases just like mine successfully, and recently. He claimed he could get me out on bond and that he knew exactly what he was doing. He seemed to know what he was talking about; and because I had no idea what was happening or what to do, I agreed to hire him.

As it turned out, that was the worst mistake I could have made. When the bond hearing came, he made fundamental arguments that were not very compelling and did not refute the arguments made by the district attorney. It felt like an ambush as I sat there and watched my attorney come unprepared to the bond hearing citing basic rules for the judge to consider granting bond, to which the judge responded that she did not need him to rehearse the laws to her and dismissed his arguments and did not grant me a bond. I was stunned that he did not once refute or argue their points, which were easily refuted and were against even common sense. Their arguments were false and misleading, and even a law student should have been able to show they were without merit. But my new attorney simply allowed them to make false statements and did not challenge them because he came unprepared. This was a shadow of things to come.

Once he was paid, which he required before he did anything, he simply showed up and did not investigate, did not look through all the evidence, and did not prepare or defend me. He simply got paid and then showed up for the hearings and went through the motions. He also did not go through any of the evidence with me before the trial and wanted me to simply plead guilty to avoid having to prepare for trial. He was paid to go to trial, and his price reflected that. However, he never had any intention of defending me or fighting my case. The truth of the matter was that he had not tried any cases like mine in thirty years, was not familiar with the current case laws and statutes, and did not prepare or look through the evidence that would have exonerated me. These facts certainly reinforced that he never intended to take my case to trial.

The attorney repeatedly asked me to take a deal up to the day of the trial and tried to have my family convince me to do likewise. He also agreed to a request by the prosecution to exclude a large number of text messages before the trial that had information that refuted the prosecution's claims and would substantiate my own. But without consulting me, and without even bothering to look at the texts in question, he agreed to exclude them from being used in the trial. What kind of attorney does something like that without knowing what the text messages contain? It makes sense that the prosecution had a reason they did not want those texts to be used in the trial and that was because they would have contradicted the testimony of the witnesses for the prosecution and shown them to be lying about the facts of the case. I was not aware of the texts before the trial started; however, during the trial when I learned of the text messages in question and brought them to my attorney's attention, he told me he could not use them. Later when I questioned why they could not be used, he told me he had made a deal before the trial to exclude them at the prosecution's request.

Again I felt as though my attorney had sold me out and was working against me and not for me. And if that was not bad enough, the expert who was hired to show video evidence that proved the prosecution and several of their key witnesses were not being truthful in their testimonies, died the night before my trial of a massive heart attack. This ultimately prevented us from using the video evidence we had at trial because his replacement was unable to get the equipment working before the judge told us to move on.

NO BOND, RETURN TO JAIL

After the bond hearing, I was led back to the holding cell in the courthouse feeling deflated, confused, and frustrated. I had so many questions going through my mind as I sat in the cell. What just happened in there? Why did I not get a bond? How was I going to survive in jail until a trial? Why was my attorney not prepared for what the prosecution was claiming at my bond hearing? Was he unable to do anything more? Were all attorneys this bad? Would I be made to endure the awful jail conditions for months, perhaps even years?

My sister, my mother, and my wife were there at the bond hearing. It was the first time I had seen them since I had been incarcerated. It was bittersweet to see them briefly as I was led into the courtroom for the hearing; but as I left, I could not look in their direction for fear of losing control of my emotions. The feelings I had when I was first taken from my home came back to me now that I was faced with the prospect of being locked up for an indeterminate amount of time in jail. That moment was my lowest since this experience began. I thought I had hit rock bottom when I was arrested. But now that I knew how bad the jail conditions were and that I would have to endure those for a lengthy period. That was the lowest point in my life!

When I was arrested, I was not sure I would make it through the first day in jail. The only hope I thought I had was getting a bond. Now that my bond was denied, it seemed like everything that could go wrong had gone wrong. Nothing seemed to be going my way, and the fact that I did not do the things I was accused of did not seem to matter to those who were intent on keeping me locked up. The thought of not seeing my children or my wife for a prolonged period was almost too much to bear. I felt overwhelmed with grief as my new reality set in.

As I sat in the holding cell, it was all I could do not to break down and cry as I listened to those who had committed crimes come back from their hearings with a bond to get out of jail. Some who had murder charges and similar charges to mine were being released. How does that happen in a fair and just system? A person can murder someone, be accused of it, or have a lengthy prison record and receive a bond but I cannot. As I sat there, I began to realize for the first time that the justice system I thought was just and fair was not. My entire life I thought the legal system was fair; and if you were innocent, you were going to be fine. Experiencing the legal system firsthand, any faith I had in the system was now gone. I also felt as though I was being treated differently by the judge who was African American because I was White and educated.

The common theme that I saw with my judge was this: if you were Black and from a poor and uneducated background, with very few exceptions, you were going to get a bond and would receive a lenient sentence. I saw it repeatedly. Those who were with me in the holding cell that day who were there for a bond hearing, most if not all, were granted bonds. All were Black and had committed crimes that, in some cases, were considered much worse than those I had been accused of. Many had a history of crime going back many years, and yet they still received a bond. I had never committed a crime or had any legal problems in my lifetime, had a job, family, and home, and still could not get a bond.

My family, who were present in the courtroom for various proceedings, witnessed firsthand a man being given a bond after he was accused of shooting the victim in the face during a robbery. The prejudice I felt from the very start was being felt every step of this process. I was being treated differently and more harshly than those who had a history of crime and were of a different race. Sadly, race seemed to play a role in how the wheels of justice worked. My judge being of African American descent, and responsible for increasing the penalty for the types of crimes I was accused of, made it seemingly impossible to get fair treatment. That day I prayed that the Lord would help me endure a trial I thought I was not able to endure.

RESIGNED TO TIME IN JAIL

Now that I knew I was going to be there for a while, I realized that I needed to reach out and talk with some people. However, it was best to keep a low profile and observe others at first before trying to talk with them. I also wanted to get a feel for the people around me and who they were. One I had observed since I arrived was an older Black man who seemed to be distraught and would walk by himself making circles around the dorm. In speaking with him, I learned he was married, and he was not able to speak to his wife. They had little money, and he was illiterate, so he could not reach out to her. Feeling a desire to help him, I offered to write a letter for him to her. He immediately agreed and told me what he wanted me to say to her. Then I went to my cell and wrote the things he requested.

The next time we came out, I read the letter to him. He was grateful and his eyes were full of tears as I handed him the envelope, complete with a stamp, so he could mail it home to her. It felt good to help him and to enable him to talk to his wife for the first time in months. Knowing he was also hungry, I bought him some cookies and chips, so he had something to eat besides the poor food we were given. He was stunned I would do that and told me he could not pay me for them. I just smiled and told him he did not need to and walked away. I was not aware at that time that what I had just done never really happened in jail or prison. Everything had a price in the jail-prison world. Rarely does anyone do something or give something for free. So my offering without expecting something in return was a rare thing. It took a little time for people to see that is just how I was, and not a fraud or me putting on a show.

The next week this kind man received a letter back from his wife. She was so happy to hear from him that she wrote to him immediately. So, for the next several months, I wrote letters and even a poem for her, which she framed and put on the wall of their home. Each time he received her response; he would bring the letter to my cell and I would read it to him. This changed his whole demeanor as he went from an incredibly sad countenance to a happy and looking forward to the mail being delivered each day. He was so relieved now that he could talk to his wife and know she was okay and stood by him. I felt grateful I could be of help to him, knowing how hard it is to be apart from those you love. I missed my wife and children terribly, too.

Another person I connected with was the man in the cell next to mine. He claimed he was falsely accused also and related some of the details to me over time as we began to speak to one another. He said he had noticed I was quite different from the others we were locked up with. He also said it seemed like I did not belong there. I told him I, too, was being falsely accused and understood how he felt. We got along well, and he and I would talk regularly. Shortly after we began speaking, he became extremely sick and went to see the doctor. His symptoms were a rash, fever, and no appetite. They took blood and performed some tests on him. Afterward, they gave him some medications, and he became even more sickly and ill. After a few more weeks, he went back to the doctor because he kept getting progressively worse. It was then that he found out that they had been giving him the wrong medications.

Another man with the same last name on our floor was being treated for AIDS, and the medications he was supposed to be receiving were going to my new friend and were making him extremely sick. This medical mistake was indicative of the medical care received in jail/prison. The standard of care is much lower than in the free world, and it seemed like those types of mistakes were made frequently. My friend said he did not have AIDS, and the drugs he was given were making him extremely ill. If he had not gone back to see the doctor, it might have been much worse. But from that point on, I was hesitant to seek medical care because of the inferior quality of care I witnessed with others among other things.

Over time others approached me curious as to why I was there because they perceived me to be different, too. I did not have tattoos, did not curse, and was polite to others. This made me stand out and piqued the curiosity of other people. Many approached me for advice or help with their case, falsely assuming I might be able to help them somehow. I quickly gained a reputation for my willingness to help others and was asked for help in letter writing, legal paperwork, food, religion, and even relationship advice. This helped me to gain favor in the eyes of the gang members who also sought my help and were friendly toward me as a result.

BOOKS RECEIVED BRING INSIGHTS

During this period I also received books from my family. Books were the best way to pass the time, and my family began to send me many books to help me learn and grow in my knowledge of the gospel and other relevant topics. I had read the *Book of Mormon* and the *Doctrine and Covenants;* but for the other standard works, I had only read parts and needed to read them fully. Before my incarceration, I had begun to read the scriptures again, but now I was spending the majority of my day in them. I cut out most TV watching in jail and spent most of my days reading from the scriptures and other books that had a profound impact on me. I started to see things I had been doing in my life from a unique perspective.

One of the blessings of my time in jail was the time I had to ponder about my life and the choices I had made. Reading these books helped me identify issues I never knew I had. I started to see how my lack of taking responsibility for my actions had affected my life in negative ways. It was also apparent that I was harboring negative feelings towards my Father and Stepfather for their treatment of me over the years. During this period of humble discovery, the Lord was helping me to discover the problems that led to the destructive behaviors that gave me jail time. For the first time in my life, I focused on myself, why I did what I did, and the behaviors involved. Suddenly, the answers seemed so clear and straightforward. This awakening was exciting for me; it was as though a light came on, and all the problems I had been struggling with were spoken about in each book I read.

My family members were inspired to send the books they did because they were exactly what I needed to read and gave me the answers I was looking for. This happened consistently during my time in jail. As a result, I had many sacred experiences where the Spirit strongly confirmed the answers to the questions I had and the truth of things by the feelings that washed over me from head to toe. Ironically, some of my greatest suffering came in my time in county jail, but it was also the place of my greatest spiritual outpourings of the Spirit. Many times I felt inspired by the things I read, and they led to great discoveries about myself and the things the Lord wanted me to do. One of those things I felt I needed to do was to forgive my Father and Stepfather. Both I felt had abandoned and wronged me in many ways growing up. I often felt unloved and unwanted by them. I hung onto that hurt and pain all those years until I went to jail. Then I read that the Lord required me to forgive them to be forgiven myself. Knowing I had much to be forgiven of and that I had made awful mistakes also, I realized I could no longer hold onto the things my Father and Stepfather had done.

CALLS TO PARENTS LIFT BURDENS

I decided to call both my Stepfather and Father while in jail and tell them I forgave them for the mistakes they made where I was concerned. I prayed sincerely that the Lord would help me to forgive them for all that had transpired in my life, knowing it to be the right thing to do. It was not easy to dial the numbers; but once I said I forgave them, peace and comfort came over me and confirmed I was doing what was right. Neither my Stepfather nor my Father were supportive when I was arrested. My Stepfather distanced himself from me and made comments like it was not his fault I ended up in jail and not to blame him for what happened to me. He also disowned me and removed me from his will and from receiving any help from him. Those things were very hurtful to me, but I needed to forgive him—and I sincerely did.

My Father made comments to my siblings that were hurtful to me and hard to let go when I was arrested, especially in light of the lack of any meaningful relationship with him over the years. But after I told my Father that I forgave him for the mistakes he made in the past, I was able to begin to build a relationship with him again. His new wife also was supportive and instrumental in helping the relationship develop. She had a son who had been incarcerated; thus, she was understanding and empathetic to what I was experiencing and willing to help in any way. I was grateful for that support and more importantly to have given the burden I had been carrying over to the Lord after so many years of carrying it by myself. That burden had handicapped me in my relationships and had made it difficult for me to trust and give my full heart to those I cared about.

The next thing I felt led to do was to make sure I had confessed every sin I needed to confess to the bishop. Reading the words of the prophets and learning in greater detail what were sins and what things I might have missed over the twenty-plus years of my life where I had been away from the church, I carefully reflected on the things I had done. I wrote anything I felt I may not have confessed or might have forgotten. I prayed that the Lord would help me to remember all I needed to make right and was able to recall the things I had forgotten and had yet to tell the bishop. As a result, I wrote everything and told my bishop that I had not purposely withheld these things but had taken time to reflect on what came to my mind that had not been resolved over the years. This was a cleansing process for me, and I wanted to be clean and resolve everything. I prayed and pondered until I felt the list was complete. Then I mailed that list to my bishop to be sure I had confessed all my sins. I knew the process was complete after sending the letter. Interestingly, after I sent the letter, I forgot the things I wrote within a brief time. The reason that is interesting to me is that while I was thinking about my past and praying for help to remember, things were brought to my mind that were specific; and I could remember with great clarity the circumstances and situations that I needed to repent. However, once I wrote those things and sent the letter to the bishop, they were forgotten. To this day, I do not recall much of what I wrote. For me, it is a blessing to have those things removed from my mind; and I feel the Lord blessed me in that regard once I had fully repented. Truly, the Lord forgives and forgets and allows us to do the same when repentance is complete and sincere.

INSIGHTS INTO PERSONAL ACTIONS

The last part that I needed to understand and work on was how I ended up in jail. After reading several inspiring books, I realized I struggled with behaviors and coping mechanisms learned back in my childhood and teenage years. One of those behaviors was a propensity to hide my mistakes and weaknesses from others. This behavior was a result of my experiences with my Father and Stepfather. As a child, I learned that sharing these kinds of things was not always a good idea and it led to bad outcomes. At least they seemed to for me because they were related to many of the hurtful experiences I had as a child and young man.

I would call my wife from jail and tell her the things I was figuring out and share the joy and relief I felt by acknowledging these things and starting to work on them. I felt the Lord's help as I prayed for strength to overcome these things and to change those behaviors. Over the next several months, I figured out many of the reasons why things had happened the way they did and how they came to be a problem. Now the next steps were to work on overcoming the weaknesses. I identified and worked to ensure that I lived my life in harmony with the gospel to help me avoid those same mistakes again.

SELF-DISCOVERY BRINGS CHANGE

Another problem that became clear as I went through this period of self-discovery was the recognition of my poor self-esteem. This was a problem I had struggled to admit throughout my life. Thinking back to when this began, it correlates directly to many of the things that took place in my formative years. Several instances came to mind to explain why my self-esteem was not very good as a child. The first instance was the time I told my mother of my Father's infidelity. The day I told her, my parents had the worst fight I ever remember them having. It was a physical altercation, with screaming and yelling, plates being thrown and broken, and threats hurled back and forth. Because my bedroom was directly below my parents', I heard everything that was said and done. That night I found myself hiding in my room scared my Dad would come for me next because of what I had told my Mom. I was traumatized that night; and to this day, I still remember the feelings that I had and how scared I was.

The thing that stands out most to me about what happened was the thoughts I had while listening to my parents fight. These thoughts included the following: 1) I never should have told my Mother what I saw that night. 2) Telling them everything was not a good idea. It is still hard for me to recall the events of that night without feeling some of the emotions I felt that day. 3) But even more painful and memorable was the night my Dad left us for the first time. He came home early that day and said he was going to drop something off to a neighbor. Then he just left and never came back. When Mom came home later that evening, she found a note he had left for her, telling her he had gone. That was the worst night of my childhood. Seeing my Mom break down into tears in a way I had never seen before overwhelmed me with guilt for what I thought I had done. All I wanted to do was to make it right somehow, but I could not. I felt helpless and at fault for her pain. After my aunt arrived to comfort her, I went to my room and listened to her cry, and I hated myself for what I thought I had caused. I thought at the time if I had just not told my Mother what I had seen at the gym, my parents would still be together. But now they were not because I told Mother everything, and it was all my fault my Dad left and my Mom was hurting.

The first time my Father left, he was gone for only a brief time and then he came back to try to work things out with my Mom. During that time, he promised me he was not going to leave us again, but he did. He had a choice between us and the woman he was seeing, and he chose her. That day was the second worst day of my childhood because I stood in the driveway of our house begging my Father not to leave, and he did anyway. How could he leave his five children while they were crying and begging for him to stay? That day I felt completely rejected and unloved. Being so young and not yet aware of how adult relationships worked or the other dynamics at play, I could only take that as he did not want to be with us, and it seemed like it was all my fault. I felt responsible for all the hurt and pain we were going through. More than that, I remember feeling unwanted and unloved. Though I now know I was not to blame for the events that happened when I was young, at that time I blamed myself for everything that happened and did so for many years afterward.

Many other difficult and traumatic experiences happened during my parents' divorce that hurt me and affected how I felt about myself. One, in particular, left me emotionally scared for years afterward. It happened one evening when my younger brother and I had gone to see my Father for a visit. He was staying in one of those motels you pay to stay for a week or more, and I remember it being in a rundown part of town that was scary to me. That night we ate takeout and for the first time in my life, we were given apple beer to drink. That was weird to me because we had never had that before and also because it had a negligible amount of alcohol in it. But later on, I realized why he had wanted us to drink it. It was because he wanted us to fall asleep. I woke up in the middle of the night and found my Dad had left us alone in the shady hotel while he went to visit the other woman. Being in the middle of the night, and not sure if my Father was going to return at some point, I panicked and was unsure what to do. I decided not to call my Mom because I was afraid that telling her what happened would lead to another fight or worse. Instead, I got back into bed and hoped that my Father would return. My younger brother also woke up, and I told him that Dad would be back soon and to go back to sleep. So we both lay back down and hoped that when we woke up, he would be there.

When morning came, Dad returned, but the fear and the trauma never never went way. He had abandoned me many times, and that fear of him leaving was very real for me going forward. As a result, I did not trust that the people I loved would not leave me. I still struggle with that same fear today. During this period while my parents were going through the divorce process, I did everything I could think of to bring them back together. My feelings of guilt and my desire to have my family back together drove me to extreme behavior. I would threaten my Mom that I was going to run away and did but never for very long. More times than not I would go next door to our neighbor's playhouse and go into the attic and cry and wish my Dad would come back. I also began acting out in school, getting into trouble and fights, and even destroying school property and being kept after school in detention. It was all done to get my parents' attention and let them know I was hurting, but that still did not bring my Father back. I tried everything I knew how to do, but it did not change the situation; and the guilt I felt never went away either.

After the many hard and traumatic experiences I had as a result of my parents' divorce, I learned through painful experiences that telling my parents things during this time was not a good idea. My Mom would confront my Father about anything I told her, and my Dad would talk negatively about my Mom as a result. Because I loved them both, I just decided not to tell them things the other did or said. That was how I dealt with things during that time. The fear of telling the truth and it leading to bad outcomes has been my experience so far. That would only get reinforced when my Mom married my Stepfather. That also led to another behavior getting reinforced when my Mother remarried. That behavior was characterized by my only saying things that were good or that cast things in the best light. I would not mention anything that could be construed as bad or negative for fear of reprisals, fights, or it being brought up constantly in the future. Telling the truth, or the whole truth, usually ended up hurting me more than it helped. Of course, I now see how faulty this thinking is, but at the time it was how I survived my teenage years.

STEPFATHER SAYS ONE THING AND DOES ANOTHER

I was optimistic about my life getting better when my Mother met and started dating my Stepfather. From the start, he told me what I wanted to hear and made promises to gain my trust. He told me he would not interfere in my relationship with my Dad and would allow me time to adjust to him as my Stepfather, and many other things to help me adapt to all the changes. It seemed like things were going to be better, and I chose to trust him. But as soon as he and my Mom came home from their honeymoon, he came to my room and informed me I had two weeks to start calling him Dad and to get used to it. From that day on he continued to break all the promises he made to me before he married my Mom. He also started lying, abusing me physically, and even once sexually. As I was accustomed to doing, I blamed myself for all the abuse I suffered at his hands, as if somehow I deserved it or that it was my fault that it happened. I was also mad at myself for trusting him and telling my Mom to marry him. The frustrating part was he seemed so genuine and sincere when we met him, and for the entire time he dated my Mom. But after they married, he completely changed; and we all saw that he had a lot of anger and bitterness inside him.

I also witnessed a dark side to him that he hid from everyone until they were married. That dark side came out when others were not around and could not account for the things he said and did to me. Then when I would tell my Mom or others what he had done, he would deny it and blame me instead. But it all happened; it was all true. The fact that I chose to trust him and then he did what he did to me made it hard for me to trust anyone going forward. I had been hurt so many times now by those whom I should have been able to trust. I no longer trusted anyone, no matter what they said or how sincere they seemed. To this day actions speak louder than words to me. I do not trust when people tell me they will do things; I trust when they do what they say they will do. I am also very hurt when they do not keep their word. The years of trauma and abuse and being lied to left deep scars in my heart and emotions that did not heal. I remember feeling as though I was not worth being told the truth, treated with respect or dignity, or being loved by anyone as a teenager.

Another factor in my low self-esteem during my childhood was my Stepfather constantly telling me I was not a good person, rehashing old mistakes, and reiterating often that I would turn out to be just like my Father. Whenever I made a mistake, he would mention anything I had ever done wrong in the past and make derogatory comments about me to friends, neighbors, relatives, and others. Those comments he thought were funny or made jokingly; but after years of hearing those things, I started to believe them. Even though my teachers and others who spent time with me told me positive things, I did not believe them. I was damaged goods that nobody wanted and that is why all the terrible things happened to me.

We also discovered after I came to jail that my Stepfather had been suffering from a mental disorder for some time. How long he had been dealing with it nobody is entirely sure. After speaking to my brother, we feel fairly certain that he has dealt with it since our teenage years. That would explain his erratic and nonsensical behavior that we saw while growing up; unfortunately, we found out too late to preserve the relationships that were already broken by the time I ended up in prison. Because only the Lord knows the heart and capabilities of others, I will leave it to the Lord to judge when it comes to my Stepfather.

LACK OF SELF-ESTEEM SPOILED OPPORTUNITY

My lack of self-esteem played a vital role in my quitting my school basketball team during my senior year in high school. That year I was having difficulty with my self-confidence. My girlfriend, whom I had fallen for, had dumped me for one of my friends. My Stepfather had helped destroy the relationship with her by telling her parents things about me that simply were not true. This left me feeling alone and lacking any real confidence going into my senior year. So when the basketball season started, I struggled to play well. Eventually, the coach benched me for a junior, which I felt was a big slap in the face. But because I was afraid to talk to him for fear of it going badly, as was my experience in life, I simply told him I was quitting and did just that. Now as I think back to my high school days, I wish I had told people what was going on at home. Also, I have always regretted quitting the basketball team and not sticking with it. I knew I was better than I had played and wished I had stayed and proven that to me and my coach.

Because of these difficult experiences, I have spent much of my life trying to figure out who and what I was. In my heart, I was afraid no one would want to be with me if they truly got to know me because of what I had experienced. I feared they would blame me or agree that those things that had happened to me were my fault. I had been so conditioned to be blamed for things that I just thought it would continue because it seemed that those who knew me best loved me the least and blamed me when things went wrong. That left me feeling very insecure and unsure of myself and questioning what was wrong with me.

ABLE TO SEE REALITY AND MOVE FORWARD

Sitting in my jail cell and thinking back on my life, I was finally able to see things as they really were and are now. Choosing to be humble helped me to accept some hard realities about myself that I had blamed on others for many years. Growing up in the difficult circumstances I had experienced made it hard for me to overcome certain tendencies because I was afraid to face my fears and trust in those around me. But I was also beginning to see that it was not their fault for the mistakes I was making in my life. It was my fault and mine alone. It had been easier to blame my parents or my circumstances in life rather than to look at myself and hold myself accountable.

The behaviors I learned and chose to use to protect myself in my relationships had a devastating impact on my life. Many of them were not things I was even aware I was doing. I did not stop to think about why I was doing them; I just did what I had always done, which I now realize was wrong. But there is no denying that the way I grew up had a major impact on how I thought and what I did. Though I realize now that I am still responsible for my poor choices, the things I experienced in my childhood and teenage years did play a key role in my decision-making process and what I ultimately decided to do.

SELF-SABOTAGING LIFE

This leads me to the last behavior that I identified as being a key to understanding why I did what I did, and that was my tendency to sabotage things in my life. In hindsight, I now see that when I was afraid I would fail or thought someone might reject me or hurt me, I would preemptively sabotage the relationship by doing something that would destroy it before they could hurt me. I did not know for years why I did some of the terrible things I did—things that made no sense and were not what I wanted—until I was able to step back and think about it. When I went to jail and was humbled and prepared to learn and understand why I had behaved so poorly, that was when I was able to begin understanding and admit that I was doing them. These behaviors were all forms of self-sabotage, and I did them as a form of self-defense. If I hurt them first, then they could not hurt me. In my first marriage, I found out my soon-to-be wife was sneaking out to make out with her former boyfriend and then was dishonest about it when confronted after I watched it happen. Up until that point, I had been honest and true to her; however, after she hurt me, I resorted to my destructive behaviors. She hurt me and now I was protecting my heart by doing things that would distance me from her. Then after we were married and I found out she had been cheating on me, I went to even greater lengths to protect myself by doing the same to her and detaching from her emotionally.

My subsequent relationships that did not result in marriage functioned much the same. Once they had done things to hurt me, I sabotaged the relationship to detach myself from them emotionally and withdrew to make it easier once the relationship ended. I realized that I never expected any of my relationships to last. In the back of my mind, I was just waiting for them to leave or lose interest. The only relationship that I even wanted to work on was my last marriage. She was everything I wanted in a woman, and she was better than I ever thought I could get. So when I met her and she was interested in me, too, I thought maybe this time I would try to do things the right way. For the first time, I thought I had found the right woman.

LAST MARRIAGE IS THE BEST

From the start, she was different from other women I had dated. She had a stable family with parents who were still together. She had an excellent job and education. We seemed to get along so well and had the same goals in life. She was beautiful and our conversations were easy and fun. She seemed like the whole package, and I was all in from the moment we started talking.

From the start, I was honest and transparent about myself in ways I had never been with others. For the first time, I felt a desire to want to share most things with her that I did not with other women. I felt I had never dated another who could hold a candle to her, since my high school sweetheart. This led to me wanting to be very open about things with her, to avoid any problems or misunderstandings.

We talked for weeks on the phone before we met, and she assured me there were no other men she was seeing or dating. Then not long after we began to date, I learned she had not told me about a man she had been seeing for months before we met, and that she had continued to see after we began talking and seeing each other. If she had been honest from the start about him, and the nature of their relationship, I think things with us might have started differently. But like my other relationships, once I was hurt or lied to, it was hard for me to move forward to trust her after that. To make matters worse, she was not honest when I confronted her about him after I learned who he was when flowers showed up at her apartment one day shortly after we had begun dating. This led to my pulling back and protecting myself by not giving her my whole heart and engaging in my self-sabotaging behaviors. The result of those behaviors was a relationship in which we lacked any real trust or emotional bond because we did not feel close to one another. I loved her the best I could with the lack of trust existing on my part, and on hers as well. At the time I thought I was loving her, but now I realize that real love begins with trust and opening your heart completely to that person, which I was not able to do at that time because I chose not to accept that risk. Identifying these problems was the beginning of the process of fixing them. Reading and learning the correct ways to manage issues and situations helped me gain the knowledge I needed to overcome these problems.

RECOGNIZED PROBLEMS CAN BE FIXED

There was a huge sense of relief at the realization that the problems I had been experiencing were fixable and that I could change over time with the Lord's help. The scriptures helped me to understand that nothing was beyond the Lord's ability to fix and heal. As broken as I thought I was, for the very first time I believed that I could be healed, spiritually and emotionally. I remember driving home many nights during those twenty years I had not been fully active in the church and thinking that after all the mistakes I had made, there was no way I could be forgiven. Now that I realized that was not the case, I had renewed my life and purpose again.

Excited to finally figure out why I did some of the dumb things I had been doing, I would call my wife and share these realizations with her, and then apologize for each of these destructive behaviors. I shed many tears and felt remorse for each of these mistakes and weaknesses that had hurt her and my family and children. Being able to see these weaknesses and acknowledge them was a very humbling experience. However, once I admitted that these things were a problem for me, I was able to start working on them and things began to change. As I turned to the Lord for help and began the repentance process, I felt the Lord's influence in tangible ways.

On several occasions, I remember being in my cell in the jail and feeling the influence of the Spirit run through my body starting at my head and going all the way to my toes. The feeling was so amazing that each time I was moved to tears and could only thank the Lord for those experiences and the answers to prayers that He gave as blessings to me. Once the guilt and pain of past mistakes were lifted from my shoulders, I also began to feel differently about who I was and the direction I was going. I felt strengthened by the Lord and the guilt I had carried for over twenty years suddenly was no longer there. I knew that it would take time to overcome the challenges I had dealt with much of my life, but now I knew I could do it and that the Lord could heal my heart and soul.

TESTING FOR STDS

Not long after I had gone for my bond hearing, I was called to the front of the dorm early one morning to be transported to the health department. I was not forewarned this was going to happen so, I was unsure whether I needed to call my attorney or what I should do. Once shackled, I was taken from the jail to the health department and told I was going to be tested for STDs. I knew I did not have any diseases and could only assume this had something to do with my case. Waiting for my blood to be drawn, I wondered what they were trying to accuse me of this time. While waiting for the tests to be done, the two deputies who had transported me to the clinic, after learning I was there to be tested for STDs, decided to make crude jokes at my expense. The entire time they mocked me and made the trip miserable for me. They also paraded me in front of other people who were there and made comments in front of them that were meant to humiliate me. I did not respond or say anything to them as they did these things to me; instead, I just kept my mouth shut and waited for them to return me to my dorm. Several months down the road on the first day of my trial, I finally learned the results of my tests and why the tests were done in the first place. The woman who had accused me of the crimes I was going to stand trial for had contracted herpes and had her initial outbreak just weeks after we met. The prosecution had requested to have me tested to blame me for her herpes diagnosis. However, when the tests came back negative, they instead petitioned the judge to not allow that information to be shared during the trial. The judge agreed to grant their motion, as she had all the other motions the prosecution had made. My attorney, who was not familiar with the current laws and statutes surrounding the rape shield law, did not challenge the ruling.

After the trial, my appellate attorney informed me we could have challenged the motion to allow us to introduce evidence that would show that the victim's ailments she claimed were from our encounter were caused by the initial herpes outbreak she suffered weeks later. According to the medical information we obtained, those symptoms began a few weeks before the actual outbreak, which would have coincided with the time she met the other man and me. All of the symptoms she claimed to have been symptomatic of an initial herpes outbreak. My attorney also had agreed before the trial to exclude a batch of text messages without reading the texts or asking me before he agreed to exclude them. Those texts that were excluded from the victim's phone showed she had been out a week before we met, went to a bar, got drunk, and met a man and spent the evening with him. Those messages directly refuted the victim's testimony at trial that she had never been promiscuous and had never met a man out at a bar or slept with him on the first date or encounter. The next day when the man she had spent the night with texted her, she claimed she could not remember kissing him or what they had done. That is the same thing that happened to me, except I was accused of assaulting her. It is obvious now why the prosecution wanted that batch of her text messages excluded from the trial because they showed their client to have engaged in promiscuous behavior just a week before meeting me and ended up contracting herpes from the man she met a week before me. She then tried to blame me for her infection at the trial. Why my attorney agreed to exclude those text messages without bothering to read them or question why the prosecution wanted those excluded is anybody's guess. What I do know for sure is that he never prepared for my trial and only wanted me to plead guilty to crimes I did not commit.

CHANGES IN JAIL POLICIES

As the days dragged on into months, the jail decided to change their food policy: instead of giving us three meals a day Monday-Friday, they decided to switch to two hot meals a day, with bologna sandwiches between breakfast and dinner. On the weekends, it was the same. This amounted to a significant reduction in food and made it more challenging to get enough calories to maintain weight. I would exercise in my cell regularly by putting all my books in a bag and using it as weights. Then I would do pushups and squats and any other exercises I could think of to stay healthy and strong. This lack of food and my exercising, however, led to a big weight loss on my part. For almost the year I was in the county jail, I lost over thirty pounds. The commissary that my family provided for me was the only thing that prevented me from losing more. The stress and the lack of quality food took their toll over time and added to the difficulty of being locked up in the awful conditions I had to endure in the county jail.

A JOKE ENDS IN SUICIDE WATCH

These physical changes also led to a horrible experience I had while in jail. I had been talking on the phone and telling my wife jokingly that the food was so bad that it would probably kill me before this was all over. I was joking, but little did I realize at that time that the district attorney's office was listening to every call I made. Whoever was listening at that moment I made the statement about the food and used that as an excuse to put me on suicide watch. Literally, within an hour of making that phone call, I had officers at my cell hauling me out and taking me to the medical floor. It was 10:30 pm when they took me down, then made me strip off all of my clothes, and gave me only a paper gown to wear. Then I was put into a tiny cold holding cell directly in front of the guards to spend the night. It was the most miserable night I can ever remember. I nearly froze to death in this room and was awakened every hour and could never get comfortable on the bench I had to sleep on. Even worse, I was naked and being watched by men and women alike and felt humiliated.

When the morning finally came, I was moved to another larger cell with several others and continued to sit in an "ice box" all day until the mental health doctor came to see us. I explained that this was all a misunderstanding, and I was not at all suicidal. I asked him to call my wife to verify it all for him. He took my wife's number and called her, but she was on a flight that day and her phone was turned off. Because he was unable to contact her and he was leaving for the night, he said he would have to keep me on suicide watch until the morning when he could verify my story.

After being naked for the past day now, and exhausted because of lack of sleep, I dreaded another sleepless night in a cold room. But instead of going back to where I was the night before, I was taken to another larger room with a concrete square in one corner to sleep on, and a toilet on the other side. I was given another paper gown and a bag of sandwiches for the night. This was one of the hardest nights I spent in county jail. As the sun went down that night, I remember praying fervently that the Lord would help me to keep warm and to have enough food to curb the hunger pains I was experiencing. I had not slept in the past twenty-four hours, had only eaten a few sandwiches, and was hungry, exhausted, and cold. The room was so frigid, and I honestly worried about hypothermia because I had nothing to protect me from the frigid air blowing in.

They put another man in the cell with me who had purposely put himself on suicide watch so that when he was taken off, he could call his girlfriend. He was housed on the seventh floor where the worst of the worst are kept. On his floor, they are not allowed to use the phones at all. Now he was going to be my cellmate for the night, and I was unsure about him from the start. After talking to him briefly, I learned he had been on suicide watch often and knew how to get a few "extras" because he was friendly with several of the guards who worked on the medical floor. One of those extra items he requested for us was what they called a turtle suit. It looked like a green life jacket and provided about the same coverage on your body, but it was something to help keep you warm. But by the time the sun went down, it was all I could do to keep from chipping my teeth as they chattered and my body shivered with cold.

I tried to keep moving to keep my temperature up; but after a while, my bare feet were so cold I could not feel them, so I sat down and prayed for help to make it through the night. I prayed with all my heart for the Lord to help me keep warm and for some food because I was hungry and needed the food to stay warm. That is when several miracles happened. One of the guards who came on for the night shift agreed to give us a few sheets that we could wrap up in and some extra bags of sandwiches to go along with them. I knew the Lord had softened this man's heart because we were not supposed to have anything given to us, but he did. He offered us both the very things I had prayed for, and I felt the Lord had answered my prayers.

I was not alone that night in that cold empty cell. I felt that the Lord was with me, and even protected me later from the man in the cell with me who tried to get too friendly when I was trying to lie down and rest. The next morning the doctor came back and released me from the suicide watch, and I was able to get my clothing back and was moved to a cell where I could sleep with blankets and bedding. After that experience, I stopped complaining about things because I realized things could be worse. I never again wanted to experience that cold, hungry experience and appreciated what little they provided for us in a new light. I returned aware now that I was being monitored closely and that anything I said could and would be used against me. The message was received.

WAITING FOR THE TRIAL AMID CHALLENGES

As the summer months approached, the temperatures in the jail increased. Air conditioning worked sometimes and then oftentimes did not. Opportunities were few to leave our cells because of staffing shortages leaving us for days at a time with no way to shower or to get clean. We also were not allowed to shave or have razors, so my beard was beginning to grow. Not being accustomed to having facial hair, my face itched and was uncomfortable. It was a challenging time for me.

Waiting for my trial was also stressful and exhausting. My attorney would come to visit and instead of working on my case and following through on things I asked him to look into, he came painting the worst possible picture and telling me if I did not take a deal, I would spend the rest of my life in prison. To this, I responded that if he would simply look into the case, and investigate the things I told him about, that the prosecution was not aware of, he would be able to defend me against their attacks. He claimed because of the large amount of evidence, he was unable to bring it to the jail to review before the trial.

At the trial, I saw the evidence and saw no reason it could not have been brought to the jail for me to review. If he had done so, I would have been able to advise him on things that I knew of that refuted many claims. However, by his actions, it is clear his goal was to get me to take a plea, so he did not have to prepare for trial. Not only did we learn he had tried only one case like mine thirty years ago but also did we learn he lied about his knowledge of current case laws and statutes. Because of the gross misrepresentation of his capabilities and knowledge, we were left unaware until the trial was over. But his insistence that I take a plea and his dreadful outlook added to my stress and worry as I sat helpless in my cell awaiting the trial. What helped me during this time was seeing my children and family through videos both at the jail and at home.

Their visits helped to keep my spirits up and to know that they were well and being taken care of. My bishop also came several times to visit and encourage me to continue to stay close to the Lord during these difficult days.

At one of these visits, he brought a letter from the Prophet, President Monson. I had written to him while I was at the jail. The reason I had done so was because of a blessing I received from my bishop. In the blessing, he told me that the prophet knew me and was aware of me. This had an enormous impact on me, and I felt a desire to write to the Prophet to see if he was aware of me. I also shared with him my path back to the church and my efforts to sincerely repent of all my sins. I did not expect to hear back from the Prophet; however, to my surprise, he wrote back and sent the correspondence to my bishop. The Prophet said that though he did not personally know me or my case, he did pray for all members of the church worldwide. He said that he would continue to pray for me in my efforts to change and repent. I was excited and grateful that as busy as he was, he took the time to reply to my letter and encouraged me to continue the repentance process. It buoyed my faith in the Prophet, and it showed me that he loves and shows concern for even the very least in the kingdom. Though my bishop also received a rebuke from the Prophet for what he told me, I was thrilled that I had received an answer from a Prophet of God. That strengthened my testimony of President Monson's divine calling, and that testimony only grew as I read his teachings and tried to follow his admonitions.

As the trial approached, we began to prepare for the motions hearing that would determine which witnesses would be allowed to testify. Finally, I would hear what the witnesses would claim. I had been guilty of using them and being dishonest, but I could think of no other accusations. The District Attorney had broadcast on television when I was arrested that any who had been on a date with me should contact his office to find others who would corroborate their false narrative. Several came forward, some who claimed their experiences with me had been very normal and nothing out of the ordinary happened. Then there were a few who had previously figured out I was married and misrepresented myself, and they ended up being the ones who testified against me. I could understand their anger and hurt for my dishonesty and infidelity. I was wrong to deceive them and meet them under pretenses for selfish reasons. But the disappointing part was that instead of telling the truth, they twisted their stories to fit the narrative that the prosecution put forth. In each of their stories, they took what happened and made it into something it was not altogether. Lies were told about events that in reality never took place.

Another disturbing thing that I did not learn until trial was that the detective who interviewed these witnesses knowingly lied to these women telling them untrue stories to get them to testify against me. He told them I was infecting women intentionally with various STDs, that I knew I had these STDs, and that if they did not testify against me, I would continue to infect others. None of that was true, nor did he have any proof of that. He also advised them to get tested because they probably were infected too. Then he claimed I brutally attacked and assaulted the alleged victim, and he needed their help to get me convicted. He also claimed that if enough people agreed to testify, the case would never go to trial because I would plead guilty. All of this was completely false and not based on reality. The detective said these things to witnesses because some of the witnesses said they were hesitant about testifying. This was because in large part their stories were not truthful, and they worried about being caught in a lie. I was informed after learning about the false statements made by the detective that the police are allowed to lie during interviews to secure testimony. Those lies worked to manipulate these women into giving seemingly coerced testimonies, all to try and force me to give a guilty plea. That is what the detective himself said in the interviews. They wanted to pressure me not to go to trial. Most of this evidence ended up not being shown to the jury because the person hired to operate the equipment could not get it to work in the time allowed by the judge. The judge had arbitrarily set five minutes. There was no law for how long it took to get equipment working, but the judge decided to give us only five minutes. When we could not, she said we had to move on and forgo showing the jury the evidence that helped prove my case.

THE ACCUSER TESTIFIES

The accuser was the first to testify at the motions hearing. Her testimony of what happened was so far from the truth that I thought the jury would never believe her story. Her claims of large amounts of blood loss, injury, and trauma were not at all true or supported by the facts or evidence. Later during the trial, the doctors who examined her after the incident contradicted her testimony and said there was no sign of trauma or injury. The other witnesses' testimonies followed the same pattern of false statements and truth distortion. The witnesses appeared to have been coached in what to say to prejudice the jury against me. There were two reasons why those witnesses testified against me: first, because I had been dishonest with them and misrepresented myself to go out with them, causing anger and resentment towards me; and second, because of the lies they were told by the detective. One who did not end up testifying at the motions hearing was my ex-wife, who had initially agreed to testify. Because the mediator submitted an affidavit favorable to me in a recently decided child support case, she was not called to testify. My ex-wife falsely claimed I owed her more money for past child support. However, once we met with the mediator, she was proven to have lied, and the mediator emphasized she did not have documentation to back up her claims. As a result, she was forced to accept a lower monthly payment to compensate me for the money I had overpaid her over the years. Because she was untrustworthy, the prosecution decided not to have her testify.

QUESTIONS ABOUT WITNESSES

Once the hearing ended, my family had questions about certain things that were said. The witnesses had made claims and twisted what had happened into something that it was not. Some of those who testified made the same claims of being drugged somehow and not remembering things. Not surprisingly, all their stories had been altered and details added to fit the narrative of the prosecution. They alleged that I was meeting women at bars to have a drink and then drugging and assaulting them. The truth is that I never once drugged anyone and never assaulted anyone. It was true that when we met, drinking was normally involved. The people I ended up meeting had suggested going to a bar to have a drink for the initial meeting. That is what the majority did so that if you did not like the person, you could finish your drink and leave. It was considered odd if you did not drink. Also because of what had happened previously with a woman falsely accusing me after I would not let her come to my home, I was careful to be respectful and polite and not do anything to upset or anger anyone for fear of that happening again.

It was understandable that after that hearing, my wife and family had questions that I was happy to answer. Knowing the phones were monitored, I wrote them and explained what had happened with each person who testified and set the records straight. From the beginning, I had been truthful to a fault about my part in what had happened and was forthright throughout because I knew what the truth was and had committed to doing what was right by accepting responsibility for my actions and mistakes. This helped alleviate the concerns my family had. As time went on, more evidence became known that showed I was telling the truth, and the others were not.

The result of the motions hearing was predictable. The judge allowed all the witnesses who testified at the hearing to testify at my trial. In my mind, allowing all to testify was further proof of her bias against me. Our objections that the testimonies of these witnesses were more prejudicial than substantive were denied. It seemed obvious these people were brought in to prejudice the jury because they were not relevant to what happened between me and the accuser nor to the case. If the trial were simply about what had happened with the accuser, and the facts, I believe I would still be free today. The judge also made the comment that if she were wrong, she would let the appellate court tell her she was wrong. Until then she was going to allow the prosecution every advantage and declined every motion we filed.

One thing we did after the hearing was to get the dress that the accuser wore the night we met tested for blood. Why the prosecution did not have the dress tested on their own to prove what their witness said was true is telling. Because they would not test it, we decided to have it tested instead. According to her testimony, she "bled out" for several hours while wearing this dress. With the amount of blood she claimed she lost, it would have been virtually impossible for blood not to be found somewhere on the dress. That and the fact that she also was not wearing any underwear under the dress made it highly unlikely.

ACCUSER'S DRESS TESTED NO BLOOD

When the results came back shortly before the trial, it confirmed what I had said from the start: there was never any blood. There was no trace at all of any blood on the dress, and this was additional proof that what the accuser had said happened was not true. The test results also revealed another important discovery, it was positive for bodily fluids. This further proved her story was false because she was wearing the dress during the encounter. So, if she were bleeding as a result of the encounter and had bodily fluids on the dress, there would have been blood mixed with those fluids if she bled because of intercourse. The fact that no blood was found simply proved her story was not truthful and that the nature of the encounter was not as she claimed it to be.

These revelations from the test results forced the accuser to drastically change her testimony at the trial. Her testimony at the motions hearing did not account for the clothing test coming back negative for blood. So, at the trial. she had to make several changes to her story to account for how bodily fluids were found on the dress, but no blood. Her numerous inconsistencies and lies were apparent to everyone not associated with her or the prosecution. Now that I knew what the accuser and others were alleging against me, I felt we could use the facts and evidence we had to exonerate me. At this point I still felt if we could simply show the jury what the truth and the facts were, I would be found not guilty. I still believed at that point that the truth would set me free.

TENSION IN THE JAIL

After the motions hearing, I had several more months to wait before I went to trial. But the longer I was in county jail, the worse it became. My cellmate and I got into a disagreement over him trying to touch me sometimes in ways that made me feel uncomfortable. When I approached him about it, he lost his temper and wanted to fight with me. I refused. I wanted to go home and did not want any more trouble. That caused some tension for some time between us, but then we left each other alone after that and nothing further came of it.

Other times we had tension in our dorm and gang members would threaten to harm those who were not affiliated, as their way of being initiated into the various gangs. They had to harm, or even in some cases kill someone, to become a member of these groups. There were times I felt I could be attacked or targeted by these gangs, but the Lord protected me, and in some cases prevented me from being in places at certain times to avoid being harmed. It was a tender mercy from the Lord that I escaped harm while in county jail.

MORE COURT APPEARANCES

As time went slowly on, I went back to court several more times. One time in particular, my wife brought me some clothes to wear during a hearing. In the pocket of the jacket she brought, she placed a little note of encouragement. Later back at the jail on a video with her, I thanked her for the note. I was unaware that her putting a note in my pocket was not allowed. So, when I thanked her for the note on the video, within minutes I had officers swarming my cell telling me whatever I was given to hand it over before they searched my cell. They also advised me if they found anything I would be charged. The judge was also contacted, and they threatened to hold my wife in contempt. Once again, they had been monitoring my communications; and when I said thank you for what you put in my jacket, referring to the note she gave me, they thought she had given me some sort of contraband. So, they searched my cell while my cellmate and I watched from the outside. That turned up nothing and they finally left, but not before making our cell unrecognizable. Being naive and not of the mindset of trying to hide anything, I was again shocked at how they continued to harass me for everything I said and did. They were trying their best to find something legitimate with which to charge me, but they found nothing.

MOVED TO ANOTHER FLOOR

Not long after this, I was moved to another floor. When I asked why, I was told for security reasons. I am not entirely sure what that was all about, but the door on our cell was not opening and closing properly around this time. I did say something on the phone about it being a security risk if the door did not open, so that might explain why I ended up being moved.

I went down one floor to a smaller dorm, and it was a tremendous change from where I had been. On this floor, they were even more short-staffed than where I came from. Getting out of the cell for a shower or phone call was more infrequent. This did not bother my new cellmate who liked to sleep with the light off all day long and stay up late into the night. This made it hard to read with the lights off all day, so I had to adjust what I did to pass the time. One thing that helped me was the option to rent a tablet from the jail. For a monthly fee, you could have a tablet that allows you to make calls from your cell, listen to podcasts, play a few games, or listen to music. My Mom rented a tablet for me, and it paid off during this period of darkness in our cell. Instead, I would listen to various podcasts and music to help pass the time. This, however, made the days and nights seem even longer. I was homesick and missed my family more than I thought I ever could.

At this point, I had been away for eight months, and my clothes were beginning to feel big on me because of excessive weight loss. I was anxious to leave and yet nervous about the trial because I was unsure of what to expect. I had figured it would be broadcast all over the news as everything had been thus far, but I never would have expected the things that ended up happening at the trial to happen. I was not at all prepared for how hard the trial was going to be, and how hard it was going to be on my family, too.

TRIAL SET TO BEGIN

At last, we had the hearing that would set the date for the trial to begin. My attorney asked the judge to allow the trial to start in January to make it easier for those in my family traveling around the holiday season, which she promptly denied. Then she set the trial date for early December, which was only about six weeks away. Anything was better than having to wait in jail, so I thought the sooner the better.

In the meantime, family members decided to come to the trial to be a support for me and my family. Many offered to take time out to be there despite all it would entail. I will always be grateful to those who came and their willingness to love and support my family during that tough time. There were also those in my family who were not as supportive, and that was hurtful. Having the religious background that I did, I knew the things that I did were wrong. Adultery, dishonesty, pride, and selfishness were grievous sins—and those deeply hurt and disappointed all in the family. Those who believed the things that were said by the news media and prosecution made up their mind that I was guilty before I ever went to trial. They made that determination without knowing the full story or hearing what took place. The prosecution presented a compelling case that if you were not privy to the facts, or made aware of the lies they told, it would be hard to believe otherwise.

The news also created a strong bias against me by their one-sided coverage of the case. My Stepfather and Mother were on different sides, too. My Stepfather did not support me and wanted my Mother not to use her resources to help me. He even changed his will to limit how she could spend the money she would receive when my Stepfather passed away, thus ensuring my Mom could only spend money on things he approved of, and not to help me. The vitriol that was again displayed by my Stepfather's actions on my behalf was hurtful but expected. But overall the family support was mostly positive and encouraging. Of course, you always want those you love to believe in you, especially in the face of horrendous accusations; however, there will always be those who will not. Knowing that does not always make it easier, but I understood to an extent.

I felt similarly when I heard that someone had been arrested for a crime. Before I came to jail or had any experience with the legal system, I assumed all who were arrested or went to prison were guilty. Like most who have never dealt with the criminal justice system, I assumed that it was always just and that if you were convicted, it was because you were guilty. However, after what I had experienced in the nine months in jail, court appearances, and the dishonest and false narratives that were being employed to destroy me, I came to realize that it is not always about the pursuit of truth and justice anymore. The truth was not what the prosecution was after in my case. For them, it was more about making up a story that the jury would believe based on bits of the truth mingled with many lies. Any holes in their case were filled in by false theories, and their witnesses were manipulated to tell stories that supported those false narratives. Incredibly, the story they produced at the trial was so different from what happened that at times I wondered if they were talking about me and the night in question, or something else entirely. It was truly astonishing and hard to believe unless you witnessed it and knew the truth of what took place. So those who chose not to find out the other side of the story, go to the trial, or hear the evidence came away believing what was written or what they heard from media sources. Sadly, only one side of the story was told on the news, the internet, and social media—and that was the accuser's story.

Rarely does hearing one side of the story reflect what truly took place or fairly represent both sides. I experienced firsthand how unfair and biased the process can be for those accused of a crime. This taught me to be very careful about jumping to conclusions when it comes to another's guilt or innocence. Because of how I was treated, I have more empathy for those who are accused and found guilty in the court of public opinion, without first having the opportunity to defend themselves against the accusations or present their side of the story.

Now that the trial was set, my wife, sister, and Mother began to arrange all the evidence into a very organized system of binders that my attorney could reference quickly. Each section had tabs detailing what was in each part so that even a cursory glance at them would have helped him become familiar with where things were located. I would soon learn my attorney made no efforts to become familiar with the work my family did to make things easier for him; instead, he was intent on getting me to plead guilty so his ineptitude would not be exposed.

A video expert had also been hired to display video evidence and locate segments that we needed to show the jury at various points while presenting our case. We also hired an expert to testify to the fact that there were no drugs found in the accuser's system and also about the consumption of alcohol the night in question.

Everything had been arranged, and the trial was now only a week away. I spent the last week preparing myself for what was about to take place. I knew it was going to be a tough time emotionally, and also physically. The weekend before the trial I spent fasting and praying for the truth to be revealed, that those I loved would be able to know the truth from error, and that justice might be done. I also promised the Lord that I would accept whatever the outcome was because when I had determined to repent of all my sins, I also covenanted with the Lord to accept the outcome, whatever that was going to be.

LAST FEW DAYS BEFORE TRIAL

The last few days before I went to court, I fasted and spent time writing to my family. I sought forgiveness for any mistakes I had made over the years and for my poor example to those in the family and to my children. Though I was not guilty of the crimes I was going to be on trial for, there was much I was guilty of, and many I had hurt by the choices I made. Most affected were those I loved and were closest to me. I spent much of the nine months in jail apologizing to my family for those mistakes. I lamented every day the things I did wrong and wished I could somehow make things right. As I fasted, I offered my food trays to those who did not get commissary or were hungry and in need. I also offered commissary food I had to those who went without. That was my way to sacrifice and show the Lord I was willing to do all I could to follow Him in my circumstances. The night before my trial I fasted also and prayed that the Lord would strengthen me for what was to come, not knowing beforehand just how difficult the next week would be.

Chapter 11

The Trial and Outcome

TRIAL BEGINS

The morning of my trial, I was taken to court and dressed in a suit my wife brought me. As I sat waiting to be brought before the judge, my attorney came to see me. He again asked me to make a deal and hinted that he might be able to reduce the time even further. I declined and expressed confidence in his abilities, saying I would not take any deal. He looked worried, but I had no idea why until after the trial began.

When I was led into the courtroom, I saw my family, who had flown in from all over the country, seated on one side and the accuser's family and friends on the other. I still remember the looks I received from the accuser's side as I walked into the courtroom. They, too, thought I had done these awful things to their daughter or friend. I felt sad and disappointed that so many people were affected by the choices I made to meet this woman and the fallout that came as a result. Of course, they would believe their daughter. I would believe my daughter, too. I did not fault any of them for their anger or for feeling the way they did. I was sad that so many were there because of me and suffering because of my selfish behavior.

JURY SELECTION

Before the trial began and a jury was selected, the prosecution made a motion to suppress the evidence that the accuser had herpes, and I did not. This would prove to be an important part of the case because she experienced a herpes outbreak for the first time after our date. However, she did not get herpes from me because I tested negative. This was the first time my attorney hurt my case because he was unaware of the current laws and statutes. He should have challenged this motion by arguing that the accuser's alleged symptoms that she claimed came from our encounter were more likely related to the herpes outbreak she experienced shortly thereafter. The reason for arguing this is that herpes outbreaks cause all of the same symptoms she complained about. The fact that she also had the virus made it highly likely that it was the cause of the pain and discomfort she had experienced. Herpes, I learned, is very painful and causes many symptoms weeks before an actual outbreak. Under the law, if the prosecution introduces evidence to claim I was to blame for some physical injury, and there is an alternative explanation for what may have caused it, we are allowed to show what that alternative cause might be. And in this circumstance, knowing she had herpes made it plausible that it was what had caused her medical problems, not what took place on our date. Because the prosecution claimed it was a result of the date, we were legally allowed to bring up her herpes outbreak as the most likely cause of her pain and suffering. However, my attorney did not challenge it, and so the jury was never made aware that there was an alternative explanation for the accuser's discomfort and pain. They also were never told that she had herpes, and I did not.

After the motion to suppress evidence, the judge brought in the potential jurors to select a jury. To do this, the charges were read aloud to the jury pool in great detail, describing each charge and its meaning. As I listened and saw the potential jurors' angry reactions, I was sickened by what I heard. The nature and description of the crimes I had been accused of were horrible and repulsive. This had the intended immediate negative impact on the jury pool. Selecting jury members took place in a room in the back of the courtroom with potential jurors brought back one at a time to be questioned by the prosecution and defense. Many potential jurors expressed anger over what they assumed I had done, eliminating them from consideration. Others said they had been abused in similar ways and were also excused. Then, some acted as though they could be impartial or fair but seemed to say so to be selected. To me, it felt like most were already prejudiced against me and were familiar with my case because of news and media coverage. Some angrily said they could not even look at me they were so disgusted by my presence.

Finally, we had a jury once all were interviewed, and both sides could select jurors they wanted and challenge the ones they did not. The jury consisted mostly of women and a few men. The alternates were also men. Once the jurors were selected and their names were called to be seated in the jury box, one of the female jurors selected, seated directly in front of me, turned to someone next to her and mouthed the words, "I am going to get him." As she did so, she turned to look at me disapprovingly and then took her place in the jury box. Later, when the jury rendered its decision, I learned she was made the jury supervisor and delivered the decision to the judge. That came as no surprise to me.

PROSECUTION'S OPENING STATEMENT

Now that the jury was selected and in place, the judge asked for the prosecution to give their opening statement. I was unaware that the opening and closing statements did not have to be factually accurate or true until the trial started. They can consist of whatever accusations or false claims they want to make or imply. The attorney for the prosecution had an elaborate PowerPoint presentation that was great theater and persuasive, though inaccurate. In the meantime, my attorney wrote down his opening statement on a writing pad as the other presentation was being given. I immediately thought this was odd and unprofessional. Not being prepared with more than a few lines on a notepad embarrassed him and me.

My attorney's opening statement consisted of rehashing the case facts we could prove and then sitting down. Instead of giving a motive for the accuser, or showing she had a pattern of similar behavior with other men before me, or her having had numerous instances of drinking and not remembering what happened back in her college days, he reiterated the basic details of the case. After seeing the two presentations, I was already concerned; but I kept thinking that he would get better at some point and the truth would carry us through. I felt that even a bad lawyer armed with the truth could still win the case.

ACCUSER TESTIFIES

The first person called to the stand was the accuser. The prosecution walked her through her version of the events that night. I immediately noticed her testimony had drastically changed from what she had testified to in the motions hearing. The test results that came back after that hearing from the dress she wore on the date provided us a way to impeach her testimony completely. Because no blood was found on her dress, her testimony to the contrary from the motions hearing had to change. These changes should have been easily brought to light to prove she had given false testimony both before and now at the trial. But when my attorney got up to question the accuser, he walked her through what she had just testified to and failed to properly impeach her, partly because he could not find the information he needed to ask her and was unprepared. Several times, the judge had to let the jury step out and take a short break so my Mother could show my attorney where to find the information he searched for. He was oblivious to where to find anything, and his lack of preparation was an embarrassment. Throughout the trial, I often heard snickering and jeering from the other side because of my attorney's incompetence. After he completed his cross-examination, I knew that things were not going to turn out well for me. I now saw that my attorney was woefully unprepared and not interested in defending me in the least. He also had an attorney friend he had brought in to collaborate with him, but he did nothing but sit next to me and doodle the entire time the court was in session.

Some interesting information came out during the accuser's testimony that was new from the motions hearing. She had sent texts to friends in neighboring states after the incident and told them she was in the hospital on a feeding tube because of the attack she claimed had taken place. She declined when asked if they could visit her, telling them it was not a good idea. The reality was that she had never been admitted to any hospital and had no injuries that any doctor could find. There was absolutely nothing physically wrong with her according to those doctors. She just lied to her friends and family. She also told close friends that she had horrible tears in her genital area due to the incident, had stitches inside her and around that area, and had bloody bandages she had to change several times a day. Again, the reality was that no stitches were needed or given to her, nor was there any visible trauma or harm to that area according to multiple doctors who examined her.

My sister correctly identified that she made these statements to people who could not examine her or confirm what she was saying to them. To the doctors and nurses who examined her, she never claimed to have bled at all and never brought up any of the things she claimed to have suffered to her friends and family. For those who had not examined her, or did not have access to her records, she made outlandish claims that could not be verified. Therefore, those who were her friends and even certain family members were misled about the nature of what happened. One friend of hers who testified said she was unaware that she had been lied to about her injuries and had been bringing her medical supplies to help her with her pretended injuries. To another friend, she admitted that there were no such injuries but said she felt she needed to tell people there were for the police to believe her story. The emergency room doctor saw no signs of trauma and no bleeding or anything that would support her story of being attacked or harmed in any way. He reported that nothing outside of a normal physical interaction took place. She also visited three other doctors who said the same thing. All of her claims of pain or discomfort were not seen or explained by the medical personnel she saw. She also met a man the same night she went out with me later in the evening to a restaurant and later exchanged texts that were sexual and suggested they may have dated. The reason this was significant was that she claimed she had been traumatized and did not feel comfortable going on dates or being around men during this time. However, the evidence showed she still went out to bars and possibly even dated the man she met after me that same night.

ADDITIONAL TRIAL INSIGHTS

Some other notable things came out on the first day of the trial. The detective on the case claimed that he was unaware there was testing available for up to six months after someone had ingested a drug to determine what they had taken. The testing is done by taking a hair follicle and testing it to see what drugs a person has ingested. The toxins remain in the hair for up to six months. This type of testing had been around for over 20 years; however, he claimed he was only made aware of it after the six-month window to perform the test had passed. Ironically, I was not contacted about the case until it had been just over that six-month time limit and testing could no longer be done. Was that simply a coincidence that they waited to contact me about the case until it had been over six months and the opportunity to test for the drug had passed? Even my attorney, who did not normally handle cases like this, was aware of the testing, so why would a detective who deals with drugs and assault cases daily not be aware of it? We will never know whether he was aware of the testing. Based on his other dishonest testimony and his manipulation of witnesses, I doubted he was being honest about the testing. I never believed for a second that he was unaware of the testing options available, especially because I was informed it was a well-known method for drug use that he should have known.

His videotaped interviews showed how he lied to secure witness testimony, but those videos and what he told the witnesses were never played for the jury. There were two reasons why the jury never saw those tapes: First, the person we had originally hired to work the videos died of a major heart attack the night before my trial. He was a relatively young man, and it ended up being a devastating blow to our case because none of the video evidence showed what the accuser said right after the jury saw the incident. In her interview she spoke about her tendency to drink heavily and that what she had to drink that night was not unusual for her. Second, the person to fill in for the man we hired could not figure out how to get the videos to work, and the judge gave us five minutes to figure it out, or we had to move on. She arbitrarily set a time limit; and when we could not get it working, she forced us to go on without the ability to show how the detective had misled and lied to witnesses, and also how the accuser had admitted that she drank heavily regularly and did not feel she was drunk the night in question.

The prosecution also presented a video of that night that showed the accuser went to look for her car after we left the restaurant and then later when I dropped her off to get her car. They did not tell the jury that the garage was confusing and hard to navigate because every level is the same. So unless you pay close attention to which floor you park on, you could spend an hour finding your car going to all the various levels. That happened to me once when I came to the office building attached to that same parking deck for work. I parked, did not recall what level I was on, and spent half an hour looking for my car. I had not had any drinks, nor was I incapacitated in any way and it was still difficult to find. So, when the accuser went to find her car after having several drinks, and it being dark outside, it is no wonder she struggled to locate her vehicle. After visiting several floors and not finding her car, she walked across the street and asked me if I could drive us instead and pick up her car later. While this was going on with her, I had been texting asking her where we were going and an address to get there. When I did not hear back because she was having trouble finding her car, I thought maybe she changed her mind, so I decided to leave. As I was pulling out, I saw her walking toward me and I picked her up. In our town, cameras were everywhere, yet somehow, none of the things I just described were caught on camera. That seemed strange, but I had no idea whether that was true. My attorney never took the time to investigate it.

The last claim she made that contradicted one of her initial interviews with the police was whether her phone had a password. In an interview just after her phone was recovered, the detective asked her if it had a password. She said she did it because she had proprietary information for work on her phone and had to protect it. She was then seen unlocking the detective's phone and handing it back to him. The person who found her phone also indicated the phone was locked and had to wait until somebody called the phone to answer it and let them know the phone had been found. But again at the trial, that story also changed because the prosecution claimed I had sent numerous text messages from her phone to her family and friends that evening. This was not true at all. I sent one text message because she let me send one to her friend as a joke. However, before it was sent, she read it and then sent it to her friend. The text said, "I kissed my date." She had her phone with her the rest of the time and texted when I would go to the bathroom, which I did numerous times throughout the afternoon and evening. She also told me she had to change her plans to stay longer and had texted those involved to do so. At no time other than the one message did I type or touch her phone or use it to send any messages to anyone. Any assertions to the contrary are simply untrue or said to support false narratives that would explain away the accuser's behavior.

TRIAL SECOND DAY

When the trial resumed the next day, the focus was on whether the accuser was drugged so that she could not give consent or recall the encounter. Testimony was given that the accuser went to the hospital approximately eighteen hours after she claimed to have been given the drug and vomited a blue pill on the floor. They claimed this was proof she was given GHB. However, the facts were that if the drug had been given eighteen hours before, it would have been ingested and out of her system within four hours according to the experts. So, her claim that the pill she vomited was GHB was not possible. The experts also testified that if a pill were given, her stomach acid would have dissolved the pill within a brief time; and it would not have stayed for 18 hours in her stomach still in pill form.

Furthermore, the drug experts also said that GHB does not usually come in pill form and is not blue. This further undermined the accuser's testimony and cast additional doubt on her claim of being drugged. The other interesting note about her allegedly being drugged was that in her testimony when her attorney asked her about the details around the time she claimed to have been drugged, she said she could remember virtually nothing. She also claimed she did not recall anything until she awoke several hours after arriving home. She also said that she only used the bathroom once during our time at the restaurant, and that is when she claimed the drug had been put into her drink. The fact that we were at the restaurant for over five and a half hours and had multiple drinks and glasses of water and food during that time was not brought up. I went to the restroom during that span many times because when drinking the need to urinate becomes much more frequent. Her being much smaller than I and having had several twenty-ounce glasses of alcohol and water over that span, would make it physically impossible for her to have gone to the restroom only once.

On cross-examination when my attorney asked her about those same specific details that occurred before and after she claimed to be drugged, her story changed. Suddenly, she had a remarkably clear recollection of how many drinks she had drunk, what happened at the restaurant, what she had texted to friends and family, and what happened after we left. She also was able to recall details from later in the evening several hours after she claimed to have ingested the drug, which the experts claimed would not happen if she had been given GHB. But she claimed to have no memory of what happened after she got into my car, or anything between us until she arrived back at the restaurant afterward. Once again she was shown to remember most things before and after the physical encounter, but absolutely nothing of the encounter itself. That is just not how GHB works according to the experts who testified. People given GHB typically cannot recall anything at all from the time it was given until the drug leaves the system several hours later. So, the accuser's ability to remember key details throughout the night, with the only exception being during the physical encounter, was not consistent with being drugged. In reality, the accuser was not given any drugs by me and was a full participant in the physical interaction that occurred in my car.

Another issue that was not discussed in conjunction with the pill found in the vomit was the fact that the accuser was taking multiple medications at the time for a variety of maladies. The pill could have been any of the medications she was taking at the time and taken on an empty stomach could have caused her to vomit at the hospital. The accuser admitted on the stand that she had taken several prescribed drugs the day we met for her anxiety. The drugs she took indicate that they are not to be taken with alcohol because they can cause adverse reactions or intensify the effects. The fact that the accuser had these drugs in her system in addition to the alcohol and that they specifically stipulate not to drink alcohol while taking the medication was never accounted for by the prosecution. None of these things were brought up during the trial. Only during my new trial motion were these things brought to light. My trial attorney failed to discover or research the side effects and alert the jury to them; instead, my appellate attorney did so and found that many side effects were memory loss, dizziness, slow speech, difficulty walking, or impaired judgment or motor skills. The alcohol, together with those pills, intensifies those effects. Taken together they would explain her behavior or lack of memory.

I was completely unaware that she was on any medication and would not have had drinks with her had I known that the medications she used should not be used when drinking alcohol. Again, these were the viable alternative explanations as to why the accuser claimed she could not remember things or was impaired in some way. The prosecution downplayed this, but it would explain why she might not have remembered things as clearly the next day and why she had the same issue with someone else a week before we met.

By this time, I was beyond frustrated after sitting there and listening to these falsehoods being told over the past two days. It was one of the hardest things I have ever experienced besides going to jail. Being unable to tell my side or explain what happened was almost more than I could take. I was frustrated and sickened by the outright lies being told and the outlandish and ridiculous assertions. Instead of considering the other possibilities that also could have explained why things happened, they blamed me for everything and ignored all that the accuser said and did. They would not admit that the accuser could have had any responsibility for what happened to her, even though the facts suggested otherwise.

PROSECUTION IGNORES FACTS

There were several reasons why the prosecution might have ignored the facts. The first was a personal one. After my arrest, my attorney came to see me and informed me that one of the women in the district attorney's office had been on the same dating site I had used, and we had spoken to one another. Though we never met, my arrest caused her to become very angry and vindictive, and her comments to my attorney insinuated her intent to see me prosecuted no matter what. This helped foster a relationship between her and the alleged victim because of their mutual connection to me. Even though it is highly unethical for an attorney to socialize and befriend those they represent in a criminal case, these two shared the same anger and desire to get even with me for what happened. This led to them becoming good friends who had lunch and dinner together, met often to socialize, and even attended the accuser's wedding—which took place about a year after the trial. Though the accuser claimed to have had PTSD and was traumatized by events she claimed she could not even recall, she met and married her new husband all in just over a year after the trial.

As the prosecution began to wind down its case, others I had met were brought to the stand to show a pattern of bad behavior on my part. These witnesses told stories that mixed parts of the truth with many falsehoods and distorted the facts to fit the narrative the prosecution was putting forth.

DEFENDANT'S CASE

After the prosecution had all its side testify, it was our turn to present our case. Before that happened, my attorney approached my family for an additional $5,000. We had already paid the amount he had requested to defend me, so this additional amount should never have been paid and was unethical. I was unaware he had asked for more money until after the trial ended and my family had paid him. They felt compelled to pay because they wanted him to put forth his best effort. The reality was that he was dishonest and a fraud. He saw an opportunity to take advantage of my family and dealt dishonestly with them and with me.

When the time came to present our case, my attorney made many egregious errors immediately. The expert he hired who testified about alcohol and its effects had not been sent the video to view the accuser's behavior before the trial; nevertheless, he had signed an affidavit claiming he had seen the video footage of the accuser's behavior and gave his expert opinion on it. The prosecution quickly jumped on this and pointed out that he had not seen the footage before giving his statement. This, therefore, made his statement false and undermined his credibility.

Then, because the video expert suddenly died, a replacement was brought in to work the equipment. He was unprepared and unable to show key interviews and evidence to the jury that were critical to my case. Also, because he lacked knowledge about current case laws and statutes, he did not challenge the accuser on the ailments she claimed resulted from our interaction. If he had known about the laws, he could have introduced evidence that would give an alternative explanation for her pain and discomfort because of the herpes she contracted around this time. None of those things happened, though, and so the jury was left with no alternative to explain why she had felt pain and discomfort after our date and could only conclude that I had somehow been the cause of it.

As I look back on all that took place in my trial, it is clear that many things did not make sense that the accuser and others testified. But the jury was not given anything else to attribute as causes, nothing to explain what happened and why. My attorney spent his time dealing with the facts and not telling the story. The facts proved she was lying, but the jury was never given a reason why she lied or the truth about what took place.

When I asked my attorney if I should get on the stand to testify, he told me not to do it and that we had created enough doubt in the jurors' minds. In hindsight, it was probably the right move—not because we had created doubt in their minds, as my attorney tried to get me to believe, but because he was woefully unprepared to question me properly. I would not have been able to tell the story because he would not ask me the right questions. At this point, I also did not trust that he had my best interests at heart. Throughout the trial the district attorney and my attorney had made crude jokes about pictures that were shown during the trial, commenting that the pictures belonged to women my attorney represented at a nearby strip club. I came to find out he represented strippers from a nearby club only after the trial was completed. This was not a man to be trusted, so getting onto the stand might have done more harm than good. But my side could never be told in court; however, the truth is written in this book.

We rested our case and the jury deliberated for about six hours. While they deliberated, I sat in a holding cell praying and talking to the Lord. Though I had hoped for a miracle, and for someone on the jury to see through all the falsehoods and lies, in the back of my mind I knew that I was going to prison—not because I was guilty, but because there was nothing for the jury to use to make a case for my innocence. My attorney had not told them the truth about what happened or even explained how things happened. Conversely, the prosecution told a story and gave them an explanation for why things happened and how. Though false and made up, it was at least something that would explain what happened. So they sided with them because no alternative was given. It makes sense to me; I would have done the same had I been in their shoes. I was told afterward by reputable attorneys that had I been given even competent representation, I would never have been convicted.

TRIAL DECISION

When the bailiff came to get me once the jury reached a decision, I remember feeling numb all over. Perhaps it was my way of preparing myself for what I knew would happen. The looks on my family's faces said it all when I walked into the courtroom. They also knew what was about to happen. When the decision was read, and I was found guilty on both counts, time seemed to stop. I remember I did not know how to feel or what to think. The reality of going to prison had never been allowed to enter my mind as a possibility. I hoped to the end that truth and justice would somehow find a way.

Now, I was a wrongly convicted felon, and the only thing I could do was to try to keep from breaking down altogether. I knew if I did, I would not be able to stop. The next moments after that are still foggy for me. My mind was racing with thoughts of not seeing my girls now for many years and going away to prison for the rest of my life. How could I be found guilty of crimes I did not commit? How could this happen?

WIFE DEFENDS ME

Then, the judge asked if anyone wanted to speak on my behalf before she sentenced me. My mother was going to get up, but my wife insisted she speak instead. She got up and pleaded with the judge to give us time to be together, that she knew I did not do what I had now been convicted of, and that there were no winners in this situation. It was a heroic and courageous thing she did for me. When I saw her get up, my emotions erupted, and tears flowed down my cheeks. I knew then that things between us were likely over, but I would not let myself believe it just yet.

Looking back, it was the final effort she would make as my wife before she would begin to distance herself from me and take the children to live closer to her parents. I appreciated all that she was willing to endure for me and feel that what she decided to do was the best for everyone. The judge then rendered her decision: two life sentences with parole. I was still in shock after I was escorted from the courtroom and the bailiff said my family had requested a small note to let them know how I was doing. He was not supposed to pass any notes to me, but I believe he did because he believed in my innocence. After writing the note, he shook my hand, told me to keep fighting, and took the note to my family. Even in a courtroom where almost all were against me, this kind man had been so friendly toward me and my family. He afforded us many things that normally would not happen, perhaps because he sensed that the case against me was wrong. He gave us some liberties that he did not give to others. That was a tender mercy from the Lord that he provided during that tough time.

When I returned to the jail, I was taken to medical to evaluate my mental condition to ensure I was not suicidal—a precautionary thing they do for any convicted of a crime. Meanwhile, my family was taken to a room where they could shed some tears and regroup before leaving the courthouse.

That night after the verdict was a difficult one. I cried and was anxious about going to prison. As awful as county jail had been, I could not even begin to imagine what prison would be like, and how long I would be there. I missed my family and children more than I could ever express, and the thought of not being a part of their lives almost overwhelmed me. Honestly, I did not know if I could survive going to prison for that length of time.

AFTER TRIAL, BACK TO JAIL

The day after the trial, my attorney came and had me sign indigent papers because I did not have money in the future to pay an attorney and needed the state to appoint one for my appeal. He also filed the appeal paperwork. When he saw me, he could not look at me as he apologized for what happened. I dismissed it with what was done is done. After signing the form, I left to return to my cell. I had nothing more to say to him after his performance in court.

The last few weeks before I was transferred to the diagnostic prison, where you stayed for several weeks before going to your permanent facility, I had several video visits with my family. My wife had set up a few to be able to talk. During one of the videos, she told me she had decided to move closer to her parents. I was stunned and unsure what to say without being given any prior warning. Overcome with emotions and the ramifications of her words, it took me a minute to respond. My first instinct was to question why she would leave. But as I thought about it, I realized I needed to let her do what she felt was right, and going home would provide her with the help and support she needed. Selfishly, I had hoped she would stay so I could have at least one visit with her before she left, where I could hug her and have a heart-to-heart conversation with her. But that was not to be, and she left the state shortly after the trial.

After about a month, I was told I was transferring to the diagnostic facility, packed up all my belongings, and was taken downstairs to be processed. I had two net bags full of books that I had wanted to leave at the jail to be picked up by a friend, but I was not given the chance to turn them over, so I took them with me. Once I arrived at the diagnostic center, I was forced to carry these two bags of books, plus my other belongings, while handcuffed and my ankles chained. It was almost impossible to do, and it took me a while to reach the doors after being taken off the bus.

Once inside, we were told to line up on numbers on the floor before us and remove all our clothing. We were then told to wash off one at a time and use flea and tick shampoo. The water was ice cold and very unpleasant. We also had to shower in front of an entire group of men. When I came out of the shower, I was given a towel and clothing to put on and taken to another room where I sat and waited to have my head and beard shaved completely. Thus, my prison term began in earnest.

Chapter 12

Prison and New Trial Motion

GANGS IN CONTROL

O nce we completed the medical exam, we were seen by a counselor and assigned housing. I was assigned to the cell house called B House. When I asked one of the inmates familiar with the housing units what B House was like, he told me "It's great if you like to fight." Having experienced the Lord's protection while in jail, I again turned to Him to protect me from harm in this unfamiliar environment.

After picking up our bedding, we were led down a long corridor toward the housing units. As we approached the doors, it was like a scene from the movies: fires and people yelling obscenities and threats at all who walked into the cellhouse. I was given a cell number and told it was in the top range. The cells were old, with metal bars like in old movies. They were no more than 10x12 with a toilet, sink, a small desk area, and two bunks.

The gangs each had sections in the cell house they controlled; if you were put into one of their cells, you had to pay to stay in the cell—otherwise, they moved you to a civilian area. Civilians are what they call those who are not affiliated with a gang. The problem you had if you were moved from your assigned cell is getting your mail. You did not get your mail if you were not in your assigned cell. Desperate to talk with my family, I said silent prayers that I would not be forced to go to another cell and be cut off from communicating with them. Some dorms had phones in them, but ours did not. The only way to talk with my family was through the mail. Gang members were watching the cells they controlled and would soon come to let those assigned to their cells know what they would require of them.

When I got to my cell, I was told not to unpack until the head Muslim came to meet me. I was assigned to a cell controlled by Muslims and might be moved if they did not like me or needed the cell for another Muslim. After waiting for some time, I was sent a message that I could unpack for the night and the gang leader would talk to me the next morning. Relieved and exhausted, I only wanted to get in my bed and sleep.

That night, I thanked the Lord for His help and protection. Then, after talking briefly to my new cellmate and getting some advice, I could sleep. The next day we were awakened early to go and eat breakfast. My cellmate told me to follow him and stay close. We descended the stairs and waited with the rest of the men from our cell block for the doors leading to the chow hall. When the doors opened, the gangs made sure they went first. They had someone block everyone else from going down the hall while their members went through. When the last one had gone through, the next gang stepped up. Because my cellmate became friends with the leader of the Muslims, he would go eat with them. Not sure what I was supposed to do, I decided to wait until the end to go.

When the Muslims started to go, my cellmate and one of the Muslims motioned for me to go with them. We went down a long corridor into the chow hall and were not allowed to speak or remove our hands from behind our backs. Guards stood by, yelled instructions, and threw people out of line for talking or not following their commands. Once we sat down with our breakfast trays, everyone ate as fast as possible. We were given five minutes and sometimes less to eat and then were rushed out. If you did not finish your food, you threw it out. If they caught you sneaking food out, you were punished. Though the food was slightly better than the food from the jail, there was barely any time to eat it.

Once back in our cells, we slept a few more hours before getting up for inspection. It was mid-January, and the cell house temperatures could not have been more than 50 degrees. I remember being cold all the time. I wore every item of clothing I had to try and stay warm. When time for inspection, getting out of bed into the freezing air was hard.

After the inspection, the "E" man, the name of the head Muslim, came to our cell to meet me. After a few minutes of conversation, he said he liked me, and I could stay in the cell. He also said I could walk with them to eat and go with them when we were allowed to take showers. Then he said he would call me "Ted" because I seemed like a "Ted" to him. I did not care what he called me as long as it allowed me to be where my mail was delivered. But I quickly learned why it was such a blessing to go to eat and shower with their group.

Civilians typically have no protection or help in a prison environment. Being allowed to walk with these prisoners and shower at the same time as this gang afforded me protection from their members. When showering, two members of the gang stood outside the shower area to stand guard to ensure your safety while you showered. The same concept applies when walking to eat and coming back. The Lord's tender mercy of my finding favor with the head Muslim was a huge blessing for me at this facility. Without this protection, I could have easily been hurt or worse. The Lord also blessed me with a good cellmate who had been to prison before and helped me learn how things were done here and where not to go when I left my cell. These two blessings helped to keep me out of harm's way and shield me from being extorted by rival gangs.

SURVIVAL PROCEDURES IN FACILITY

To be safe and avoid prison problems, you must learn what to do quickly. One thing I learned early on is that none of the inmates stayed in their cells during the day, which led to safety issues. The locking mechanisms on the old prison cells were easily manipulated, and most would stuff toilet paper in the holes to prevent them from locking correctly. Then, when the inspection was completed, they had a way to pop the doors, roam around in the cell house, and go into other cells.

The guards occasionally told people to return to their cells but rarely enforced the policy, so nobody paid attention to them. The SERT team (Special Emergency Response Team) would occasionally come in, and they had no problem putting their hands on people and getting them back in their cells. Most of those on this team were ex-military or special forces. They were the only ones the gangs respected. They would also shoot rubber bullets, beat people into submission if they resisted, and fire tear gas into the cell house to disperse people to their cells. The diagnostic facility is a level-five high-security prison. In level-five camps, the guards can be hands-on and use force whenever they want to subdue inmates and prevent riots.

Each cell house had two ranges, the front and back. The front range of the cell house where I was located had one guard who stood at a podium with no guards on the back range. The back range is where I was told not to go, or I would never come back. I found out why that first day. In the back range, inmates would do gang initiations by hanging a sheet up and having fights behind the sheet. Some gangs initiated their members by making them fight all the other members simultaneously. It could be a 20:1 ratio. Once you take your beating, you are in. Other gangs require you to "free pick" a civilian and beat him up. Others require you to commit murder.

Depending on the gang, the initiations vary. But these initiations took place on the back range out of the guard's sight. He rarely dared to go back there himself. The gangs controlled the place, and the guards allowed them to do almost anything they wanted. To pay them off, the gangs would give the guards food and other things on store day to maintain their freedom to do as they pleased. This made it a dangerous place for people like me who were not affiliated and unaccustomed to how gangs worked and what they did. This made it critical to pay attention to what was happening around me and limit the time I was out of my cell for any reason.

My cellmate was good to me and treated me well. He was an older Black man who had served time off and on for several years. He had been delayed in leaving the diagnostic facility for several months because of health concerns. Anytime you complained of a health problem, you had to stay longer in the diagnostic facility while the problem was treated. I was told not to complain about anything to get shipped out quickly. I had no known medical issues and was thankful for my good health. I had lost a lot of weight while in county jail, and I anticipated losing even more at the diagnostic facility—but other than that I felt good.

When the time came for showers, I was again amazed at the process and how the gangs controlled them. When we were allowed to start showering, the gangs lined up first and their members were allowed to shower while two would guard the doors. Once each gang had showered, then the civilians could shower, but they were unprotected and vulnerable to having their clothing stolen or being assaulted while in the shower. Unfortunately, many were robbed and hurt as a result. This was a great blessing the Lord afforded me to shower with the Muslims. I had to wait until the end but was afforded protection while showering and my clothes were never stolen. Though I was in a very unsafe environment overall, the Lord continued to protect me from those harmful elements.

I received no physical harm while in the diagnostic facility; however, I witnessed many people being hurt and even a gang war between rival gangs that resulted in inmates getting hurt and even killed. One of these incidents took place inside my cell. The head Muslim was playing a game of dominos in our cell with my cellmate when one of his underlings came in and whispered something in his ear. He quickly got up and left the cell and we were told to step to the back of the cell. Right after we did so, they led a man into the cell, pinned him up against the wall, and accused him of stealing from someone. Then they started beating him, and one of them removed a sharp metal rod with a sharpened end and threatened to stab him. Not sure what to do, I prayed he would not be harmed. Thankfully, they stopped and did not stab him; instead, they beat and dragged him out of the cell. That was how the gangs dealt with problems and kept people from stealing from them.

When a gang member steals from someone who belongs to a rival gang, those two gangs square off against each other. That scenario played out while I was there. After one gang was accused of stealing from another, they settled it in the showers. There were probably forty or more people who ended up fighting in the showers and many were hurt badly and sent to the hospital. This brought in the SERT team, and they went cell to cell pulling out those they suspected and throwing them in the "hole." The hole is an area where you are put for disciplinary reasons. Some of these cells are only big enough for you to stand up, and you have to stand up the entire time and even sleep standing up. Other cells in the hole are isolated, and you do not leave your cell for any reason except to shower once a week. This is not a place you want to be for any reason. After seeing these things, I only wanted to get away from this camp and hopefully go to a safer place.

BOOKS FOR STUDY AND LEARNING

Now that I knew I would not be forced to move from my assigned cell, I unpacked my few belongings. Out of the two bags of over 150 books I brought from jail, I was only able to keep eight books. They normally only allow you three books; yet somehow, I was allowed to keep eight. I do not know why I was allowed the extra books, but I suspect that the Lord's hand was in it. These books ended up being especially important to my study and learning while I was at that facility. The rest I was forced to donate because I could not keep them, nor could I afford to send them home.

Out of all the books I had, I chose my scriptures and the commentaries on *The Book of Mormon*. I had begun to read them while at the jail and wanted a chance to finish them. Unfortunately, that meant I had to donate the other 150-plus books I had accumulated over the past year at the jail. The only other things I had were provided by the prison, including one roll of toilet paper and soap. The basics like a toothbrush, toothpaste, and other toiletries had to wait until I could get them from the commissary. The jail issued me a check when I left for the balance on my account, but that took about a week to show up on my commissary account. In the meantime, I used whatever I could find to get by.

REFLECTIONS OVER THE PAST YEAR

After I settled in, I sat on my bed and began to reflect on all that had happened over the past year. The reality that I was now in a prison cell and had been convicted of crimes I did not commit was a hard reality to face. I began to think about why this all happened and what it would mean for me. I also remembered thinking about what I had done to bring myself to this point, and once again I had to acknowledge that I was the one solely responsible for being there.

I had committed adultery, lied to my wife and family, and misrepresented myself to others who thought I was someone I was not. Worse than that, I had disregarded the Lord's commandments and my faith and decided to do things my way. None of those things were anyone else's fault but my own. Had I honored my marital vows with complete fidelity and lived my faith, none of this would have happened. Though I was frustrated and sickened by the lies and falsehoods that were presented at the trial, I was the one who gave them that opportunity by the choices I made.

The biggest source of sorrow and disappointment was that I knew what was right and yet rebelled against God anyway. Being removed now from the situation I had been in for the past 20-plus years of my life, I saw how unhappy and unsatisfying my life had been over that time. The truth was I had been going from moment to moment, thinking that the things I was doing would make me happy or fulfilled. However, those feelings were always short-lived. Then the regret from those choices drove me to do other things to try to feel better about myself because I hated how I felt afterward. It became a vicious and destructive cycle that led to worse and worse outcomes.

Feelings of guilt, shame, and embarrassment led me to believe I was not someone anyone could ever love, including God. After I turned my back on Him and made so many horrible mistakes, I convinced myself not even He could forgive me.

One evening in particular I remember driving home from being with someone I should not have been with and looking up into the night sky and thinking I was going to hell, no doubt about it. There was simply no way I could ever be forgiven for the sins I had committed. That was a very sobering and devastating feeling. That is not at all what I wanted, but I was now a lost cause. As a result of that despair, I gave up any hopes I had to change or repent. What is the point I thought?

When I was finally humbled and prepared to listen, the Lord being aware of the thoughts and feelings I had, reminded me through my patriarchal blessing that He indeed still loved me and would forgive me if I were willing to fully turn to Him with all my heart and repent. When I committed to doing so in my heart after reading my blessing, the outpouring of love I felt from the Lord that day changed my life. From that moment on, I promised the Lord I would accept responsibility for my actions and confess completely and honestly to those I had hurt by my actions. That is exactly what I did with as many as would allow me to confess my faults and seek their forgiveness. Now that I was experiencing the consequences of my choices, and how painful they were, I was disappointed for not heeding the warnings I had been given. Now I accepted responsibility for my actions and refused to blame anyone else for what happened.

After writing a letter to my family to inform them of my transfer and to give them the address of the facility, I read in my scriptures and thanked the Lord for all His blessings. He had indeed helped me to remain safe in jail and now again during the first few days of my time in the diagnostic facility. He provided food for me when I was in need and led me to avoid confrontations and dangerous circumstances. I was aware of all He had been doing to help and preserve me and felt love and gratitude for His tender mercies. I had tried to live the gospel the best that I could, and I had seen the fruits of it in the blessings I was given.

After a few days, we began to go for testing on various subjects. Our aptitude was tested in English, math, grammar, and spelling. Then we had physicals and bloodwork done. These things took place over about a week, and then I had to wait to have my blood work processed. When done, I would be assigned to a permanent facility. My only hope was to go someplace where I could be safe and serve the time I had left in peace.

I was not sure if a place like that existed, but I held out hope that some of the better places I had heard of would be my landing spot.

PRAYING AND READING FOR SPIRITUAL LIFT

After just over a week, I completed the diagnostics and went back to spending my days in the cell house. Being away from there for most of the past week was a nice break. Coming back to the cell house hysteria was not fun. So to combat that, the first thing I did each day was kneel in prayer and then read scriptures. Praying and reading provided the spiritual lift I needed and helped put me in the right frame of mind. The rest of my day I had to figure out how to survive the destructive elements that were at work all around me.

To survive, I found things to keep busy. One of those things was laundry. My cellmate explained the guards come once a week to the cell house; if you throw them a dirty jumpsuit, they, in turn, throw a clean one back. However, if they did not have your size, you got whatever they had left, whether it fit you or not. Some opted to wash their own instead so that they were sure to have a uniform that fit. I decided to do that, too. My size was not common, and my jumpsuit was new, so the chances of my getting a good one back were slim. But to wash, my only option was to use the toilet. As appalling as that was, it seemed a better option than having a uniform that did not fit or was falling apart. I cleaned the toilet, then used what little soap I had to clean my uniform. Once cleaned, I hung it in our cell to dry. I had two uniforms given to me when I arrived and wore one while drying the other. I did the same with my other clothing. Because of cold temperatures, my clothes took a while to dry. Consequently, I stayed in bed until they dried to stay warm.

COMMISSARY A BLESSING

The other thing I was optimistic about that week was commissary. Each week those with money in their accounts had their names written on a sheet of paper and read aloud to the cell house. If your name was called, you could fill out a store sheet. When our store day arrived, my name was called, and I quickly filled out my list. Anxious to get some toiletries and snacks, I lined up with the others and went with my cellmate to the commissary. We waited in a lengthy line while they located the items for each person, placed them in a bag, and charged your account. My cellmate waited for me to get my store before going back. Once we had our store, he told me to take the sheet I was given and wrap it around the store bag so the items I purchased would not be visible when we returned to the cell house.

As we approached the doors, I realized why he had said to cover up the bag. The gang members were standing watch as people came back to the cell house with their store bags. Some were watching and taking note of the cells that people returned to with store. Others were forcibly taking bags from people as soon as they arrived. Because I was in a Muslim cell, the gangs did not harass us when we returned with our store, but many were not so fortunate.

After all had returned, we were called out for lunch. Upon returning we learned that many of the people who received commissary had been robbed while at lunch. The gangs not only extorted seven dollars per person from the people who were in the cells that they claimed but also robbed them of the remainder of their store after they left for lunch. This caused an uproar, and many went to the guards and complained their store had been taken. In response to the complaints, the SERT team was called, and they came into the cell house, sprayed pepper spray, and put everyone back into their cells. Then this team went cell by cell; if you did not have a store receipt that matched your ID and the items you had, your store was taken. This happened to many of the gang members, which prompted a violent response from them. They also retaliated against those they suspected had told on them.

To the civilians who complained, they tossed them out of their cells and all their belongings with them. When that happens, that is considered "refusing housing," and they are then sent to the hole. Even though it was not their choice, they were still sent to the hole anyway. Then, later that afternoon when the mail arrived and was being distributed, the gangs threw a bucket of feces and urine on the guards and sent them running out of the cell house. This was how the gangs would exert control. If you interfered with them, you suffered the consequences described, along with other retaliation.

I remember one older man in particular who had been thrown out of his cell and beaten by the gangs that day. I was in the middle of writing a letter to family as I watched this man who had to be in his 70s sit dejected against the wall with all of his belongings strewn all around him. How unfair and sad it was that he was being punished for doing nothing other than wanting to keep the things he rightfully purchased. This left a bad taste in my mouth; and in the coming weeks I, too, would have my run-in with the gangs.

Another issue we had to deal with that week was the toilets getting clogged up and overflowing into other cells. When guards would do their occasional walk-throughs, some would try to flush contraband down the toilets before they came to their cells. This would clog the toilets and cause a flooding problem for the cell block. The second week I was there, our cell was flooded with feces and urine and the smell was enough to make you sick to your stomach. Being stuck in our cells, we could only wait until the problem was fixed. In the meantime, we tried to barricade our cell from the flow of water the best we could. Along with the cockroaches and rats that were the size of cats, this old facility was full of creatures that filled the cell houses and kitchen with all kinds of surprises. At night the floors were filled with cockroaches; and in the morning, you had to shake your boots out to be sure you did not step on anything before putting your boots on. It was a filthy place, and I was ready to leave the day I arrived.

PEST PROBLEM

The pest problem was particularly bad in the kitchen. Cockroaches frequently made it into the oatmeal, grits, and soups. Other unidentified objects would show up in various foods regularly. For those who worked in the kitchen, they said they had to constantly fish insects, bugs, and rats out of the food they were preparing. There were many days when I had to remove things from my food, including a large metal object, hair, and other foreign items. Despite all this, my appetite did not diminish; and

I often found myself praying to receive the food I needed to keep warm and healthy. The Lord often blessed me with extra food on days when I was feeling especially weak, hungry, and cold.

HEAVENLY PRAYERS FOR FOOD

One of the instances stood out because I was cold, tired, and extremely hungry that day. On my way to the chow hall, I said a silent prayer pleading with the Lord to provide enough food for me to stay warm and ease my hunger pains. The entire way to the chow hall, I prayed for His help. Then as I sat down, something unusual and amazing happened. People came to me and offered me food, which rarely happened, so it stood out to me. That day I ate more than I usually did and was full when I left the chow hall. These kinds of tender mercies showed me that the Lord does hear and answer our petitions to Him. That was a very personal answer to a sincere prayer for food.

That afternoon I went back to my cell, got on my knees, and gave thanks for what the Lord had provided me. This was one of many times when I prayed for help to receive the food I needed. Each time the Lord heard my prayers and provided for me. When I left that facility after five and a half weeks, I came away with a firm testimony of the power of prayer and the Lord's willingness to answer our sincere requests. I knew that the Lord heard and answered my prayers because of the personal way He answered them.

It had been two weeks since I had arrived at the facility. I was anxious to hear from my family and waited each day for letters to arrive. Finally, the letters came, and I could not wait to read them. Sitting on my bed, I read them over and over. Letters from those you love mean so much, especially when you are in a hostile environment and fear for your safety and well-being. I appreciated those who wrote to me encouraging me to stay the course and trust in the Lord. I needed that strength and encouragement more than any other time in my prison experience. No one can understand how hard or how difficult that time is in a place like that unless they live through it.

Though I shared many things with my family that transpired while I was in the diagnostic facility, there are many things that I did not because of the graphic nature of the incidents. I will only say that the things I experienced there were enough to shake any man, and my reliance and my pleadings to the Lord were more intense and earnest than at any other time in my life.

THE CONDEMNED AMONG US

While in my second week at the diagnostic center, I also saw several inmates who were condemned to die shortly on death row. This facility housed all those set to be executed by the state. Those condemned to death were often led down the hallway we used to get to the chow hall. We were forced to turn and face the wall as they passed by. They were always surrounded by guards with guns and wore chains around their ankles and wrists. One of those times I remember turning and looking as the inmate passed by and thinking about what he might be feeling just days away from being executed. If you knew you only had a few days left, what would you be thinking and feeling? This caused me to reflect on my repentance and the great mercy and gift it was to be able to repent.

Though I was in physical bondage, my spiritual bondage was over. I had sought repentance and felt that the Lord had accepted my efforts. The guilt and pain I had carried for many years was now gone. I wondered if that man I had just seen and was only days away from dying thought about what was next for him after he died. Would he simply go from one imprisonment to another? It was not for me to say, but I knew that if I were called back to my spiritual home at that moment, I would no longer be in prison because I had fully repented of my sins. Though far from perfect or from the person I aspired to be, the critical changes I needed to make had been made. That gave me a measure of comfort, yet I still felt sorry for the men who were to be executed. I wondered if they were simply going to a place far more difficult than the facility they were preparing to depart from in this life.

GOOD PEOPLE AMONG US

During my first few weeks at the diagnostic facility, I also met some good people. In that challenging environment, many found religion quickly. When faced with very difficult circumstances, often even those who claim to be atheists quickly pray for God to help them. Many who came to our cell would ask me about my faith. Before I came to prison and before turning my life around, when people asked me about my faith, I would say I was a member of the Church of Jesus Christ of Latter-Day Saints, but not practicing. I was ashamed to tell people I was a member of the church because I feared the inevitable backlash that would come as a result. Now it was quite different for me. I was happy to share with others that I was a member of the Lord's true church and looked forward to sharing what we believe with those who were interested.

The Muslims were curious about the *Book of Mormon* and the other tenets of our faith. I had many discussions with members of this group and others who had questions about what we believed. This led to many discussions and even to my lending the *Book of Mormon* commentaries to those who were curious to read more about our faith. Sharing the gospel was now something I was excited to do, as I was no longer ashamed to tell people about the church or what I knew to be true.

DIFFICULT FACILITY ROUTINE CONTINUES

By the third week, I was beyond ready to leave. The daily grind of watching people get beaten up, stabbed, or singing/rapping in their cells day and night was enough to drive the most patient person insane. The only thing I disliked more than all of these things was the smoking and smell of wicks burning throughout the cell house. Those who were desperate to smoke would take the peels from the fruit we were given, dry them in their cells, and then smoke them. The combination of smells of cigarettes, dried fruit peels, marijuana, and the musty stale air of the cell block made me nauseous at times. Sleeping was not an option during the day because of the singing, yelling, and constantly being on guard. I

217

had hoped by some miracle that my name would be called that week to be transferred, but it did not happen. So, the nightmare would continue for at least another week.

Several things happened in the third week that made life a little more uncomfortable. The "E" man for the Muslims was transferred that week and that changed the dynamic for my cellmate and me in several ways. We were still able to go with the Muslims to eat and shower, but now the gangs were beginning to encroach on us because we technically were not Muslim. Without the "E" man, and not being Muslim, our protection was gone. They even went as far as to approach us in our cell and ask us if we were going to store. We did not tell them if we were going to store, but we knew then that they would come on store day to extort us. They had seen us go to the store the previous week and now they were going to try to cash in. We just had to decide if we wanted to pay or not, and how we could keep our store.

During this third week, I also needed to get my beard trimmed. After three weeks of unshaven hair, I did not recognize myself. It should have been easy to do, but it was not. Many times I stood waiting for hours in a line that never moved because people were cutting in ahead of me and inevitably we would run out of time for haircuts. I had tried already several times but had not been successful yet. Finally, I managed to get in a relatively short line; and just as my trim was done, the SERT team came into our cell block and sprayed everyone who was out of their cell with pepper spray because of some emergency. I somehow managed to avoid getting directly hit but struggled to breathe. I coughed for hours afterward as the spray lingered in the air. I was so tired of the non-stop foolishness that went on every day that I did not care where I was transferred, as long as I was far away from this place. As the fourth week began, my cellmate and I decided to go to the store and then hide our food in various parts of our cell: in our sheets, blankets, and in other hiding spots to avoid getting robbed. We knew with the "E" man gone, we were probably going to be extorted or our store items stolen. The gamble paid off because after returning from the store, several gang members came to our cell to get their payment. We paid the seven dollars to avoid having a problem and then hung a sheet across our cell like you do when using the bathroom and hid the rest of our food in various places around the cell. Knowing they would come back to try to rob us at some point, we left a small sac that was visible inside the desk area. When they returned to take the rest of our store goods, they would find the bag of items we left in the open and take that and leave. It worked, and the rest of the items we hid remained where we left them undisturbed.

Though we lost a significant amount to the gangs, we were able to keep enough for ourselves to get us through the week. But I grew frustrated as I sat and watched these thieves laugh and take advantage of others and then brag about how much they had stolen from people throughout the cell block. I decided at that moment, I would rather starve than give these thieves any more of my store goods. So, I decided not to go to the store again until I had transferred from the diagnostic facility. The Lord blessed me numerous times with the food I needed, and I would rely again on his help to get me through until I transferred.

TAKING A STAND AGAINST GANGS

That same week my cellmate ended up transferring to a medical center, and I was alone in my cell until later in the evening when the new arrivals came. I was nervous about who the new cellmate would be, so I prayed it would be a decent man not affiliated with a gang or a smoker. My new cellmate turned out to be a good man. This was not his first time at the facility, and he knew how everything went and quickly fit right in. Over the next several days he was gone doing diagnostic tests, so I was again left to myself in my cell where I stayed to read and get some extra sleep. My neighbors to my left were Mexican and were part of a gang but were friendly toward civilians. They even offered to let me cook with them the next store day and store my goods in their cell so they would not be stolen. The thing I learned about the Mexican people is that they look out for one another. Anytime a new arrival who was Mexican came into the cell block, he was immediately brought into the group and given food and whatever he needed. That has been the same everywhere I have been since coming to prison. The Mexicans are very giving and share all they have with those with whom they are friendly or with their fellow countrymen. I appreciated their offer but declined because I did not want any problems for me or them by having them help hide my store goods in their cell. I was hopeful of leaving anytime now and could manage another week if I had to. Though I was often hungry and cold during my time there, I took some satisfaction in knowing the gangs would not get any money from me going forward.

FINALLY ALLOWED OUTSIDE

On the Saturday of that fourth week at the diagnostic facility, a guard announced that we would be allowed to go outside for recreation. It was cold outside; but after almost a year of being inside, I was excited to enjoy some fresh air. Going outside was a big ordeal that required guards to check all our IDs and then allow us out in stages until we reached a large open grass area. There we found some basketball hoops, pull-up bars, and an area to play soccer. I decided to walk with a few men whom I knew from my cell block because walking alone was not recommended.

Going outside was nice to breathe in the fresh air, but I was not accustomed to seeing the large, barbed wire fences and an armed guard in a tower watching over us. It was the first time I remember feeling like I was a convict because of how they treated us and the high-security measures around us. I remember watching cars as they drove by and thinking about what it was like when I could drive anywhere I wanted to go, whenever I desired to do so. Now my freedoms were severely limited with no end in sight. Being outside also made me homesick for my family and wishing I were with them. As I watched people outside of the gates go as they pleased, they reminded me of how captive I was and that their lives were going on and mine seemed to be standing still. After about an hour, we were told to gather up by the exit and then return to our cell block. Some had spent the entire time gathering up items to dry and smoke, while others had been trying to find things to make weapons. It amazed me to see how the minds of some people worked. I concluded that some are just criminally minded and spend their time trying to find ways to break the rules in every conceivable way. If they spent as much time trying to better themselves, they would probably do some amazing things. Seeing that in others reinforced my desire to never fall into that criminal mindset or allow myself to become like those with whom I was locked up.

After a long weekend where the hunger pains were on my mind frequently, Monday came and again I was hopeful for a transfer. I had been there five weeks now and had already seen people who had come in with me transferred. Not having any medical issues or problems, I was poised to transfer any day now. That day came on Thursday of that week. I received word I was transferring early that morning, packed my things within minutes, and was waiting near the doors to the cell block. Anxious and nervous now about where I might be sent, I was listening to those who had been through the process and were now talking about where the good places are and places you wanted to avoid. After being led down a long corridor, we were separated into groups based on where we were being sent.

ASSIGNED TO PRIVATE PRISON

When I found out I was going to a private prison, people were giving me mixed signals. Some said the food was better at private camps and they had air conditioning. Both of those sounded fairly good to me. But the negative side was the nickname it had—"gangland." Coming from the diagnostic facility where the gangs were in charge, the last thing I wanted was to go to a camp where that was the case again. But I had to trust that wherever the Lord sent me, there was a purpose and a reason for my going there. I prayed that this would be a good place for me and looked forward to getting better food and some commissary again at my new camp.

After a long three-hour ride on a bus with our hands and feet shackled, we arrived at my new camp. It was literally in the middle of nowhere and looked much less ominous than the facility we just left. When we got off the bus, we were led into an area where we were strip-searched and given new clothes. The white scrubs we were given were much better than the jumpsuit I had been wearing for the past month. After getting dressed, our pictures were taken for our new IDs and then we were led into an office where the officer in charge of drug enforcement asked me if I had a drug problem or any tattoos. We were then issued our bedding and other clothing items, as well as the things we brought with us. All items were searched. While this was taking place, people who were locked up in the segregation area next to where new arrivals were being processed began asking people if they needed any methamphetamine before we went to the intake dorm. This is where all new arrivals go to complete paperwork and to receive a dorm assignment.

INTAKE DORM AN IMPROVEMENT

The intake dorm was ice cold, but there was plenty of room for us because we had only about twenty people in the group and about fifty bunks in the dorm. We finally had a phone and TV and were fed a meal that tasted so good I could have eaten ten of them. Not being rushed to eat was a welcomed change, as was watching the news after almost six weeks.

That evening I was able to call my family and let them know I had been transferred, and they were as relieved as I was to finally leave the diagnostic facility. Not yet sure what to expect from this new camp, I was anxious to see if it was going to be better than where I had been. Honestly, I had hoped to stay in the intake dorm with only twenty men because it was quiet and peaceful. But that only lasted a few days and then I went to my assigned dorm.

The next morning after having some delicious biscuits, jam, and eggs, I was already happy with the new food—it was a significant improvement. The head counselor then went through the paperwork we needed to complete: our phone list and visitation list. Then we were allowed to take a shower and relax that afternoon. Tomorrow we were going to be sent to our permanent housing, and I hoped to be placed in a good dorm with some quality people around me. I had heard this camp was full of gang members and that certain dorms were nothing but gangs; however, I prayed that I would be put in a place where I could focus on my spiritual goals and begin the process of appealing my case.

ASSIGNMENT TO DORM

As we packed our things and prepared to go to our dorms, a list of where everyone was assigned was passed around. I was to be housed in Building 4, which was a place for those who had life sentences; however, the dorms were cramped and crowded. I had been hoping to go to the newer, larger buildings that I had heard about—Buildings 7 and 8. Though it is not what I had hoped for, I prayed it would be a good fit for me.

Once all the bags were loaded onto the cart, we headed down the hallway toward the various buildings. As we arrived at each building, those who were assigned to those dorms went into their assigned areas. When we arrived at Buildings 3 and 4, which were the last stops before exiting the building to head to 7 and 8, those who were in this building with me grabbed their things and went inside.

As we waited to go to our dorms, we said our names; and the officers pointed to the dorms we were to go to. There was one inmate assigned to my dorm, and he entered first and dropped his things on the first open bunk. As I entered, I looked for an empty bunk; but after walking around, I found none. When I walked out to inform the officer there were no other bunks available, she told me to step aside while they figured out what to do. I was anxious by this time and wondered if I would end up in an undesirable dorm. While wondering why my luck was not particularly good, she came back and told me to load my things onto the cart outside because I was going to Building 7! Relieved and excited, I loaded my things back on the cart and went to 7. I had heard of this building while in the intake dorm, about how nice and new it was. Those who had been assigned to go there were happy about it because of the good reports we heard.

After entering the building, I understood why people liked these dorms. The buildings were relatively new and much larger and more spacious than the older building we had just exited. Once inside my new dorm, I found an open bunk in the front and put my things on it. Immediately, several people from around that area came over and began talking to me. Right off the bat, I was asked what drugs I preferred because I could get anything I was looking for in there and not to worry. When I responded I did not use drugs, they were a little surprised and confused. White men my age had a reputation for drug use. My not using drugs had them a little off balance, and then they asked if I was a religious man. I told them I was, and it made more sense to them. After seeing some of my books, they asked if I was a Mormon and I indicated that I was. This led to a conversation and opportunity to debunk false ideas several had about our faith: how many wives we had, and so forth. The latter is a quite common misconception among those I talked with.

After unpacking my things, I was told what to expect in the dorm and how things operated: receiving commissary, inspections, and dorm rules we were to follow. As I looked around, I saw a lot of various gang elements and a mixture of non-affiliated people who were my age and also did not have any tattoos or markings. I was immediately drawn to these men, and we began talking. These men made up the group of people with whom I spent the next two years of my life.

It took a little while after I arrived in this building to recognize just what a great blessing the Lord had given me by putting me in this building. What I thought was bad luck turned out to be a great blessing. The building I would have been in was ridiculously small, and I later learned that it was a place I would not have enjoyed. Conversely, the dorm I ended up in had several Christian men with whom I quickly bonded. We became good friends during the first two years I spent there. The Lord knew where it would be best for me and put me in that spot. This was yet another example of how the Lord's hand was present throughout this experience. Often what I thought was just bad luck was the Lord directing my path to what He knew was a better situation.

After only a few weeks, I was summoned to the mail room to pick up legal mail. We had to sign for it; so after showing my ID and signing, I was given a legal document from the Superior Court. But instead of this having something to do with my case, it was a civil lawsuit filed on behalf of the accuser against me and the internet dating site that I had used to meet her. The lawsuit made many of the same claims the accuser made in the trial, plus new and even more outrageous accusations that never came out during the investigation or previous court proceedings. She wanted twenty-five million dollars from the lawsuit. When I finished reading it, I was sick to my stomach and unsure of exactly what to do. It stated I had thirty days to respond to the allegations.

Without an attorney at that time, I called my Mom and asked her what I should do. She said she would go online and answer the claims for me. Then we would figure it out from there. At this point, I was wondering what else could go wrong. How could I pay for a lawsuit and would they target my wife in this? The sickening feeling in my gut made it hard for me to function because I now worried that those I loved would be harmed by this new development. I was also amazed at how quickly the lawsuit appeared after the trial. Within only a few short months, I was served with a lawsuit that I never saw coming. The amount was also surprising, and the fact that five law firms were representing the accuser also got my attention. I had no idea what to do and had no money to pay for an attorney, so I began to stress about what this would mean. I knew that the standards for civil lawsuits were even less than a criminal suit. The fact that I had been convicted probably made it seem to them like it would be a slam dunk to win the case. All I could think about was how I felt like they were piling on now and everything that could go wrong legally now in fact was.

CIVIL LAWSUIT

This news about the lawsuit made everything more challenging as I tried to adapt to my new surroundings. So far, I had made a few friends in my new dorm and was trying to get used to being right in front of the sports television. On the weekends, the television is left on until 1:30 am and turned back on at 6:00 am, leaving me five hours when no people were standing around my bunk talking or cheering. The volume on the television was turned up, making it hard to sleep. I also had people in the dorm who accused me of being an undercover police officer because I did not use drugs or participate in gambling or other nefarious activities. This led to them looking me up on the internet and then sharing my charges with the dorm. Some even tried to extort me into doing things in exchange for keeping my charges a secret. I am innocent and have nothing to hide, so I refused to let them manipulate me. No matter what they said or threatened, I was not going to be compromised just to fit in. I was not a criminal on the outside and would not become one now on the inside. Others tried similar things the first few months I was there, and even those men who liked men tried to con me into appeasing them. I firmly declined to do what they wanted and let them know that would never happen. In prison, fear and intimidation are used by people to get what they want. I refused to be bullied or intimidated and turned to the Lord for protection and help to make it through daily. This was a time when I ended up relying heavily on the Lord for protection and help to avoid dangerous situations.

Maintaining my spiritual foundation was key, so I was careful to read my scriptures and pray daily. I did my best to keep the commandments knowing that if I were obedient, the Lord would once again deliver me from those who would harm me as he had in jail and at the diagnostic facility. In this, my faith was beginning to be firm and unshaken. Many times looking back, the Lord protected me through the help of others—through direct inspiration and by softening the hearts of those who conspired against me. My faith was firm, and the Lord protected and blessed me. Knowing that made it easier to trust in Him and not to be persuaded by others.

As a result of increased faith, it did not take long for people to notice I was different than most. I had many in jail and the diagnostic facility who told me I did not seem to belong there. In my new dorm, this same thing began to happen. People would randomly come up to me and tell me that they could tell I did not belong in prison. They could just tell by the things I did and said and how I carried myself. I understood what they meant because I also felt I could tell the ones who were who had committed a crime and the ones who were innocent of wrongdoing. When you live in close quarters and hear and see what people do daily, it does show you their "fruits." As the scriptures say, "By their fruits ye shall know them." (*King James Bible*, Matthew 7:16) Though many try hard to fool or pretend they are something they are not, living with them day after day reveals their true selves over time.

After several months of getting acclimated to my unique environment, I could not help thinking about my new trial motion and also praying my new attorney would be better than the two I had previously. Though public defenders did not inspire much confidence from people generally because of poor pay and the sheer volume of cases they manage, I had hopes that the Lord would bless me with someone who could bring forth the truth and tell my story about what happened.

Several weeks after the lawsuit arrived, my new attorney scheduled a call that I could take in the counselor's office in my building. When it came time for the call, I was called into the office. While the counselor sat in the room with me, I spoke to my new attorney. My first impression of her was not a good one. She seemed bitter and negative and did not inspire any optimism about my case having any chance of being overturned. She seemed intent on spending the time on the phone telling me not to get my hopes up, that her initial review of my case yielded not a lot of things we could argue, and that I should not expect any miracles. After the call, I was shaken and depressed. I remember feeling like I could not seem to catch a break, and once again had an attorney who was not going to help me or look into the case. Instead, she seemed determined to take from me any hopes I had of getting justice. My sister had a different take on her. She seemed to think she was a "bulldog" and would be a good attorney for me. That was not my impression, but perhaps that was just her way of not getting my hopes up only to be dashed later if it did not work out. Though I preferred someone who would be optimistic, she at least did not just tell me what I wanted to hear or fill me with false hope, as the other attorneys had done.

My new attorney advised me not to respond to anything I was sent for the civil lawsuit. Though my Mom had responded to the initial complaint, no real damage was done. She did say it was unusual to get a civil lawsuit filed so quickly after a trial. According to her, normally it takes about six months to file a civil lawsuit because they cannot begin the process until the criminal trial is concluded. So there appeared to possibly be some impropriety on behalf of the district attorney's office. If they had indeed released information to the attorney who filed the civil suit before the case was completed to help them file the suit before the two-year window to file expired, legally this could be problematic. Once the trial ended, there were less than four months before the statute of limitations expired, leaving them short of time unless they had been given information early. My attorney, after checking with civil attorneys she knew, seemed convinced that this was the case and began to look at my case differently.

To help me with my lawsuit, my Mom reached out to the internet dating site and talked with their legal team to discuss the lawsuit. Because they were a party to it also and had the means to pay for legal representation, she inquired about the possibility of us providing valuable information to them in exchange for help with my case. Knowing these attorneys to be very capable, my Mom knew that they would want the information she could provide. This was a dangerous move for her, however, because she could face legal repercussions if not done carefully. This was a stressful time for my Mom and me because of the ramifications of all that was happening. I did not want my Mom to suffer for trying to help me, but I felt helpless to do anything to stop it. While all this was going on, my attorney was made aware of the civil suit and contacted the attorneys for the internet site about making a deal with them in exchange for information. They were able to agree, and a meeting was planned around the time I would be back at jail for a hearing on a new trial motion.

RETURN TO COURT

The first time I transferred to go back to court, I had no idea I was going. I was called up to the front of the dorm at 8:00 pm and told I was transferring that night. I was not told where I was going until just before I boarded the transfer bus. Because I was unaware of any court dates, nor had I received any word from my attorney, I thought I might be transferred to another prison facility—which I hoped was not the case. Before I left my dorm, I called my family to let them know I was leaving and had no idea where I was going but would contact them as soon as I could. Then I said goodbye to my friends and was taken to the intake where arrivals and departures take place and prepared to leave. I would soon learn the whole transfer process is exhausting. You do not get any sleep, ride on a bus for hours with hands and feet shackled, and eat a minimal amount of food. You are also forced to use the restroom standing up with hands cuffed and people all around you.

My first time on the bus, I was directly across from the toilet and had people literally feet away using the bathroom on and off the entire trip. It was uncomfortable and gross, and I swore not to sit anywhere near that area of the bus again. Once I arrived at the county jail, memories came flooding back of the hard and challenging times I had there a year and a half earlier. Things were still the same, and I saw many guards I recognized and they recognized me and said hello. There were several who had been kind to me in my time there and they treated me well upon my return.

After being booked back into the jail, I was taken to the court return floor where those who are returning from prison are taken. It is a quieter dorm because those there are accustomed to prison life and know what to expect. It was more laid back than the dorm I had been in while there previously, and I appreciated the calmer atmosphere.

This was my first opportunity to meet my new appellate attorney handling my appeal. She came to see me before I was taken in front of the judge to discuss what would be taking place in the hearing that day. My attorney had discovered that the prosecution had failed to turn over all the medical records of the accuser to us during the trial as was required by law. The fact that those records were not turned over and that the prosecution denied they existed indicated they might be trying to hide something from us.

During the hearing, my attorney argued that these records had been there the entire time but were never handed over. We needed to be able to see what information they contained and why it had been kept from us. In the end, the judge sided with us and ruled in our favor. She was going to review the records in chambers; and then if they contained things about our case, she would decide how to proceed. It was the first time the judge had ruled in our favor, so I was grateful for the work my attorney had put into my case thus far.

The next day my attorney came to visit me in the county jail to discuss our strategy and to answer my questions. She had been very thorough in her investigation of the facts of my case, and I was pleased that she was looking into everything for me. She said she would continue to investigate all areas where she felt there were issues with my case and update me as things happened.

I ended up spending a week back at the county jail and endured disgusting food and freezing temperatures that were the norm each time I was there. When I was told I was transferring back to my prison, I was ready to go. The next morning as we were getting ready to leave, a very large Black man was brought in who was on his way to the diagnostic facility. The problem with this man was that he must have weighed nearly 600 pounds, did not fit into any of his clothes, and was already sweating profusely. I felt bad for the man as he sat uncomfortably with us waiting to leave.

When the time came for officers to load us into the van, they put us all into a small holding area in the center of the van. I had the distinction of sitting next to this huge man while on the trip back to the diagnostic facility. The drive was about an hour, and I immediately regretted getting in the van first. Within just a couple of minutes of being squashed like a sardine, the sweat and smell coming from the large man began to overwhelm us all. We started banging on the window for the officers to turn on the air because it became hard to breathe. I felt bad for this poor man who had his clothes falling off him and was dripping with sweat. The whole side of my body that was up against him was wet from his sweat. It seemed like the longest hour of my life! When we finally arrived at the facility and the officers opened the door, they had to spray some air freshener into the van because it smelled so bad. We all were then allowed to step out of the van because we were nauseous and wet with sweat. My hands and feet were also swollen and sore because of wearing hand and ankle cuffs.

When I arrived back at my prison facility, I thought the process to get back to my dorm would be easy. I was wrong! We were taken to the intake dorm, and we had to wait five days before being put into our permanent dorm. However, the dorm I was put into was not the dorm I left. It was in Building 3 instead and a much smaller dorm. I was put above a man who smoked nonstop day and night. Discouraged, I prayed that night that the Lord would bless my body to overcome the fumes I was being forced to breathe and to help me get back to my dorm.

MIRACLE PUTS ME BACK IN BUILDING SEVEN

The next day by divine providence, as I was heading back to my brick masonry class that I had been attending before I left for court, I saw the two sergeants from Building 7 where I had lived the past two years. Having always gotten along well with these officers and having had a good rapport with each of them, I said hello. They asked me where I had been moved to. I told them I went to court and upon returning had been put into Building 3. Then I asked them if there was any way I could come back to my old dorm in Building 7. They said I could and agreed to move me later that day.

As I walked away toward my class, I marveled at how often the Lord continued to help me in ways I could never predict. Some might see me running into the sergeants as just a coincidence, but I had learned that it was more than that. The Lord was directing my path and helping me as I put my trust and faith in Him.

After returning from my brick masonry class, an orderly from Building 7 came and told me he was there to bring me back to Building 7. I told an inmate who had come back from court along with me and who was also from Building 7 that I had met the sergeants from our building and had asked to return to that building. When I told him they had agreed to bring me back, he also wanted to return, so he had gone to see them when they called us for lunch. The officers agreed to move him with me. Relieved, I quickly packed my belongings and loaded them onto the cart, as did the other inmate. Both of us returned to our respective dorms. He and I remained friendly and would say hello whenever we ran into each other after that, and he thanked me for helping him get back to his dorm. Later on, that would prove to be a big benefit; however, for now, I was happy to help and glad to be back in my old dorm.

Once I settled into my old dorm, I figured out why they had not put me back into the dorm when I returned from court—it was full. However, the day I spoke to the sergeants in the hall, a bed had just opened up that morning, enabling me to come back. I felt that the Lord had opened the way for that to happen. Trusting Him and the process resulted in the blessing. I did not complain when I was sent to Building 3 and was willing to stay there if necessary. But after learning that my bunkmate was a heavy smoker, and I could foresee it was going to be difficult to stay there, the Lord allowed me to return to better circumstances.

Once I returned to my dorm, I hoped to get my old bunk back because I had made a deal with a friend to take it until I returned. He also had held onto a few things for me while at court. However, when I went to ask him to trade bunks with me, he said he had decided to stay in my old bunk. No one wants to give up a bottom bunk after having it for a while, so I understood and did not make an issue out of it even though he had promised me I could have it back. But then I noticed he had withdrawn not only from me but also from everyone else, too, and started using drugs heavily.

After about two months, he asked to talk to me and said he wanted to apologize. I was curious, so I came to the table and sat and listened. He said when I left for court, he was told why I was in prison and what I had allegedly done. He said it made him upset, and he decided then he was not going to give me my bunk back because he did not want to make my time any easier after what he thought I had done. But after watching me these past months, he realized he had made a mistake. He said there was no way I could have done the things they said. He said he could tell I was not like that and apologized. I frankly forgave him and told him I appreciated the apology and encouraged him to get sober so he could get home to his son.

After that talk, I thought a lot about how the things we do and say show what kind of people we are. The actions and words speak loudly either to our condemnation or to our innocence. I had many who told me that they knew I was innocent because of the things I did and said, and also by what I did not do and would not say. It was another reminder of why a good example is so important.

RETURN TO COURT AGAIN

Six months after my first court date, I was again told I was returning to court, packed my bags, and left for county jail. Each time the experience was long and extremely unpleasant; however, it got easier because I knew what to expect.

When I arrived this time at the jail and was taken to the court return dorm, the officer who had been in the dorm I was in while at trial was now the officer for the court return dorm. He recognized me immediately and made sure I had a cell to myself in a quiet corner of the dorm. He had always been good at helping me and had again looked out for me as much as he could. It was the first time in three years I had been by myself and I loved every second of it.

The first day I spent a lot of time on my knees thanking the Lord for the blessings I had received and for the help He had given me. I also had the chance to just talk to Him and pour out my heart about all that was on my mind in ways I could not in my prison camp. For the time I spent back at county jail, I loved the fact that I had a cell to myself and that I could talk with the Lord aloud and in private.

I was back in court this time to set the date for the new trial motion. The agreed-upon date was July 3rd. For the first time in this process, I knew when I was coming back to court. I was not excited about spending the holiday in county jail or missing the burgers we would receive in our prison camps. However, I knew this was more important and would do whatever was necessary. Finally, the date was set, and I was now anxious to get back to court for a do-over.

MEETING FORMER MEMBER

After my court date, I ended up staying for two weeks in jail. During this time, I met a man who had been a member of the church back in his youth. He told me his story and his difficulties with drug abuse and alcohol. This led to his incarceration and eventually to making significant changes in his life. One of the changes he made was to make God a priority again. He said the moment that he decided in his heart to do that, things started to change in his life. Shortly after he had begun to repent, he was summoned back to court where something happened he had not expected. As he shared his story, I felt I could relate to how much his life changed for the better once he decided to repent. The miracle that took place for him was now going to enable him to be released from prison within the next year. He had over twenty-plus years remaining on his sentence until this miracle took place. It was amazing to hear the story, and we ended up riding back to the diagnostic facility together before he was taken back to his prison facility.

I do not know what became of him after that, but I hope he continued to make changes in his life and eventually made it back to church, a goal he set before being released.

JAIL LACKS NECESSITIES

The two-week stay in the frozen cells at the county jail was miserable. After only a week, I was already tired of being extremely cold and hungry. Without a commissary and with the minimal food they served at the jail, I lost fifteen pounds in just two weeks. So, on the first Saturday morning I was there, after reading my scriptures, I got on my knees and asked the Lord to provide me with enough food to be warm and to temporarily relieve the hunger pains.

Not long after I prayed, the orderlies came and began to deliver lunch trays. When they opened my door to give me a tray, they told me the inmate two doors down had instructed them to give me his tray. Shocked, I took the two trays, went inside my cell, and sat on my bed. Then I immediately got on my knees to thank the Lord for providing the additional food.

Over the past three years, I have prayed often for the food I needed, and each time the Lord heard my prayers and provided what was needed and more. Some of those prayers were answered in what I felt were miraculous ways. Today was one of those miraculous ways. The man who gave me his tray did not know me and had no idea I had prayed for another tray. He never spoke to me afterward, so it was a one-time blessing. I also knew that no one gives away food for free in jail; otherwise, you starve. For these reasons, I knew the Lord had provided a miracle and I was filled with gratitude. Feeling content and warm for that one day was a great feeling.

RETURN TO PRISON AND HONOR DORM

Upon my return from court, I was sent back to Building 7; however, this time I was put into dorm DD, instead of GG. This was an honor dorm for those who tried to follow the rules and spend their time in a more peaceful and quieter environment. I had been asked before if I wanted to go into that dorm but turned down the opportunity because of the friendships I had in GG. However, now that many of those friends had gone home, I decided to go into DD and see if I liked it. It was impressive! The dorm was quiet and clean. You could hear a pin drop after 10 pm. After just a few days, I was kicking myself for not moving to DD sooner but was happy to be there now.

Also during this time, I started to experience some health problems. I had pain in my lower back and sides, and at times a fever, nausea, and diarrhea. This went on for several months as I went back and forth to the doctor for tests until they finally put me on antibiotics. However, when the medicine did not work, they suggested maybe nothing was wrong at all. I did not trust in the medical care I was receiving and instead prayed that the Lord would help me to know what was wrong and provide a way to get treatment, if necessary.

In my last few days before going back to court, I told my family what I truly felt and had come to know in my heart over the past three years of my incarceration. God was in charge, and I had finally learned to trust in Him, His timing, and His direction for my life. I no longer sought to have things done in my way or time frame, and that is how I was approaching this new trial motion—come what may, I was putting it in God's hands.

NEW TRIAL MOTION

This time I was prepared and ready to go to court. Knowing I was going was both good and bad. The anticipation is sometimes hard not to think about, and I had been anxious leading up to this especially important hearing. But at least I could have everything ready to get some rest before leaving. When I arrived back at the jail, I went back into the court return dorm, but this one had no working televisions. That was the first time this had happened because all the other times I had been there, the television was working. There were good and bad aspects to this. The good part was that there were extended periods with little to no noise. The bad part was that several inmates took it upon themselves to sing as loudly as they could to one another, and that was almost worse than the TV being on. But I was again in a cell by myself, and that was nice to have some alone time again.

On this trip, I ended up going to court on three separate occasions. Trips to court are tedious, long, and freezing in a holding cell with my hands cuffed listening to stories from the others waiting with me. On the first trip to court, my case was the last one the judge heard that day, and my attorney told the judge that we were going to need a full day to present my new trial motion. However, the judge put my case to the end of the docket, leaving little time that day to present our case.

When I was finally called into court, it was close to 6:00 pm. Everyone was exhausted, and my sister and brother had been there all day waiting and were also tired. The judge had my attorney start the new trial motion with the medical expert because he was only going to be there for that day.

The medical expert was able to testify about several of the assertions made by the prosecution. The first was to debunk the theory that the accuser was given a drug at the restaurant. The accuser claimed to have thrown up a blue pill at the hospital more than eighteen hours after the alleged incident and claimed it was the GHB she was given the night before. The medical expert explained that once a pill is swallowed, within a brief time it is broken down by stomach acid and sent into the bloodstream. Therefore, he said there is no way a pill could survive in pill form fully intact eighteen hours after it was ingested. So, the prosecutor's claim that it was GHB she threw up at the hospital the next day was not possible.

The next thing the medical expert clarified was the accuser's ability to function and remember what she did about the night in question. At the trial, the accuser claimed she could remember certain details in great clarity from that night, including how many times she went to the restroom, how many drinks she had, when certain things took place, what she texted to people, what I did and did not do, and how she got home. So, in essence, she was able to remember most of that entire night. However, according to the expert, this was not consistent with someone who had been drugged. To remember details throughout the night but then have no recall about the physical interaction that occurred in the middle of the events she claimed to remember is not typical for someone who has ingested GHB. He said that someone who had taken that drug would remember nothing of the night, beginning shortly after the drug is taken, until at least four to five hours later when the drug was out of the system. His account disproved her story and her claims to remember so much of what happened that night. When he finished his testimony, the medical expert had completely undermined the prosecution's entire case. He did this by supplying solid facts and evidence that proved that the pill she claimed was GHB did not normally come in pill form, nor the color blue as she claimed. He also showed that the pill would be ingested quickly and that it would have caused total memory loss for the time it was in her system, or approximately four hours. I was grateful for the truth being told and was optimistic that the remainder of our case would go as well.

After the expert's testimony, the court adjourned until the following day when we continued to present our case. My attorney called the prosecutors to the stand to question them about the timing of the civil case and how much they knew about it. She was trying to get them to make a mistake and admit to making a deal with the civil lawyer or something that showed they had an agreement to help one another on the case. Each one took the stand and lied about what they told the accuser and claimed she had inquired of them and they simply helped her as a result. If they had told her to seek civil action or provided help, this would have resulted in a Brady violation and my case would have been overturned. They knew this and were careful to make sure to say it was the accuser who had inquired about civil action and that she had contacted and hired the attorney on her own.

The civil lawyer also took the stand and with a smug look on his face, denied he had sought information on my case from the prosecution before he was allowed to by law. He also claimed not to have a deal to pay the prosecution for the referral if he won the civil case. Then he made this statement: "I would never do that; that would be against the law." Even as he said that he had a grin on his face and smiled at my attorney. The cover-up was on, and they all were careful not to implicate each other or themselves. In the end, my attorney was unable to get them to make a mistake and had to simply infer that there was some impropriety with how the civil case came to be. We knew there was; we just could not prove it.

Next, my former attorney who represented me at my trial was called to the stand. My appellate attorney had over four hundred questions to ask him about how he managed my case and his knowledge and competency with current laws and statutes. He admitted over and over on the stand that the things he did were wrong and not due to a strategy, but rather to not being aware of the laws and his incompetence. He admitted to not reading the texts that he agreed to exclude at the trial; and when told what was in them, he admitted that it was a mistake to exclude them. He also admitted to not being aware of the current laws and statutes, and that it was his incompetence that led him to do what he did. When he finished testifying, my attorney seemed very pleased with the answers he gave. Afterward, she commented that she had never had an attorney admit that he had no idea what he was doing and had no strategy. The mistakes he made were due to ignorance of the law and a total lack of preparedness. My appeals attorney proved I had been given ineffective assistance of counsel for my trial. As happy as I was that the trial attorney admitted to these things, I was also angered by how blatantly he had lied to us about his abilities and how many cases like mine he had tried.

He admitted on the stand that what he said was untrue. All the money he took and the lies he told to take advantage of us were egregious and upsetting. When he left the stand, I thought to myself how sad it was that he had sold his integrity and soul for money that would never bring him peace of conscience for what he did to me, my life, and my family.

The next person to testify was the accuser. The prosecution had tried desperately to keep her from having to testify again, but the judge had no choice but to have her testify to show how incompetent my trial lawyer was by not asking the questions that were relevant to my defense and not being aware of the laws and statutes. My appellate attorney argued that she needed to be able to bring up issues that my previous attorney thought were off-limits because of the law. One major point that she wanted to make was that there was another explanation for the accuser's pain and discomfort she claimed to have suffered as a result of the physical encounter. By law, we are allowed to present an alternative explanation when the prosecution claimed that I was to blame for her pain and discomfort. In this case, it was the fact that she had recently contracted herpes from someone other than me.

Another point the attorney wanted to question her on was the texts that had been excluded from the trial that showed she had a similar experience with another man just the week before. That week she went out drinking, met a man, slept with him, and then did not remember what happened the next morning. The accuser was brought to the stand, and my attorney began to question her about the events that happened that night and about the medications she had taken that day. She claimed that the medications did not say they could not be taken with alcohol, which was untrue, and my attorney was able to show proof of that with warning labels. She also was able to show that the effects from the pills would be intensified with alcohol consumption and lead to unpredictable side effects, including possibly memory loss. She also questioned why she had been taking these medications to begin with, and she claimed to have a medical issue that required them. One of the issues she had, as revealed in the texts, was hemorrhoids. She had suffered from them for years before I met her. Of course, this contradicted her testimony that as a result of the physical encounter with me, she now had hemorrhoids.

The texts showed that to be a lie. She also claimed the fifteen medications she took were only for physical issues. However, my attorney was able to prove she had been seeing a psychologist before she ever met me, which she had also lied about by claiming she had begun to see her only after the encounter because she had developed PTSD (post-traumatic stress disorder). However, the texts indicated that she had been seeing the psychologist long before the incident between us occurred. My attorney discovered that one of the medications she was taking was primarily used to treat schizophrenia. It also had an off-label use for a stomach disorder, which she claimed was what she used it for. This, coupled with the records that were withheld from the psychologist, led us to believe the medications she took were for the mental disorder, not the off-label use she claimed. These were the records we discovered after the trial that the prosecution tried to keep from us, that the judge said she would review in her chambers to determine if there were things relevant to the case in them.

Then my attorney moved to the pain the accuser had been experiencing. She was asked to tell the court what her symptoms were. After she finished, my attorney told her that she had described every symptom that people who are having an initial herpes outbreak describe. The attorney then made the accuser admit she had herpes and also admitted this could have been the cause of her symptoms. Of course, she denied that; but it was clear to everyone there that it was probable that the herpes was to blame for the problems she had. My attorney then reiterated that I did not have herpes and could not have given that to her. The attorney moved on to the text messages. Here she did her best work. She was able to show that the accuser had gone out to a bar, got drunk, and then called me that night wanting me to meet her—which I declined. Then she met another man, kissed him, and most likely slept with him and did not recall any of it the next day. When the man texted her the next day saying how much he had enjoyed himself, she claimed not to remember what had happened. Ironically, she did the same thing to me the next week. She tried to deny that it had happened, but my attorney made her read the texts aloud to the court and confirm that they were hers and were accurate, which she did. This showed she had lied and had a propensity for this kind of behavior. This also contradicted her previous testimony where she claimed she had never kissed a man whom she had just met.

Her texts also showed that she had lied to the police, to her friends, and to her family about the extent of her injuries. She led them all to believe that she had stitches in her genital area, that she had been hospitalized for a week on a feeding tube, and that she had injuries elsewhere. She also admitted to a friend that she had lied to the police to get them to believe her because up to that point, she felt they did not. She also claimed that because of the trauma she experienced, she had to change her look and decided to cut her hair. But the texts revealed that she had been planning to cut her hair for months and had talked to her friend about donating it. Lastly, the texts revealed that after the incident when she claimed to be traumatized and sitting at home afraid to go out, she was in fact out at bars drinking and hanging out with friends as she had before. Each of these lies and confessions were in the texts to her family and friends that the prosecution tried to exclude from becoming known. But now they were my redemption and revealed the true nature of what had taken place. Finally, the truth was known and heard by all who were in the courtroom that day.

The accuser's own written texts were the most compelling evidence that this trial was all done to convince people that something terrible happened, when in fact it did not. I felt vindicated and grateful to my attorney for bringing the truth to light and exposing the lies and falsehoods. Though it might not change the outcome, for me, it was proof I was innocent and that an injustice had been done.

At this point in the hearing, the judge began to speed up my attorney and even stepped in and did not allow her to question the accuser about other things, claiming she had already covered those areas. It seemed to me like the judge began to protect the accuser because she was caught in so many lies and her story was falling apart. I am convinced that the prosecution and the judge knew the truth but were content to allow the injustice to stand, rather than admit their mistakes and allow me to have a fair trial. In my mind, there was no other plausible explanation after all that came to light.

When that portion of the new trial motion was over, I thanked the Lord for a competent attorney and for answering my prayers for bringing the truth to light. That was my main concern from the start, that those I loved would come to know the truth, regardless of the outcome. Now I felt that this had been accomplished and I was now willing to submit to whatever the Lord had in store for me.

UNUSUAL NEW ROOMMATE

My family stepped up while I was at the jail for a month and ordered me a few books to read and also sent me a few postcards and funds for the commissary. Letters were no longer allowed, so postcards were all that could be received. For the next two weeks, I was alone in my cell reading *The Book of Mormon* and then the other books when they arrived. I was able to go to the commissary during this time, so I had a few snacks to eat when the meals were not enough. The extra food helped keep me warm and full.

After two weeks I ended up getting a cell mate. He was from a federal low-security prison and had to come to the jail to resolve his case. He was a nice man, and we ended up having many conversations. He noticed me reading the *Book Of Mormon* and asked about the church. I shared the story of Joseph Smith and the Restoration. He was a Baptist and had a very lax view of religion. The way he practiced it was vastly different from what I was used to. He admitted that for him religion was something you did on Sunday; and the rest of the week, you did not think about it. He held a leadership position in his congregation, and I asked him to explain how they managed situations where people had transgressed the commandments, and what they did to correct them. He admitted that not much is done, aside from the confession of the sin. It was interesting to me because it seemed there were no consequences for mistakes made, and that even people in leadership positions were allowed to stay after making serious transgressions. When I told him how the repentance process worked in our church, he seemed amazed at all we were asked to do. I then referenced the scriptures to show that we were simply doing what the Savior required to ensure a true and honest repentance.

He also told me of the seemingly lavish lifestyle they had at his low-security facility. They did not have fences or gates. They had softball fields, fishing ponds, workout facilities, classes, fire pits, outdoor leisure furniture, and organized team sports. They also had access to the internet and computers. They ate like kings and their commissary was amazing. I could not believe all the amenities they had; it seemed more like an all-inclusive resort, rather than a place of punishment. He was in shock at how bad the food was in the county jail, and I could understand why after he told me what they were used to eating. He also missed all his recreational activities and leisure time outside. He was there to resolve his case and had hoped to avoid doing state prison time. I told him after going to his all-inclusive low-security facility, he would not do so well in the prison system here. He was honestly terrified of it after I told him what he could expect if he went to state prison. He was due in court early the following week and immediately called his attorney and said to do everything he could to avoid serving time here after his federal sentence was over.

When it came time for his court date, this inmate was anxious to go, but when he returned, he was relieved and happy. The judge had ordered him to serve a concurrent sentence to his federal time so he would be spared time in state prison. He did not realize how lucky he was, but after our talk about state prison realities, he had an idea at least.

He left a few days later before I was transferred back to my prison camp. I appreciated having him the last couple of weeks I was there because the stories he told about his all-inclusive prison resort made me laugh until I cried. After all, it seemed so lavish and like a reward instead of a punishment. He ended up leaving me the last few snacks he had, and I wished him the best for the rest of his life. I knew I would never talk to him again but hoped that he and his family could be together again soon.

MEDICAL ISSUES

While I was at the jail for a month, I also decided to have the doctor there see if he could explain why I had had medical issues for the past several months. He asked me a few questions and did a few tests and then surprised me when he told me what the issue was: I was normal. When he told me, it made sense; but it had never happened to me before I came to prison. It ended up being a great blessing to have stayed that entire month in jail because I was able to see the doctor and receive assurance I was healthy.

The next week I transferred back to my prison camp but knew I would be returning one last time in a few months for closing arguments for my new trial motion.

BACK IN PRISON WAITING FOR COURT AGAIN

Over the next several months as I waited to go back to court, I began to help my youngest daughter prepare for her upcoming baptism. Feeling a desire to help her understand what getting baptized means, and the commitments a person makes when baptized, I spent time in the scriptures and wrote what those things were to my daughter and had a book sent to her so she could understand what it all meant.

Shortly after my incarceration, my second-oldest daughter was baptized and my wife told me that right after she came out of the water, my daughter told her she had a really good feeling inside that made her happy. When I heard that, I knew she felt the confirmation of the Spirit telling her she had done the right thing and that the Lord was pleased with her. I wanted my youngest to experience that same joy and feeling at her baptism, too.

The classes I had taken in prison thus far I had completed and graduated. I had taken a computer technology class that focused on Microsoft Word, Excel, PowerPoint, and other applications. I had used these extensively in my work before my arrest, but they were working with an updated version, so I was able to learn a few new things and keep my skills sharp.

The other class I took was a brick masonry class. We went outside each day and learned how to lay bricks and make fire pits, mailboxes, and porch steps. It was a fun class, and I enjoyed being outdoors each day. I was fortunate to have completed that class before my last court date. If you miss more than two consecutive weeks while in class, you have to retake the class. Because I was gone a month before my last court date, if I had not finished it, I would have had to start over.

After going back to closing arguments, I planned to get into the horticulture class so I could grow some of my vegetables while being outside each day.

FINAL COURT APPEARANCE FOR MOTION

Four months passed before I was finally alerted to when my next court date would be. The weather was getting cold outside; and as the time approached to leave for court, a nasty ice storm hit the entire state. All transfers were canceled the night I was to depart, and the next day I had my family calling my attorney to figure out what to do. She said they may still get me if the weather improved, so I waited to see what would happen. Sure enough, that night another man and I were called out from my dorm to tell us they were transferring us that night. With my court date the next morning at 9:00 am, I knew I was either going to be late or miss it altogether. I figured they would move it to the next day and did not expect to go to the courthouse, but I was wrong.

When we arrived at the jail, the guards said the judge still wanted to see us; and we were rushed inside, changed into a jumpsuit, and taken to a transport van to go to the courthouse. Normally, we would be taken to our court return floor and be given socks, T-shirts, a sweatshirt, and toiletries before being taken to our cells. But because there was no time, they simply put us in our jumpsuits, with nothing on under them except our underwear. We did not have socks, shirts, or sweatshirts either. Nevertheless, they took us over for our court appearance. The temperature outside was extremely cold, and I could not stop shaking with cold that entire day. I froze while waiting to go into court; and on top of that, we had not eaten, nor did we get any food before racing over to the courthouse. Once there, we did receive the standard two sandwiches and a pint of orange juice, but it was hardly enough to make a dent in my hunger pangs and cold.

After waiting all day to see the judge and for my attorney to present closing arguments, we were led again to the van to return to the jail. At that point, I was tired, hungry, and frozen, and my wrists and ankles were bruised and swollen because my bare feet chafed against the metal cuffs. It was a miserable day, and things only seemed to be getting worse.

Once we arrived back at the jail, it was late once again; and, of course, we missed dinner. We also had to wait to be booked in, which we were not before we were rushed to court earlier. So, while we sat and waited, I said a prayer petitioning the Lord for a good roommate, a meal to help me get warm, and a safe environment while at the jail. Because I had suffered that entire day, I prayed with great intensity and even to the point of tears. I was exhausted and just wanted to lay down, to eat, and to get warm.

Once the booking-in process was completed, we were told the court return dorms were both full. We would have to go into the general population instead. I was taken to the top floor where the worst of the worst are housed in the general population. At that point I figured my day could not get any worse and prayed that somehow it would work out—all the time knowing that the general population in the jail can be extremely dangerous, especially on the floor I was going to.

When I arrived at the cell I was assigned to, I found my cellmate was an orderly and had just been given some home-cooked food from one of the guards. He had tuna salad sandwiches and fresh apple pie he had already split into two containers. He asked me if I would like to have some of the food, and I wanted to cry. He had no idea how difficult the last 24 hours had been for me and how hungry and cold I had been all day. However, the Lord knew and had sent me to his cell to be blessed with food I could not have had anywhere else in the jail that night. Once again, what I thought was going to be a tough situation the Lord turned into a huge blessing. The man I was with was also a Christian who was trying to do what was right and had been robbed the night before by some gang members. He told me he had prayed for a good roommate. We were blessings for each other.

KIND ROOMMATE SHARES FOOD

Amazingly, my roommate and I had both prayed to have a good cellmate, as well as for food and protection. The Lord blessed us both with all we had prayed for. Before I went to bed, I thanked the Lord for the blessings we received.

As I tried to get warm after eating and getting into bed, I thought about the events of the last twenty-four hours. First, getting transferred the day I had court and being rushed to the courthouse with barely any clothes on in freezing temperatures. Then, having only a couple of sandwiches for that entire day and being cold and shivering the entire time. Spending over 15 hours in hand and ankle cuffs while being last to be seen by the judge—with my wrists and ankles raw, cut, and bleeding because I lacked socks—was traumatizing. Then, exhausted, cold, and hungry, I had to wait once I arrived back from court to be booked into the jail. At this point, I thought the worst was over; then I was told there were no beds on the court return floors, and we had to be housed in the general population on a floor where the worst of the worst are housed. So, I remember thinking I was going to be in trouble. Then the miracles happened. I was put with a man who was an orderly and he had just given me not one but two portions of tuna salad and two portions of hot homemade apple pie. A guard had just given him the food as I arrived in the cell—Miracle Number One.

The Second Miracle was that this new cellmate was a Christian man who had prayed for someone like me to be his cellmate. Before I arrived, two people tried to rob him the day before while he was alone in his cell. He was the only one in that dorm who was not a gang member, and he prayed he would get a cellmate who was Christian, too—Miracle Number Two.

The Third Miracle happened as I was trying to get on the kiosk to secure my password for the phone, but the kiosk in the dorm was not functioning. This left me with no way to use the phone to contact my family. This good man put his code into the phone and then allowed me to call my family a few times over the weekend to find out about my daughter's baptism and to let them know how things went in court—Miracle Number Three. People in jail normally do not do these types of things. I rarely saw such generosity or kindness in my time there. These things did not happen by chance. The Lord put me with someone He knew would help me and provided me with the necessary food and assistance I needed. My cellmate also shared several commissary items to help me until I transferred that following Tuesday. We also had several talks about God and my faith—which he had many questions about—and what prison was like. He was one of the best cellmates I had to that point in jail or prison.

YOUNGEST DAUGHTER BAPTIZED

The next morning, after reading my scriptures, I sat in my cell thinking about my youngest daughter. In just a few hours she was going to be baptized by my brother-in-law. It was another occasion where I would be absent, and I was feeling disappointed and saddened at missing another milestone in her life. So, when I prayed that morning, I asked for a blessing on her, that she would know how I felt about her, and a few things I wanted her to know. Those things were that I loved her, was proud of her for being baptized, and hoped that she would always remember me. I spent the entire morning silently asking the Lord to help her to know these things.

Because her Mom requested I not contact her at that time, I was not able to find out about the baptism until my Mom left after attending the baptism to visit my sister. So, when I called, she was able to tell me what had happened. She said my wife had been very cordial and gave her a hug when she arrived. Then she told me all went well, and she was grateful to attend. Mom said my daughter looked beautiful. My brother-in-law then asked to speak with me. He told me that when he put his hands on my daughter's head to bless her, he felt impressed to tell her the things I had asked the Lord to share with her. They were the same words I had used. I knew immediately that the Lord had heard and answered my prayers and told my brother-in-law the things that I had desired my daughter to know.

After thanking my brother-in-law for being there to bless her, I again was struck with how much the Lord had blessed me and my daughter. During that weekend, I felt I could see the Lord's hand in my life more plainly than ever before. The miracles He provided me, and the direct answers to my prayers were a powerful witness to His awareness of me and His willingness to help me when I needed it most. This was a testimony to me that if I remained obedient, which I had been striving to do since the day I read my patriarchal blessing, He would bless me and provide for me.

MIRACLE AVOIDING CAR ACCIDENT

Tuesday morning as I prepared to leave the county jail for perhaps the last time, I felt impressed to pray specifically for my safety that day. I had never had an impression like that. But I got on my knees that morning and did just that. Later, as we were being loaded into vans to return to our prison camp, I was just about to board the one van when I was told instead to get into the other van. This ended up saving me from severe injury and possibly even my life. About thirty miles from the prison, as we were traveling down the various two-lane roads that led to the camp, we had just gone through a four-way stop literally seconds before when I looked back at the van following us and saw a car run the stop sign and hit the prison van broadside. The car missed us by just seconds. When the car hit them, one of the passengers in the front seat was ejected through the windshield and onto the road almost being hit by another car. At that moment, all of the people in the back of our van began yelling at the officers to turn around because of the accident. Once the driver realized what had happened, he turned around and raced back to the other van to assist. The van had massive damage to the side and back, making opening the doors to get to the prisoners difficult. The police arrived within a few minutes, and we watched them work to open the doors of the van and render aid to those in the other vehicle. Not long afterward, life flight helicopters were on the scene to send those with serious injuries to the hospital. Inside the back of the van, the injured prisoners looked bloodied and battered. Several appeared to have serious injuries and were taken to the hospital. All of us in the back of the other van were stunned as we watched them load the injured into waiting ambulances and rush them off to medical centers. Everyone was shaken and all said prayers for the welfare of those we witnessed being taken to the hospital.

The warden arrived while the injured were being treated and first came to check on us, then went to help those in the van. One of the officers in the front of the van hit had head injuries and was also taken to the hospital. As I witnessed all that was taking place, I could not help but think back to that morning when I was given the impression to pray for protection. Even though I was OK, I was still shaken by the realization that I could have easily been in that van and that could have been me who was being taken to the hospital. Again, the Lord had preserved my life for a purpose that only He knows. I felt grateful to have followed the impression I was given that morning. That prompting ended up saving me from serious harm and even perhaps saved my life.

It was the third time now that the Lord had preserved my life. The first was the accident I had at age eighteen when I was miraculously unharmed after being hit broadside by a truck going sixty-five miles an hour. The EMT who was in the vehicle behind me said it was a miracle I was not killed. Then when visiting my in-laws, I was taken to the hospital for a gallbladder problem when the doctor discovered my appendix was about to rupture. I would have been driving the next day if I had not gone to the hospital that night. Most likely, I would have died if my appendix ruptured, and I was not able to get to a hospital in time. Then this last incident in the prison van where I was spared a life-threatening accident was another great blessing. Why my life had continued to be spared I was not sure, but I knew that the Lord had a purpose for me, even though I was not sure what that was.

When we arrived at the prison, the guards were visibly upset about what had happened to those in the van. They quickly processed us and took us into the intake dorm. Once settled, we were all sent to medical to get an evaluation. All were upset about what had happened, but we also were grateful to have been spared injury. After calling my family to let them know what had happened and that we had been fortunate to escape injury, I went to bed early that night, remembering to thank the Lord for His protection from harm.

The next day the warden came to see us and asked if we were all okay. We also were visited by the prison psychologist to ensure we did not have PTSD or trauma of any kind. More than anything, I was grateful to have been spared injury and that I was done with court transfers for the near future.

MOVE TO DIFFERENT BUILDING

After a brief stay in the intake dorm, I was sent to Building 6. My dorm in Building 7 was full, so I was put into a kitchen dorm until a bed was available in my old dorm. There were good and bad aspects to being in a kitchen dorm. The good part was that those who worked in the kitchen were allowed to bring back some tasty food they cooked, so you ate well. The not-so-great part is that people were going in and out all night long to work. As a result, the dorm was noisy all night long. Because my bunk was close to the front, I did not sleep much at night. One of the men from our dorm worked in the officers' lounge and made salads all day. He was allowed to bring back two salads at night and would sell them to anyone who wanted one. I would buy them because they were the only real vegetables and meat I could get and because they tasted so good. I ended up spending Christmas in that dorm and then in early January a bed became available in Building 7, and I was moved back there.

CHRISTMAS SEASON

During that holiday season, I did the twelve days of Christmas for my Mom and children. Each year since coming to prison, I tried to do something different and special for my family. One year I had portraits made for each of my girls by taking their most recent pictures and having an artist here draw me into their picture so it would look like a current picture of us together. Another year I had pictures of my children sent to my Mom and had her create a picture puzzle with all the pictures of the girls together. The pictures were of memorable moments in the girls' lives, and something I thought would be special to have for years to come. Another year, I wrote poems that were framed. The next year I had personalized jewelry sent; and for my oldest daughter's graduation, I teamed up with her Mom to give her a graduation gift of a ring with her birthstone and a necklace from both of us. It was always my goal to give meaningful gifts and things that they can look back on and appreciate for many years to come. I hoped that each year the things I gave my family were meaningful to them.

Soon after moving back into my old dorm, I had an experience with my oldest daughter that was very special to me. It all started the day before I spoke to her when the commissary made a mistake on my order and gave me thirty dollars worth of phone time instead of the three dollars I had ordered. They had never done that before, and I was told there was nothing they could do about it. Irritated about the mistake, I called my Mom that day and vented my frustration. However, she said something interesting: "Maybe it happened for a reason." That ended up being the case because the next day when I called to speak to my daughter, she did not have funds on her account. So, my having thirty dollars because of a mistake turned out to be a blessing. Those funds enabled us to have many calls and one of the best conversations that I can remember up to that point. Then on the final call, she said some things that brought tears to my eyes. She told me I was the best Dad; and that even though other dads are physically present with their daughters, I was more a part of her life than her friends' dads were. She also thanked me for all that I had taught her and told me how grateful she was. To hear her tell me those things made everything worthwhile. I had always wanted her to know and feel how much I loved her, and to have her acknowledge that meant the world to me. I will never forget that day and the feelings I had when she told me those things. As a Father that is as good as it gets.

FAMILY VISIT

My Mom and oldest brother came to visit me a few weeks into the new year. They had come to visit me every year now at least once for a three-day visit. I looked forward to seeing them and having a few snacks from the machines that we do not normally have access to. Each visit I asked my brother for a Priesthood blessing and for guidance in the things the Lord would have me do. It meant so much to have family members sacrifice to see me and spend time with me. My sister and two other brothers had also been to visit me during my time in prison. Each visit was an emotional boost and a chance to speak openly about things that I felt uncomfortable sharing over the phone. The support and love from my family was invaluable. They had been a steadying force and influence; and their advice, counsel, and prayers made life here just a little more bearable.

Not all of my family relations remained strong and supportive during this time away. For many reasons, my relationship with my now ex-wife had become strained. For reasons she had not disclosed to this point, she stopped talking to me, and I only had communication with my children. It was the opposite of what I would have expected to happen with her. I had anticipated that she would be angry and distant at the start, and then over time might have been willing to speak to me about issues relating to raising and teaching our children. What I found was that she did the exact opposite. She was supportive and loving at the start, and then over time became angry, hurt, and distant. This is where the situation was at this point, and she would not discuss anything with me now. This was disappointing; and though I had expected her to feel that way at the beginning, I did not think she would cut me off years later.

Based on the little bit of information I could get from the children, I suspected that my ex-wife had come to her own conclusions about things that happened that were not entirely accurate or true. Because she would not speak to me about her suspicions, she was left to her own conclusions. Based on what I had been told, those were not accurate conclusions; however, I had no way of helping her understand what took place. One honest discussion would have helped her to understand things clearly, but she would not allow me the opportunity. Knowing that everyone grieves and handles things differently, I tried to be supportive and respect whatever she asked me to do. Though it was hard not to know what was happening in the lives of my children, I did my best to stay connected in all the ways I had available to me—email, letters, and phone calls.

Chapter 13

Prison And New Trial Decision

NEW WARDEN

This was also a turbulent time at the facility. A new warden came to the prison in the past year, and things began to go downhill quickly. Issues that had never been a problem before suddenly became big problems. The facility became inundated with drugs, tobacco, and people making their alcohol. Homosexual behaviors that were more in the shadows before became more openly practiced and endorsed. The guards became very lax in enforcing facility policies; things became chaotic and dangerous before long. Gangs began to take control of dorms and violence increased as rival gangs tried to control the drug and tobacco trade. Others worked with hackers on the outside to crack the security on the tablets we had been issued to get on the internet, use social media and other platforms, and download movies and pornographic material. They then would offer to hack others' tablets for a fee and then download these same items at outrageous costs ranging from $150 to $300. Before long, many had their tablets hacked and accessed things they could not use. Little was done to curb what was happening because of low officer staffing and guards after the last warden left.

My dorm, which had been an honor dorm up to this point, now became like most other dorms where people did whatever they wanted and could get away with. When the warden left, the staff in our building changed also. The new unit manager failed to discipline or maintain the high standards we were accustomed to in our dorm. This led to the deterioration of the dorm, and we no longer looked like an honor dorm. Things became increasingly more challenging as the conditions in the prison deteriorated overall. In just over a year, most good officers had quit or were fired, and the new staff ignored the nefarious activity that now permeated most dorms. As I awaited the response from the court on my new trial motion, I prayed I could endure these new conditions and not compromise my standards to fit in.

FATHER GIVES VIEW OF BREAKUP

While waiting for a response to my new trial motion, I asked my father what had happened in his relationship with my mom and why he had decided to leave our family. I had questioned why and often blamed myself for his not wanting to stay with us. As an adult, I needed answers to let go of some of those questions that had haunted me for years. Going into it, I was not sure what to expect. My Father had never told me much about why he left but quickly blamed my Mom for all that had happened. Being young, I did not understand all that took place, but as an adult, I was prepared now to know what had happened and why.

So my Father wrote me a letter, explaining what had happened between them from his perspective. This included some indiscretions involving my mother. My Mom had been compelled to tell me about an incident when I was twelve because my Father told me something had happened, and I had questions about it because of the proximity of it happening when I was born. I was seeing a counselor then and wanted to know what took place. The counselor encouraged my Mom to tell me, and she did. Based on what she said, it was a minor incident; it did not justify my Father using it as an excuse to do what he did. However, after reading what my Father had written, and confirming this with my older brother, it was clear my Mom had not disclosed the more serious incidents that had also occurred. Though nothing she did excused his behavior, I could see that the trust between my parents had been broken years before, and my Father used that as an excuse to do what he did years later.

In a way, I understood how breaking that trust and never fully resolving the issues surrounding the incident could lead to problems later in the relationship. In almost all of my relationships, the person I was dating had either cheated on me early on or lied about things initially, which led to a lack of trust. Coupled with my skepticism of people, that only justified my fears and kept me from getting too close to anyone for fear of being hurt. I also used that as an excuse not to put all my trust and hope in one person because I had never had a relationship where I was not burned. I thought it was better never to get too close than to hurt like I had all those times before. What someone else does never justifies doing it back to them; I realize that now more than ever. But at that time, that was exactly what I did to avoid getting hurt by them. It is a very destructive behavior, and my parents had both used it on one another at various times in their relationship. I learned the same behavior. I know other deeper issues between my parents helped to drive their behaviors, but the lack of trust and the relationship not based on mutual love and respect for one another were two of the biggest reasons why things were not right from the start.

After reading my Father's letter, it was also clear that he was less than truthful about events that took place and took little responsibility for what he did. I could understand his feelings about what had happened with my Mom, but not once time did my Father apologize for what he did and how it ultimately affected each of the children. No matter what my Mom did, that did not justify his behavior and breaking up our family. I had hoped more than anything that he would, at some point, apologize sincerely for the trauma he had caused in my life and for not being there for me. After telling him how hard it was for me after he left, and how I felt unloved and unwanted by him and my Stepfather, I expected he would feel a need to say at least he was sorry. But he never once said those words to me. He seemed intent on rationalizing what he did and denying he did anything wrong. It was hard for me to read and hear from him, but at least I now knew where he stood and why, from his perspective, he did what he did to our family. My Father has never taken responsibility for his part in my parents' divorce, and I promised myself that I would never do the same in my life. I would accept the blame for my mistakes and suffer the consequences. Also, I would ensure that my children knew I took responsibility for my actions. Instead of justifying my mistakes, I would acknowledge them and seek their forgiveness.

My parents are good people, and both had challenging childhoods and difficulties in their own lives growing up. Knowing that it was my responsibility to let the Lord judge, I knew I must let go of the hurt and pain I suffered for many years and love my parents for who they are now and for all the efforts they were making to help me. Both stepped up and supported me during this trial; by letting go of past hurts, I could see them differently and love them for the good they both have. The Lord allowed me to forgive and let go of the past, so I was determined to make the best of the time I had left with them and appreciate all they brought into my and my children's lives.

JUDGE DENIES NEW TRIAL

Several months had passed since I had last been to court when my attorney emailed me to say the judge had denied my new trial motion without explaining why it was denied. I had expected her to deny my motion, but her not indicating a reason was unsurprising. It had been made abundantly clear during my new trial motion that grave errors had been made and an injustice done. However, instead of correcting the mistakes, the judge intended to let an innocent man stay in prison, though they all knew the truth about what had happened.

CASE NOW BEFORE APPELLATE COURT

Now that my case was on its way to the appellate court, I was finding ways to use my time effectively. So, I joined our unit's soccer team and played goalie. I had played soccer growing up but had never been a goalie before. But as it turned out, I was fairly good. It was another way to get outside and exercise; I enjoyed it. I also got into the horticulture class to get outside to grow vegetables and soak in the summer sun.

During this time, I was also interested in researching the various Christian denominations and their beliefs. Talking to so many people of different faiths and not always understanding all their beliefs and why they believed what they did, I decided to learn more about these other religions. I wanted to speak to those of different faiths about their beliefs, and having that knowledge was important to avoid offending them. My mom sent me information on the leading Christian religions. Then, I spent the better part of several weeks writing the information in a format I could refer to when I needed to remember it easily. It was a worthwhile project and benefited me greatly as I knew more than most people I spoke with about these different faiths. Most were unaware of their church history, where they came from, and how they evolved. Only the Church of Jesus Christ of Latter-Day Saints believed in keeping a detailed history and personal records. I quickly learned that for many, church was just a Sunday activity that required little more than showing up on Sunday, and then afterward not thinking about it much until the next weekend. By comparison, I found that in our faith, we are one of the few who ask for daily devotion, service, and faithfulness in word and deed. The knowledge I gained through doing this research was helpful for me, but I was also able to share basic principles with those who knew little about their faith. This was a great benefit to others as well.

Around this same time, I began to experience pain down my left leg and in my lower back area. I went to see the doctor to find out if I had hurt myself while exercising, or if there was something else going on. When the X-rays came back, the doctor determined it was probably my sciatic nerve and suggested some exercises that I could do to alleviate the pain. After several weeks, the pain began to dissipate, and I continued to stretch and use the exercises moving forward to ensure the pain did not return. One of the challenges of prison is to stay motivated to exercise and stay active. It is quite easy to get lazy in prison and neglect to get proper exercise and nutrition. Though I had been exercising regularly when my back began to hurt, I had not been stretching as much as needed. The doctor's prognosis helped me get into a stretching routine before my workout, and it was never a problem again.

As fall came around, I had an opportunity to play softball. I ended up playing first base and batting cleanup for our team. I had not played in several years but found I could still perform above average. Playing sports in prison is not like playing in the free world. The stakes are much higher in prison, and the tension and trash talking is legendary. Once the game is over, the next week the winning side relentlessly taunts the losers and overstates their performance. Knowing these things before signing up, I was hesitant to play. But after lobbying from my dorm, I decided to try it. Luckily, I could still play well and hit the ball hard, and my teammates were excited about getting me to play.

Our team was one of the better ones in the compound, and we made it to the semifinals where we blew a ten-run lead and lost to the eventual champions. After the season, I was voted to play in the All-Star game at first base. I was the only one on my team who was voted an All-Star, so I heard the grumblings from certain team members who had high opinions of their play. I had not sought to be on the All-Star team but enjoyed the experience. Though the trash-talking and taunting went far beyond anything I had ever seen or heard, my goal was to remain humble and do my best. I will admit that, at times, it was hard not to respond to the absurdity of the comments. A few times, I felt compelled to set the records straight after listening to what was said. However, overall, I did a good job of keeping my head, being complimentary to others, and downplaying my stats. The best part was the exercise and the competition because I had always enjoyed competing in sports since I was young.

As the new year began and my birthday was approaching, a new challenge was coming that would change the entire world for years to come. It would also change how the prison functions and our everyday lives in ways no one imagined. A new worldwide pandemic began in China and has now spread to the West Coast of America. We had just received word from the Department of Corrections that until further notice, all visitations were suspended and would be until further notice. The world was beginning to shut down, and life in prison would change drastically as the COVID-19 pandemic paralyzed the entire world.

Chapter 14

Pandemic

When the news first reported a new virus circulating in China, I do not think anyone thought it would be something we would have to worry about. However, as time went on and the number of people infected and dying continued to rise, the prison systems went into lockdown mode. Once the first virus cases were reported in the United States, our facility suspended all contact with the outside world. It started by first suspending visitation and education. Initially, the lockdown would be for a month, but as time passed, the lockdown became indefinite when the cases became widespread.

Within weeks, rumors circulated that the prison would lock down the kitchen and send only sandwiches three times a day until the lockdown was lifted. The virus spread to most parts of the country by late March 2020, and a prison guard from a facility nearby us tested positive for the virus. This prompted officials to set up a quarantine dorm for those at the highest risk for serious infection, and three people from my dorm were moved to this dorm by the end of March.

By the first part of April, education classes were suspended, and we were stuck in our dorms 24 hours a day. Cloth masks were distributed, and we were instructed to wear them whenever a guard entered the dorm. We also had to wash our hands often to prevent infection. At that point, I had not heard whether there were any infections in the facility, but it was only a matter of time. The outside world was also experiencing lockdowns with businesses, churches, and schools moving to remote learning and working. The world seemed to be coming to a standstill while the medical experts tried to figure out how to deal with the virus.

Our facility had our first confirmed virus cases during the first few weeks of April. More quarantine dorms were set up for the most vulnerable people, and many more from our building were moved to these special dorms. The idea was to keep them isolated to prevent exposure to the virus. So, an entire building became a quarantine center. Those who lived there were not among the most vulnerable and were put into other dorms, including ours.

President Nelson, Prophet of the Church of Jesus Christ of Latter-Day Saints, asked everyone worldwide to observe a 24-hour fast on the upcoming Friday to petition the Lord for relief from the virus. So, after our meal on Thursday night, I began my fast. Right after I opened my fast, I was told that we would have pizza for lunch the next day! I had not had pizza for five years and could not believe this would happen on the day I would be fasting and could not eat it. What were the odds of that? I struggled momentarily with the temptation to save my pizza for later and eat it for dinner. Still, I did not feel right about that and decided to give my pizza to an inmate who gets little commissary help and would appreciate it.

When I handed over my pizza to him, he thought it was a joke and asked me twice if I was serious before he took it and thanked me. Then, I headed to the showers so as not to have to watch the others around me eat their pizzas. While in the shower, I felt peaceful and happy instead of disappointed. I knew The Lord was pleased with my sacrifice to give up something I wanted to follow His prophet. Though the sacrifice was only food, it was a major sacrifice because I truly wanted that pizza! But my willingness to give it to someone else to preserve my fast gave me a feeling that my Heavenly Father was proud of me. Feeling this impression, the sacrifice was worthwhile. Later, I learned that pizza was a way to keep people happy during the lockdown because other prisons were experiencing riots and unrest because of the virus and being locked down.

My attorney emailed me the next week to let me know that the courts had shut down and were not reviewing cases until further notice. She said she could not give me a timeframe of when they might resume. It was all based on what happened with the virus. So, now everything was in limbo with my case, and the outside world was restricted just like we were.

By the end of May, we had been locked down for three months. We had yet to have a major outbreak like some of the other prisons, but some were sick and isolated in the "sick dorm" where all who tested positive were sent. I finally had a chance to get out to my garden after three months away and found it doing well other than an abundance of weeds. I was fortunate to be one of a few from our horticulture class who was allowed to water the gardens for our class, enabling me to pick my ripe produce. Getting outside in the fresh air and picking vegetables was a great blessing. I found ripe tomatoes, jalapeño peppers, banana peppers, green onions, celery, onions, cilantro, and basil.

Knowing I would have a lot of vegetables to pick, I took a large bag with me and brought my produce back to the dorm. After giving some to others, I made a delicious fresh salsa that tasted better than anything I had eaten recently. That day, I was so thankful to leave the dorm for an hour to pick the fresh items in my garden and to make fresh salsa, which I then shared with those around me. There is nothing like garden fresh.

By mid-June, the virus hit our facility hard. Unfortunately, the dorms that were set aside as quarantines for the most vulnerable had a serious outbreak with over 100 people becoming seriously ill, resulting in more than 20 deaths. Many more were hospitalized. The virus had spread to 4 of the 8 dorms on the compound by this time, but ours had not been hit yet. I knew it was only a matter of time before we, too, would have an outbreak. I just prayed that it would not be too severe and that I could overcome the virus.

APPELLATE BRIEF PREPARED

My attorney emailed me to say that my brief for the appellate court had been completed and that she would send me a copy to review.

There was still no timeframe for when the courts would be back in session, but the brief was ready when the courts finally resumed activity.

Within a week, the brief arrived, and I could read what my attorney put together. She did an excellent job of detailing all the issues we identified, truthfully laying out the facts disproving the prosecution's claim. Reading the brief about that time in court and the things that took place there was difficult, but I was grateful for my attorney's work. I prayed that those on the appellate court who reviewed the information would see through the lies and false narratives and right the injustice that had been done.

PANIC WORSENS—AS DOES ANARCHY

As the pandemic worsened, conditions in the prison deteriorated also. Many officers quit, were fired, or got sick and were no longer coming to work. This led to a lack of rule enforcement and anarchy in the dorms. Every kind of debauchery that could be thought of was being done, and only a handful of people in my dorm resisted getting caught up in it. My workout partner, his bunkmate, and I were a few of the holdouts who were not breaking every rule during this time when there were very few staff, and little was being done to curb the behavior. I believe the prison allowed people to do as they pleased to keep things from becoming unglued. With tensions high because of virus concerns among inmates and the prolonged lockdowns, the prison felt like a tinder box waiting to explode. Maintaining lofty standards was difficult for those trying to follow the rules, while everyone around us tempted us to participate in their wickedness. An attitude of "They don't care, so why should we" ruled the day.

Frustrated at how perverse and unruly things had become, I struggled with how to cope with my new reality. Not leaving the dorm anymore and sitting inside with little to do were major issues that led to fights, lack of patience, and substance abuse amongst the inmate population. As my environment became even more challenging, and the days seemed longer and longer, I turned to the Lord for help to endure and for some relief from the evil being perpetuated all around me.

APPELLATE BRIEF FILED

By September, my attorney emailed me to let me know my brief had been filed, and I could expect to receive an answer sometime between November and March of the following year. Finally getting to this point was exciting and scary. I felt a pit in my stomach as I thought about how the ramifications of their decision would affect my entire life. During this time, I tried to stay focused on staying healthy and on the things I could control.

By mid-September, several dorms in our building were quarantined with confirmed virus cases, but there were no cases in our dorm. The weather had begun to turn cooler, and that was a welcome relief because our air conditioning had been out for the past week, and the colder temperatures cooled the dorm.

STATE'S RESPONSE TO APPELLATE BRIEF

I received the state's response to our appellate brief in the last week of September. I was amazed at the even more blatant lies and false assertions in the brief, more than had been done during the trial. Outright lies and falsehoods littered every page, making it difficult not to be frustrated at how ridiculous it was. The only solace I took from reading it was that if time were taken to read the transcripts and testimony given at the trial and new trial motion, the truth would prevail, and their lies would be revealed. But I admit I was surprised at how they had just thrown all truth and facts out the window and resorted to outright lies that were twisted into the worst possible narrative they could make up. Somehow, it was okay to ignore the truth completely and viciously accuse me of things that had never happened. The justice system was anything but just in my case, and I struggled to maintain any confidence in the system the more experience I had with it.

STIMULUS PACKAGE COMING

During this same period, I received word that a stimulus package sent out to help people impacted by the lockdowns in the free world was also available to prison inmates. At first, I was skeptical when people began to talk about it, but after my Mom researched it, she said it was legitimate. So, she sent me the paperwork, and I filled it out and sent it in. The amount offered was substantial and would allow my family a break from having to help me over the next year or more.

COVID HITS THE DORM

Right after I submitted my stimulus paperwork, my workout partner said he was feeling sick and could not exercise with me. A few days later, I was sick, too, as were most of the inmates in our dorm. COVID had finally hit us, and many in the dorm were suffering from mild-to-moderate symptoms. A few had severe illnesses and had to sleep sitting up just to be able to breathe. I lost my sense of taste and smell and had terrible body aches, fever, and congestion.

The one thing that saved me was some pills given to me by another inmate when he left to go home. They were prescription-strength cold and flu pills for congestion. Those, coupled with some Ibuprofen, enabled me to rest and sleep. Without them, I am not sure what I would have done. It was a tremendous blessing that I had those, and one I attributed to the Lord because I felt He had blessed me with those pills months before the virus appeared. I was sick for two weeks before the symptoms ended, and I finally started to feel better. It was a long and hard two weeks of bed rest.

REQUEST FOR DAUGHTER'S BIRTHDAY

As December approached, I had an idea for my youngest daughter's birthday. I emailed the family and asked them to reach out to her so she would have many cards and people wishing her a happy birthday. Because of the virus, I knew she would not have a party, so I hoped this would cheer her up and make her feel loved and special on her birthday.

The family responded to my request with an outpouring of love, cards, and gifts. Knowing the difficulty everyone was experiencing because of the virus lockdowns, I knew my daughter would not have a typical birthday like she was accustomed to. But when I spoke to her on her birthday, she had so many cards and gifts from family that made it special in an unusual way.

During the previous Christmas season, I participated in the "Light The World" initiative the church encourages members to engage in. The year before I had sent my Mom, my wife, and my two youngest girls emails and letters every day during the Christmas season to remind them to focus on Christ, emphasizing the meaning and purpose of the holiday. For my wife and girls, the letters were designed and colored for a distinctive touch, and I hoped the messages would inspire them. For my Mom, I sent emails each day with messages about Christ. The best part was doing it for others every day, taking the focus off of what I was missing and making the season more about those I loved.

FAMILY IDEAS FOR CHRISTMAS

I wanted to do the same for my oldest daughter during Christmas. Each day, I sent her emails encouraging her to remember the Savior during the holidays and serve others while enjoying the season. Without money to spend and no way to be physically present, finding ways to show my children and family how much I loved them was a challenge. I hoped that the time and effort I put into all I did for them would convey that from me.

RIOTS IN FACILITIES

In early December 2020, the prison system began experiencing riots in facilities across the state. Officials in our facility feared that seeing what was happening in other prisons would encourage people in our prison to do the same, so they turned off all televisions and all access to email and phones to curtail contact with the outside world. It only lasted for a day until the news stories about the riots went away, but the frustration and anxiety were real, and our facility was no different.

CHRISTMAS IDEAS IN FACILITY

By mid-December, I had been thinking of ways to help a few around me get something extra for Christmas. My friend and workout partner, blessed with $10 per week for essential items, never asked me for anything, but I knew he would appreciate a little food and a good set of scriptures. My Mom ordered me a nice set with all the standard works for the church in one book. Because my friend and I had many conversations about our faith, I felt he would appreciate having a copy to read. So, on Christmas, when he left his bunk, I put the scriptures, some food, a letter with my testimony, and an invitation to read the scriptures on his bed.

When he came back, he seemed surprised and curious. He sat on his bed and read the letter. He sat there for what seemed to be an eternity and then came over to talk. He thanked me for the food, and then, with some tears in his eyes, he thanked me for the scriptures. When he did so, he told me two years ago when he moved into the dorm, he would not have read the *Book Of Mormon*. But after getting to know me, and reading some books about the church, he changed his mind and said he was now willing to read it with an open mind. Several times I shared talks with him from General Authorities that touched his heart and also some books to read about the church and its leaders. Along with our conversations over the past two years, these things prepared him to find the truth for himself. I prayed that as he read, he would be led to know the truth as I had been.

Some others around me did not have family support, so food was always a welcome gift. I ordered some extra items at the commissary that week and planned to pass some soups and other goodies to those without. On Christmas morning, I had so much fun delivering the food to those around me who were without it. They were surprised and grateful for the gesture, and it made my day to be able to help those around me—even in that small way. Then I called my family and girls to wish them a Merry Christmas as I had done every year since I had been in prison. This year, I gave them some individual gifts and a 500-piece picture puzzle with photos of the girls at important moments in their lives. My goal was to give gifts that would last many years and remind them that I loved them and thought of them often.

As 2020 ended, I was optimistic of receiving good news surrounding my appeal, and some relief from the pandemic that kept us locked down for most of the year. I watched a football game on New Year's Day and went to bed around ten that night. The past year had been a tough one, and I was ready for the hope of a better year ahead.

STIMULUS BEGINS TO ARRIVE

As the new year began around mid-January, I received my first portion of the stimulus payment. I was surprised when I first saw the amount on my account, then relief and gratitude for the gift. It had been hard to rely so much on my family during my incarceration. I disliked ever asking for or talking about needing things. I felt uncomfortable asking and would sometimes go without so that I would not feel like a burden to them. I know this was due in large part to my growing up in a home where we were often reminded by our Stepfather of the burden we were on him and how much money he spent taking care of us. Since then, I have been self-conscious about being burdensome and have tried to make sure I contributed in some way or completely independent of others.

Now that I had some money that did not come from my family, I felt a small degree of independence that I craved and felt I could spend the money on things I needed and not feel restricted by the limited funds I had. It was good not to have to depend on others, even if it would only last for a brief time.

COVID RESTRICTIONS BEGIN TO RELAX

By February 2021, the prison began to relax some COVID restrictions because cases had declined. They even allowed us to go outside for recreation. Education classes also started again, but I had already completed my horticulture class and had no other classes to take because I had taken most of the offered classes.

I also knew that soon I would be hearing from the appellate court. For the past six years since the trial, I hoped and prayed that the true nature of what took place would be realized and I would be released. Now, as the time drew near, I hoped that someone other than the judge, who seemed determined to believe a lie, would see through the lies and reverse the decision.

APPELLATE DECISION ARRIVES

The day the decision came from the appellate court caught me completely by surprise. That day I had a scheduled video visit with my Mom; but when the video came on, my older brother was also there dressed in a shirt and tie. Neither let on that they had something to tell me until a few minutes into the call. My attorney had called to inform them that the appellate court had rejected every issue we had raised and had declined my appeal.

At first, I was so stunned I could not say anything, so I just sat there as my brother and Mom tried to console and comfort me. My brother then offered to give me a blessing, which I accepted; afterward, we talked, but I was still in shock. I thought the appellate court would see what we had presented and allow me to have another trial. How could they possibly reject every argument we had when they were based on the truth and the facts? Once again, I felt blindsided as the reality of what had happened slowly sank in.

But unlike when I was first tried and convicted, this time, I knew that the Lord was in charge and that every injustice I suffered would one day be made right. The past six years spent studying the scriptures and the experiences I had gone through taught me to trust in the Lord and not rely only on my understanding.

So, as difficult as it was to hear that the Court denied my appeal, I did not feel helpless or in despair. I felt comforted knowing that the Lord knew of my innocence about the conviction charges and that one day, my reward for enduring whatever He allowed me to go through would be worth it. The hardest part was realizing that I would miss so much of my children's lives, milestones, and events that are so important to share. My greatest regret is the pain and the absence that my choices caused. Not being there for my children and the hurt they experienced and have expressed is the hardest part of this entire experience. I hurt more for them than I do for me.

TIME FOR MORE REFLECTION

After receiving the news, I spent the next couple of days reflecting on what my life course would now look like. In the blessings I had been given, I was assured that I would be free again one day, and I still felt that would be the case. The hardest part was not knowing when or how that would happen. My family was also looking into hiring an attorney to review my case to see what, if anything, more I could do to fight my conviction.

After sincere consideration and prayer, I needed to allow the Lord to help me go forward. There were two issues I felt were the most critical in the decision to be considered: First, I felt we had spent enough money, time, and effort with worldly powers to try to secure my release. I had been trusting too much in the arm of flesh and not enough in God, who has the power to do all things. It was now time to trust more in the Lord and His timing and not to spend more money on attorneys who had taken advantage of us more than they had helped us.

Second, was the effect a new trial would have on my family and children. Knowing how traumatizing the first trial was and the vitriolic nature of the prosecution, I knew the effect a new trial would have on my children, who were now much older. These effects would be even more profound and difficult for them to endure than during the first trial. The way the prosecution put me all over the news and internet telling salacious lies and false narratives, I feared it would do more harm than good, and I did not want that for my family or my children. They had all been through enough, and I did not want them to spend any more on an attorney on my behalf.

Before making this decision, we fasted as a family. The decision I felt was right was confirmed by others in the family. We needed to allow the Lord to take over and put our trust and faith in Him. That is the answer I felt was right, and that is what I expressed to my older brother and my Mom in advance of a call they had planned with the family. Ultimately, the decision was made not to pursue any other legal remedies because of the cost and the very distinct likelihood that it would also fail. The chances of getting my case overturned at that point were less than five percent. But more importantly, I felt it was not what the Lord wanted us to do, so I decided to move forward and wait on the Lord to provide me relief.

While talking to my sister-in-law, she suggested that I begin writing my history and record all that had happened in my life and all the changes, blessings, and miracles that had taken place throughout my incarceration. Over the past six years, I have spent hours on the phone and in emails relating my experiences to family and friends. Now, I could make it available to all who desired to read it. The thought intrigued me, and after taking some time to pray and think about it, I felt that suggestion was what the Lord wanted me to do. It felt right, and I became excited at the opportunity and time I had to put into this important project.

Chapter 15

Patience in Suffering

B y May of 2021, we were informed we needed additional booster shots for COVID-19 and that a resurgence had begun because of new virus variants. Lockdowns were being contemplated again in the world and remained in place in prisons all over the state.

DELAYED DENTAL TREATMENT

During this time, I had a cavity that needed to be filled, but treatment had been delayed because of the pandemic. The dentist had not been working in the facility since the outbreak and had only recently returned to work. Her absence created a backlog of work to be completed. I was on the waiting list and had been since 2018 to get my cavity filled. Now, after three years, I was concerned that I might lose the tooth if I waited much longer.

I submitted another medical request to have my cavity filled, hoping that being persistent might pay off. Then I prayed and asked the Lord to bless my body and teeth and let me fix them before it was lost. Knowing that the medical care in prison was substandard at best, I tried to take care of my body in every way to avoid having to use the medical services. Doing everything I could, I then put my trust in the Lord to help me get the tooth fixed and remain healthy.

Not long after submitting the request, I received correspondence indicating that I was on the list and would be seen as soon as possible. Not knowing how long the wait would be, I prayed again for a miracle.

Then, the miracle happened. I received a callout to see the dentist only a few weeks later. When I arrived in the medical unit and had my tooth examined again, the dentist said that I would have lost the tooth had I waited any longer. Knowing that the Lord had blessed me before with health and protection, I felt He had once again made it possible for me to get my tooth fixed before it was too late.

Afterward, as I walked back to my dorm, I reflected on how blessed I had been to maintain my health and teeth in these conditions. Time after time I received blessings and been protected. I was confident if I did my part, the Lord would help me as He had done before. Knowing all that had to happen for my tooth to be saved, I still marveled at how the Lord accomplished this latest miracle. After waiting three years to be seen, I knew there was no way that my tooth could survive that long with a large cavity in it. Nor should I have been able to be seen that quickly with the backlog that the dentist had after I submitted my request only weeks earlier. But as had been the case many times before, the Lord made it possible for me to be seen before my tooth was lost. I should have waited another six months; the Lord continued to open doors to help me receive the care I needed.

By September 2021, COVID had returned to the facility, and many dorms were locked down. The frustration of being locked inside essentially a large warehouse day in and day out, hardly leaving our dorm, was difficult to deal with. Everyone felt the urge to go stir-crazy. Before COVID, we would walk to the chow hall, exercise outside, walk to class and have much more freedom. Since the pandemic, these liberties have been rolled back to virtually nothing, leaving us to struggle with little to do and too much time to fill. With people flush with cash because of the stimulus checks given to all prisoners, most spent their time using drugs or buying movies or other illicit materials for their tablets.

TOO MUCH TIME, TOO LITTLE TO DO

I focused on writing my history, studying the scriptures, exercising, and reading from good books. The challenge was that those who were using drugs were now staying up all night, making noise, and keeping others from sleeping. They were also stealing power cords for the tablets while others slept, disrupting my usual study time by playing loud music and being disrespectful. This led to increased fighting and dangerous dorm conditions. I was also getting angry at those with no regard for others and frustrated with the smoke and scent of the burning wicks that littered the bathroom area. The dorm began to smell like a bar, and I worried about secondhand smoke exposure and the effects these toxins could have on my body. The guards seemingly allowed people to smoke anywhere they pleased, making little effort to stop it. I felt trapped and helpless to do anything because the staff brought in most of the contraband, so asking them for help seemed pointless.

DORM CONDITIONS DETERIORATE

None of the issues I described were a big problem in our dorm before the pandemic. When the pandemic hit, older more vulnerable people were placed in a quarantine dorm, and those in that dorm were swapped out with them. This brought a bad element into our dorm, and it was never the same. That change coupled with a change in our unit manager, who did not like the idea of an honor dorm, allowed anyone to be placed in it whether they smoked, used drugs, or were disruptive. Honor dorms were a refuge from the violence, drugs, and disrespectful behaviors that were commonplace in other dorms because they were held to a higher standard, with dorm rules that were strictly enforced. There was very little to no smoking, drug use, or noise tolerated. The overall cleanliness exceeded that of other dorms by a wide margin. My dorm was one of the last few honor dorms on the compound, and when that changed, it became inundated with drugs, violence, gangs, and every vice imaginable. Inmates even made their own wines and liquors that they sold for extravagant amounts.

Things you never thought could go on in prison were commonplace, and most were willing to indulge in these activities. The depths of depravity that some were sinking to were beyond anything I had ever witnessed or thought possible. To me, it felt like the system had completely broken down because of limited staffing, the pandemic, and gangs exerting control.

CHANGE DAMPENS SPIRITS

As a result of the changes that took place in our dorm, and the denial of my appeal, I began to struggle with everyday challenges. At one point, I wondered if I could get through all the time I had left if things continued as they were. Many times I questioned if I could. Feeling disheartened about the circumstances I found myself in, I wondered if I was making a difference anymore or if my life still mattered.

These feelings were amplified by the challenges I was having with my two oldest daughters and ex-wife, who were not speaking to me at the time for assorted reasons. I had tried to speak with my ex-wife about teaching the children important skills and about topics they would soon face but received no response. The more I tried to help, the more I felt pushed away and ignored. In one of the two emails she sent me during this period, she mentioned that things we had previously discussed were added burdens that she did not have the time to do or implement. Understandably, she was busy with work and trying to raise the girls, and I knew how challenging that was. However, I also knew that life is always challenging and busy, and I felt that teaching children these fundamental principles should be the priority. Recognizing such a limited window to teach them, I felt the importance could not be overstated. I worried we were missing our chance to prepare them for the challenges that were soon to come or already experienced. I took her hesitancy to speak with me about what she was teaching and how she was raising the children as her way of saying she no longer wanted to collaborate. My efforts to reach her to discuss these issues resulted in her suggesting we go back to email communication. After she suggested emails, she made no effort to communicate further. She knew more than anyone of my desires to help and be there for our children, and yet I felt she did not see the point of including me since I was not physically there to help. Knowing the importance of both parents being involved and how vital that was to the children's well-being, I lamented not being there. But when I tried to impress upon my ex-wife what I went through as a child with a Father who was not there for me, it seemed to fall on deaf ears. Knowing I could not force things, I was resigned to allowing her to do as she saw fit and let the consequences of not addressing issues beforehand play out.

This was a difficult situation for me to accept. Knowing the challenges the girls would face in their lives, I felt they would not be prepared if we did not talk to them about what they would experience and help them to know the best path to follow. My ex-wife's tendency to avoid difficult conversations left me wondering if she had talked to the girls about the subjects that I knew would be issues in the coming years. I was also concerned about my ex-wife because she had changed to another religious denomination. I was concerned that their values and morals would suffer leading them to make some of the same mistakes I made and suffering the same heartaches. Having done all I could, I prayed very earnestly for their welfare every day.

Prayer did not relieve the feeling that I was failing my children. Feelings of inadequacy and regret for my life choices that took me away from my family overwhelmed me at this time. That and my limited communication with my children only heightened those feelings.

All of this happening simultaneously negatively impacted me in several ways: Being one who likes to fix things, I felt helpless because I could not help my children how I needed to. This, coupled with my dorm issues, made my life very challenging, and at times, I felt overwhelmed. This prompted me to turn to the Lord for guidance and comfort. Knowing the Lord to hear and answer my prayers, I petitioned for my children's welfare and happiness and the ability to endure the challenges I faced in my current circumstances. I learned that the only road to lasting happiness was following the Lord's plan and keeping His commandments.

Having gone contrary to the Lord for many years, I knew better than most what happens when we decide to live our lives independently of God and His laws. So, I redoubled my efforts to live the gospel so that the blessings would come. I knew that was the only way to endure and endure however long I was to be here. This knowledge motivated my every effort to teach my children and help them know what leads to happiness in this world and what will only lead to problems, pain, and misery.

RACIAL TENSIONS INCREASE

By 2022, people who had been flush with money from the stimulus checks were running out of money. With no money to pay their debts, fighting began to break out in dorms everywhere. With every store call came threats of violence to those who could no longer support their habits. The tension was palpable. There was also a higher level of racial tension because of riots and police shootings that had been taking place in various places around the country. Though relatively few in comparison, people of color were being convinced by the news media that there was a concerted effort on behalf of law enforcement to discriminate against them, and they took it out on the Caucasian population in prison, as the racial disparity in prison was overwhelmingly African American. White people began to be targeted by both officers and fellow inmates because of what they were seeing and hearing on the news. This only worsened the tension and led to anger and bitterness toward one another because of what was taking place outside these walls.

Then, in February 2022, Russia invaded Ukraine, and that had a significant impact on me. For the first time in my lifetime, I was able to watch a war on television being waged on another country and see the devastating effects it had on families and innocent people. Never before was a war so visible to the whole world. The images of watching the men put their devastated wives and children on a train to leave the country while they stayed to fight for their freedom was heart-wrenching. It made me rethink my approach to things in my life and helped me see that I also needed to put those I love first and find ways to serve and love them and others.

DIFFERENT PERSPECTIVE ON LIFE

That shift in focus provided an opportunity to see things from a unique perspective and to see others with greater empathy and compassion. It also helped me realize that others who have not been taught or experienced the same things I have, are living the only way they know how and do not know any differently. This was evident in the two countries at war, each being taught differently and adhering to their own beliefs, expectations, and training. Knowing this about others helped me have more patience with those who struggled in my dorm and understand their weaknesses and shortcomings. I resolved also to renew my efforts with my children and love and encourage them through their struggles and successes.

More than anything, my desire to maintain my relationship with the Lord helped sustain and drive me to continue to do all the necessary activities each day that helped maintain my testimony. Over the past seven years, that has been the key to keeping me focused and dedicated to following the Savior.

As the fall of 2022 approached, the world was in greater turmoil than at any other time in my lifetime. Political unrest was being felt around the world. Economies were dealing with record inflation, high prices for energy driven by wars, bad economic policies, and natural disasters. The country also faced rising crime rates and greater social divisions because of changing morals and values. Truly, this was a time spoken about in the scriptures when the whole world was in commotion; and without a spiritual foundation, many people were struggling with depression and unhappiness in their lives.

SPIRITUAL FREEDOM

For all these reasons, I am so grateful that the Lord helped me to repent and change my life. These changes helped me deal with all I have gone through and continue to experience. With the help of the Lord, I have learned I can endure any trial or circumstance. Though I might have many more years in prison before I secure my freedom, I know that if I continue to follow the Lord and keep His commandments, one day I will again be physically free, just as I am now spiritually free. This experience has helped me in ways I could never have imagined when this all started, and what I have been through has taught me things I could not have learned any other way.

Though I would never want to go through an experience like this again, I can now say I have changed and become a different person. My knowledge of God and of what truly matters has been enhanced and fortified. My gratitude to the Lord for rescuing me from the life I was living cannot be adequately expressed. I am a better man for having endured what I have been through so far; and I know that if I hold out until the end, I will be prepared for life beyond these walls and for an opportunity to serve the Lord in whatever capacity He sees fit to bestow upon me.

Most importantly, the past almost eight years have taught me that God truly does live and is in the details of my life. He has blessed me in every way, answered my prayers, and shown me through sacred experiences and tender mercies that He loves me and keeps His promises. This knowledge has made it possible to endure the challenges I have faced and gives me hope that one day, all things will be made right, and all wrongs and injustices that have occurred will be corrected. I know that God is real, and I hope after reading my story, you will know it, too.

Chapter 16

Post-Covid Conditions Worsen

EXPECTATIONS UNFULFILLED

W hen the government finally lifted the COVID restrictions nationwide, I anticipated life returning to what it used to be before the pandemic. Things like outdoor recreation, visitation, and educational classes had been largely cut back or nonexistent during the crisis. I hoped they would be restored to previous levels now that life was returning to normal. However, what happened instead was not what I anticipated. The prison deteriorated further in most areas since the end of COVID-19 and into October 2023. When I first came to prison, inmates were allowed outside to the large recreation area at least twice a week for several hours. That allowed us to play various sports including basketball, volleyball, softball, soccer, and cornhole. Others could walk around the fields, jog, or do calisthenics for much-needed exercise. However, when COVID hit, all outdoor recreation in the large yard ended, and the only space to exercise outdoors in the future was what they called the "small yard," a small enclosure next to our building about the size of a half basketball court. It looks like a large dog kennel, and it is called that by many inmates because it is small and cramped. That is the extent of most of our outdoor time except walking to and from the chow hall to eat.

Without adequate exercise outdoors, many inmates struggle with poor health and suffer from conditions like high blood pressure, diabetes, and heart disease. Because of overcrowding, dorms provide little room to move around, and exercise can happen only when people sleep. As a result, I get up at 3:00 am four to five days a week to exercise and ensure I have the necessary space and equipment. Some think I am crazy to get up at that time just to exercise; however, for me, it is a lifestyle and a necessary thing to avoid health problems and to be able to defend myself, should the need arise. But even more than those things, I enjoy exercise and feel better afterward. When I don't exercise, I feel sluggish and weak and have difficulty avoiding extra weight. Knowing how poor the food and health care are in prison has also been a key motivator in keeping my body healthy and strong. I find that by doing my part to stay healthy, God provides me with the other things I need to maintain good health. My experience has been that if we do our part and trust in God, he will do the rest. This even applies to how we take care of our bodies. Though working out in the dorm requires a lot of discipline and effort, my overall health and well-being have paid off. Unfortunately for others who lack the motivation, the lack of outdoor recreation and the limitations of the small yard has led to a huge increase in health problems and medical care for many.

Visitation has also been a major factor in the well-being of inmates and has undergone major changes since the pandemic. Before COVID, visitors could come for four hours on any given day on the weekends or holidays to visit loved ones. During and after the pandemic, visitation was first completely cut off for a period and then resumed but reduced to only two hours wearing a mask and seated behind a plexiglass wall with no physical contact. Physical contact was also allowed again, but other changes were implemented that further complicated the process. One of those changes required families to sign up for visits through email and to receive confirmation of their visit before arrival. On top of the required background checks, birth certificates, driving records, and other personal information to be approved for a visit, visitors must wear certain clothing and endure stringent admission procedures. These and other additional steps have only discouraged people from coming to visit. One inmate commented to me that he believed the prison was deliberately making it harder for people to visit to do away with in-person visitation completely. After close to nine years of life here, I, too, suspect the worst because more often than not, our worst suspicions end up being fairly accurate. As a result, I am very hesitant to have people come because the process is difficult, costly, and requires great time and effort. Though my family has been willing to do whatever it takes, I know it is not easy, and they are often frustrated with the process.

Another factor is when an inmate enters the visitation area once loved ones arrive. Typically, it takes fifteen to thirty minutes to get into the visitation room from the dorms. Once you arrive at the door leading to visitation, the officer opens the door and leads you into a small room just outside the visitation area and performs a strip search that includes body and clothing. Once dressed, you are led into the visitation room, sign in, and go to the assigned table where your family is waiting. So the two hours you were supposed to have usually ends up being only about an hour and a half.

FIRST FAMILY VISIT IN THREE YEARS

The first visit after all of the changes occurred was when my mom, sister-in-law, and oldest daughter came to visit. I will always remember that visit for several reasons: First, my daughter, whom I last hugged when she was twelve, was first to enter the visitation room while I sat waiting at the table. It had been almost nine years since I had hugged her, so I was anxious to finally put my arms around her and tell her how much I loved her.

Then, the moment came when I saw her walk into the room, and I could hug her for the first time in years. I struggled to contain my emotions and could not. Years of pent-up heartache and longing to be with her overwhelmed me, and I broke down and sobbed on her shoulder. My sister-in-law followed her in, and I was grateful to be able to see her after many years. But then I noticed that my mom was missing. It was only after we sat down that I found out why. She had been stopped from entering because she was wearing open-toed sandals which are not allowed. So, she had to go to a nearby store to purchase some acceptable shoes. Upon returning, she was told she could not enter until she returned her electronic watch to her car and left it there. So, after 30 minutes, Mom finally entered the visitation room and told us what had happened. Her frustration was evident; she said there was nothing on the prison website about the restricted clothing and her electronic watch. Her point about the prison website made sense; unless someone comes regularly, that person may not be aware of all the current rules and restrictions. The lack of information, what is restricted, and what is not is another reason people are discouraged from visiting the facility. The entire system is dysfunctional and broken. From top to bottom, this prison does not operate smoothly on any given day. Visitation is another area that is run like everything else—haphazardly and inconsistently. After close to nine years in prison, I have come to expect nothing different, but my family and others who come are shocked at how disorganized and inconsistent things are. For me, I have come to expect nothing less.

MAINTENANCE PROBLEMS

Another area that has directly impacted inmates since the COVID-19 outbreak has been facility maintenance. Before COVID, the buildings were all in good working order, and the air conditioning units and utilities functioned properly. But after COVID, nothing in the buildings functioned properly anymore. For example, my dorm has not had a fully functional air conditioning unit for over a year. Living in an area that has excess summer heat makes air conditioning necessary! Repairs have been made repeatedly on the unit but to no avail. When we asked the maintenance person employed by the prison about the problem, he told us he had explained to his boss what needed to be fixed. However, prison management refuses to spend the money to fix it properly. Instead, they do short-term, less-expensive fixes that usually fail within days. After repairs are often made, water drips from the air ducts overhead onto dorm beds. Then, not long after that, the compressor and other components freeze up because of clogged filters.

Other preventative maintenance is not being done to maintain the units. Starting in October 2022, the air unit we had that operated on two compressors had only one working. That was the case until the spring of 2023. As temperatures outside began to rise, our dorm temperatures rose with it. By June, the temperatures inside the dorm were in the upper 80s to low 90s. Attempts were made to fix the unit, but nothing worked. Whenever we asked someone about the status of the air, we were told parts were on order.

That was the case until August 2023, when families of those in my dorm began to get involved by emailing and calling corporate offices and complaining about the dorm conditions. After receiving several complaints, a licensed air conditioning contractor was hired to fix the problem. He took pictures and said additional parts were needed, and again, we were still waiting for parts. In the meantime, dorm temperatures rose into the mid-90s during the afternoons—suffocating the dorm with heat and humidity. During this time, prison officials mocked us and said that state camps do not have air, and if we wanted to go to a state camp, they could send us to one. They also offered to send us to other dorms if we disliked our place. These were all veiled threats because of the complaints made to their corporate office on our behalf. Finding a good dorm like the one we live in is hard to find in prison, so no one wanted to go. However, we all suffered without air conditioning the entire summer. Large floor fans were finally brought in; however, they did little to dissipate the heat and humidity. One part has yet to be fixed, and parts are still on order as of October 2023. We have no idea when or if it will ever be fixed. Thank goodness cooler temperatures and the open outdoor vent have temporarily improved the conditions. Nevertheless, instead of fixing problems, management uses less expensive means, and parts constantly break down.

FOOD SIZES DECREASE

Changes were also made to the food we received since the pandemic ended. Because food costs increased, prison management changed the menu to give less expensive options and smaller portions. Since I arrived in prison, the food portions have been slowly decreasing, and the costs for commissary are increasing each year. Most portions now given would barely feed a small child and do not feed grown men. As a result, inmates increasingly try numerous times to go through the lines for more food. Prison management, in turn, has posted guards at the door to turn away those who try to go through more than once. This has led to many confrontations between guards and inmates who claim they have not yet eaten, though in reality many of them have and are still hungry. There have always been those who try to get more than one tray no matter how much food is offered; but since the pandemic has ended and food portions are at their lowest point, the problem has escalated to new heights.

Compounding this problem is the steady rise in commissary costs. Understandably, costs for all have escalated because of inflation and other market pressures. Prisons are not immune to these cost increases. However, also known among those familiar with prison life are the exorbitant prices charged for commissary items. Some examples illustrate how much they have increased since my arrival almost nine years ago: Peanut butter was $2.18 per container; the cost for the same item today is over $5. Cheese was also $2.25 per container and now is nearly $5! Soups, the main source of money exchanged among inmates, started at $.25 per soup when I first arrived. Now, the cost is $.61 per soup. Cereal started at $3 and now is close to $8 per bag. Most items have increased over 300 percent, with the largest increases in the past two years. With the increased costs and the lack of food offered by the facility, inmates have turned to stealing, extortion, and taking extra trays to compensate for lack of funds or commissary. Many live in fear of being harmed because of the desperation some have to feed addictions or get what they want. With food and commissary being the main source of currency, the combination of less food being served and higher commissary prices has led to more dangerous circumstances for everyone.

COVID RELIEF FUNDS BRING DANGER

Another factor affecting life in prison was the COVID-19 relief checks sent to all Americans, including inmates. The influx of funds has led to some dangerous circumstances, especially among those who struggle with drug addiction. For almost a year and a half, after the funds were received, dorms were inundated with drug use and people running up debts that eventually they could not pay because they ran out of money. Not normally being accustomed to having money, some went overboard and increased debts in the hundreds or thousands. Knowing that people had COVID-19 money made the dealers more prone to lend money on credit because the money came from the government. But when those running up debts with multiple dealers overpromised on how much money they had, payment was exacted in other ways. The price for nonpayment in prison can range from being beaten or stabbed to removal from the dorm and even death. Most of those who deal drugs are affiliated with gangs and have people all over the prison and in other prisons, so there is no escape from paying one's debt. I have witnessed more beatings than I can recall and could see what would eventually happen before it did. Sadly, those who sell the drugs prey upon those who have addictions and then take advantage of them to take their money and force them to pay. I have heard many call their loved ones to petition them for money to save them from the penalty they knew was coming for nonpayment. In the end, the COVID relief funds greatly benefitted some and relieved the burden for a time from families sending funds to their loved ones in prison. But for those with addictions, the COVID money created more addicts to substances like synthetic marijuana or "strips" as they are called, and to methamphetamines, some laced with other more addictive chemicals that make stopping virtually impossible. COVID has changed many things in prison, but the biggest thing it did was create more addicts by being locked inside the dorm flush with money to spend and nothing else to do other than get high, read, or exercise.

EDUCATIONAL CLASSES DECREASE

Educational classes also changed dramatically after COVID. Before the pandemic, classes were held regularly by teachers who tried to help inmates learn the material and showed some concern for those they taught. If you did not go to class, teachers held you accountable and would give you a disciplinary report. Privileges such as commissary and phone were revoked after COVID-19 changed our lives. Many teachers left during and after COVID, leaving many classes unavailable because they had no one to teach them. With the new staff came a different culture that did not hold people accountable and allowed for cheating on tests, thefts in the education department, and a general lack of control in the classes. They also allowed inmates to sign in and leave if they did not want to attend a class. Because state and federal governments pay for the facility to offer these classes, each member's signatures were required. But instead of teaching classes consistently, teachers often just called inmates to class to sign the roster sheet and then leave. If actions speak louder than words, what they are saying is that they want to make sure to get paid, and they do not care if you learn anything. Though everyone here knows the educational classes offered are more about making money than helping inmates learn a new skill or become rehabilitated, it is even more obvious now after COVID.

LACK OF SECURITY CONTROL

The last, and perhaps most important, aspect that has changed since my arrival and after the pandemic is facility security. Prison staff turnover is extremely high because of the conditions and circumstances that must be managed daily. That has and probably will always be the case. However, the lack of institutional control and willingness to allow inmates to do as they please have been steadily getting worse from the time COVID started until now. Several aspects, in particular, have made prison life more difficult and dangerous. The first thing that happened when COVID hit to keep the facility from rioting and tensions from overflowing was the staff beginning to look the other way regarding drug use, smoking, and fighting among inmates. Staff did not seem to care as long as the infraction did not lead to serious injury or bodily harm. Before COVID, smoking, drugs, and fighting brought discipline and solitary confinement. During COVID-19, inmates could smoke whenever they wanted, and drugs flowed more than ever into the dorms. As a result, fighting happened daily with no repercussions for those involved. At the time, management attributed the increased fighting to the COVID crisis. the lockdowns that we were experiencing, and were trying to pacify inmates by giving them what they wanted. The problem with that approach is that now that COVID is over, the inmates are refusing to return to the status quo and instead continue to do what they have done the past few years since COVID. Though the staff have tried to roll back some of the things they allowed the previous few years, it has not made much of a difference.

Another aspect that has made it more dangerous is the use and carrying of weapons by inmates. Not long after COVID restrictions were lifted, we were going to eat lunch and were required to go through a metal detector before entering the gate to enter the chow hall. We were required to go through the detector because there had been numerous attacks on the compound recently using various weapons. As people were preparing to go through the machine, the warden and security staff advised people that if they had weapons, they should drop them before going through. When I walked through, a giant pile of weapons was on the ground next to the metal detector. But even more surprising is that nothing happened to those who were carrying the weapons on their body. The weapons were left on the ground where they were dropped, and as people left the chow hall, they grabbed the weapons to take back to their dorms. I could not believe what I was seeing! But seeing that firsthand shows me they are not serious about the safety of the inmates in the compound. Knowing this has only emboldened others to do the same, and the problem has only worsened over time. I could understand the reasons for not enforcing things as harshly during the lockdowns.

Still, the unintended consequence of relaxing those policies is inmates taking advantage of relaxing the rules and not wanting to return to the disciplined way it was before.

Chapter 17

Relationships Healed

W hen I wrote my story, I often spoke about my relationships with my Father and Stepfather and used what they did as examples of things I did not want to repeat. I did so by trying to express my feelings and the experiences that most affected me in my youth. I wanted people to understand what I felt and, subsequently, how I chose to respond to those feelings. At times, those feelings were bitter, harsh, and even unforgiving. But this experience I have been through these past nine years has taught me that the greatest healing balm for past hurts is forgiveness, so I want to share how that healing balm has helped heal those relationships and what they now look like today.

MY FATHER

First I want to talk about my Father. Over the last nine years since coming to prison, I have been able to rekindle my relationship with my Father and his wife. They have been very supportive, loving, and gracious in their concern for me and my family. Speaking on the phone two to three times per week has allowed me to get to know my Father in ways I never have before. I have grown to understand and appreciate him differently than I did when I was younger. His great sense of humor, insights into situations we speak about, and his willingness to share what happened between him and my Mom from his point of view have helped me move past old hurts and love him for who he is and who he has become. I have recognized that my Father is trying to do his best to love me; that is all I ever wanted from him. Having him be a part of my life in such a critical way I never thought would ever happen is all I ever wanted before my life changed and I came to prison. One of the greatest blessings I now have is my relationship with my Father, which means everything to me.

Of course, there is an amazing woman behind every great man, and I consider his wife one of those. During my time here, she has helped heal many relationships in my family through her efforts and very kind and thoughtful gifts. Her consistent and genuine concern has paved the way for others to reconnect with my Father, build back their relationships, and strengthen them. I am so grateful to know my Father has someone like her with whom to share the remaining years of his life. Their support and love during this time in my life have been a blessing. I have learned that forgiveness and allowing people the opportunity to change and grow is the way to move forward and have a strong relationship. Because I have seen and experienced many changes in my own life, I now try to allow others the same chances to grow and become the best version of themselves that they can be. That is how I now see my Father and his wife, for who they are now and the good they do to me and those in my family. The past no longer affects my relationship with my Father because we have forgiven each other and moved forward together.

MY STEPFATHER

My relationship with my Stepfather has been different, too. I was pretty critical of him in my story, and harsh at times in my assessment of him over the years. Sadly, all the things I expressed were real, as well as how I felt at the time. But not everything that happened was bad; there were many happy memories, too. Though what I shared in my childhood was mostly of things he did that hurt me, he did much to help me by what he taught me. I also want to point out that we came to realize that he had been struggling with mental health challenges, for how long no one is quite sure. It is possible that they affected him as far back as my teenage years or before. But whenever those challenges for him started, I felt it was important to share some of the good he did and some of the positive things he taught me along the way. Along with my Mother, he taught me how to cook. I also learned to make pies from scratch, casseroles, and sauces. I also learned to can vegetables and fruits and make jams and jellies. He taught me to work hard, paint, and make house repairs. He taught me how to plant a garden and care for a yard. He also taught me to appreciate my labors' fruits and be self-sufficient. I have always appreciated these things and felt it important to share how much they have impacted me, especially now that he is gone.

My Stepfather passed away not long ago at the end of 2023. I did not get to say goodbye, at least not how I had hoped. I had tried to make amends with him years before but did not receive a response to my repeated requests to talk or reach out. I sent him several letters expressing my sincere forgiveness for what he had done and asked for his forgiveness in return. I was not the perfect son and was guilty of many faults in our relationship, for which I was genuinely sorry. I had hoped one day to talk with him in person to say all these things, but I know now that he knows how I feel.

Forgiveness is not easy; for some, it takes time to get to where they can forgive and move forward. For me, it was recognizing that I, too, was broken, made mistakes, and needed God's forgiveness to change and move forward. But to do that, I had to allow others the same opportunities. When I did so with my Father and Stepfather, that's when the healing began, and the burden I carried for years was lifted. I now understand that is what the Savior meant in the Bible when he speaks of His burden being easy to carry. When we let God judge others, we allow Him to carry the burden instead of us, freeing us from judgment and condemnation. After years of carrying such a heavy burden, I now feel free and at peace with my Father and Stepfather. Letting God be the one to judge others allows us the freedom to focus on what we need to do to become the best people we can be.

Chapter 18

Conclusions

Writing this history has greatly benefited me, and I hope it will also benefit those who take the time to read about my experiences. I tried to emphasize the choices and consequences of those choices, rather than the circumstances that started the choice process. I learned in my own life that one poor choice leads to other poor choices, and ultimately to the wrong path if we seek happiness and success. The opposite is also true. If we choose to do good, it is easier to keep choosing that path and, in the end, to find peace and fulfillment. The part I did not understand or realize when it was happening is how important even the smallest decisions are to the path we take in our lives. Every decision a person makes directly impacts their path; I have found no exceptions.

FIRST TRUTH LEARNED

While writing about my life and talking to those who are imprisoned around me, I realized that my experiences are not unique but are the experiences of so many who lose their way because of difficult childhoods, substance addiction, abusive parents, or inadequate teaching of proper or healthy ways to live their lives. This inevitably leads those not taught to make the right choices to more heartache and misery. Regrettably, if the parents themselves were never taught, the children never learn and perpetuate the cycle.

The common denominator in all these instances is that those here, at some point, felt unloved, unwanted, and unneeded and were not taught how to be successful in their lives. This leads to a lack of self-esteem and confidence, and an inability to trust that others can love us, especially when we do not even love ourselves. When this happens, the neglected often seek to find fulfillment in unhealthy and destructive ways because it is easier and requires less emotional commitment, vulnerability, and trust. People deficient in these areas often want to have relationships, just not the vulnerability of having to put all of their trust and heart into them. Because they never properly learned how to have loving, healthy relationships, they instead sought unhealthy and destructive ones. These kinds of relationships rarely last and often lead to even more instability and emotionally distant relationships.

My life story follows that same format. I grew up in a home where my parents struggled from the start to have a healthy and loving relationship because of the choices they made from the beginning. Over time because there was not a healthy foundation, the relationship failed and ended in divorce, affecting all in negative and unhealthy ways. This led me never to see what a true loving relationship looked like; instead, I saw a hollow substitute that was never real or heartfelt and full of anger, resentment, and betrayal. Their relationship ended in divorce, and it left me feeling empty, unloved, and unwanted.

The experiences that I had as a result of my parents' failures and what transpired afterward when my Mother remarried affected my life for the next thirty-one years. Issues of trust, neglect, abuse, and violence made it hard for me to have healthy and loving relationships with others. Feeling like those I loved rejected and left me also affected my self-esteem, which impacted my relationships in devastating ways. I did not believe people could love me or that they would not leave me at some point. My lack of trust in others and the belief that they would also leave me led me to distance myself from people for fear of losing them and being heartbroken again.

Instead of giving my heart to one person, I would have relationships with multiple people for short periods so that I would never give my heart to any of them. Then, if I began to get close to them, or them to me, I would sabotage the relationship so that it would end. This kept people at a comfortable distance from me and allowed me to break things off before I could get hurt or rejected. This destructive behavior was how I dealt with my unresolved feelings and fears that were brought about by my childhood experiences.

This is how I felt about my life for thirty-nine years until I came to prison and realized the truth about what was happening in my life. I had spent my entire life blaming my Father and Stepfather for every mistake and terrible thing that ever happened to me. While It was true that the things they chose to do negatively impacted me and my decision-making process, I ultimately realized that every choice I made was entirely my own and mine alone. No one forced me to make the decisions I made. I did that all by myself, and the mistakes were my fault, too. With the realization of all these things also came a renewed sense of self-worth and confidence that I have changed and become the person I should have been all along. Through a thorough and true repentance process, I once again had the proper respect for myself and confidence that God loved and accepted me.

SECOND TRUTH LEARNED

The second truth I realized about myself is that I had held onto all the pain and hurt I had suffered all those years earlier and had never forgiven my Father and Stepfather for how they treated me and the choices they made. Holding onto that hurt and pain caused bitter and resentful feelings that negatively affected my relationships. The biggest impact it had was on my trust in others. But this also was a choice I made not to trust people largely driven by my choice not to forgive or resolve my feelings. Instead, I chose to bury them and pretend that I was okay and that I was not struggling with trust or abandonment issues. However, that was a lie.

THIRD TRUTH LEARNED

The third truth I understood was that there is one source where pain and hurt inflicted upon us by others can be healed, and we can become whole again in body, mind, and spirit. That is through the Atonement of Jesus Christ. He is the only one who can heal a broken heart and a wounded soul. His is the only power on earth or in heaven to heal any earthly pain or sorrow inflicted on this earth and make us whole again. I experienced the power of the Atonement of Jesus Christ in my life, and it changed my heart and desires and healed the broken soul and mind that had been the cause of so much suffering and grief in my own life and in the lives of those I loved.

I came to understand these three truths only after I was humbled by my life's circumstances, which allowed the Lord to help me begin to see what was causing me and those I loved so much pain and suffering.

KEY DECISION MADE

The three truths learned led to the decision to turn to the Lord wholeheartedly and trust in the promises given to those who fully trust in Him.

The result has been nothing short of miraculous. I never thought I would have the courage to face and repent of all my sins, but the Lord gave me the strength to do so. I never thought I could survive even one day in jail, but I did for close to a year. Then, I thought I would not make it in prison, but now it has been almost nine years, and He has blessed and preserved me this entire time. Without the Lord, I would never have changed who I was and would be lost to this day. Because of His mercy and willingness to bless those who choose to repent, I am now free from my past sins and have progressed even in this difficult environment.

LIFE MESSAGE

I hope this history illustrates the message of hope in the midst of great suffering. We are responsible for how our lives turn out because we make the right or wrong decisions that directly lead to the path we travel. Though the choices others make can impact our choices for better or worse, we still decide for ourselves what path we will take, regardless of what others decide they will do.

Lastly, I hope others can see that as lost and broken as I once was, you are never too lost or broken to return and be healed by the Atonement of Jesus Christ. He loves us despite our weaknesses, sins, and poor choices. He is aware of the difficulty in each of our lives and will reach after us hoping that one day we will reach back and find our way back to Him. As Alma did in the *Book of Mormon,* I feel that I was one of the vilest of sinners, and yet the Lord saw fit to rescue me and help me find my way back. I know He will do the same for anyone who truly desires to repent and change their life.

If anyone has a question about whether God is real or if He loves us, I hope that after reading about my life and the miracles and blessings God has given me, you have received the answer to that question for yourself. If you are struggling with the problems I dealt with in my life, I pray that you will also choose to turn to our Savior and seek His help to change and heal. His is the only power on earth who can make that happen.

LDS Faith Terminology

References within the manuscript refer to the following sources: Church and *Bible* Scriptures, including *the Book of Mormon, Doctrine and Covenants, Pearl of Great Price; King James Version of the Bible (*New and Old Testaments): Genesis, Hebrews, Mathew, Mark, Luke, John, Acts, Corinthians, James, Daniel, Psalms, Timothy, Titus, Hebrews; *Joseph Smith Translation of Bible; Pearl of Great Price.* Source: Church of Jesus Christ of Latter-Day Saints Church of Jesus Christ of Latter-Day Saints Legal Department https://www.churchofjesuschrist.org/search

Aaronic Priesthood: As a result of the failure of the Israelites to observe the gospel law administered by Moses under the authority of the Melchizedek Priesthood, the Lord gave an additional law of performances and ordinances and "confirmed a priesthood also upon Aaron and his seed, throughout all their generations" (D&C 84:18) to administer it. This priesthood was of lesser power and authority than the priesthood of Melchizedek. It was used to administer the outward ordinances, particularly as characterized by the ceremonies of the law of Moses.

Apostle: The word means "one sent forth." It was the title Jesus gave (Luke 6:13) to the Twelve whom He chose and ordained (John 15:16) to be His closest disciples during His ministry on earth and whom He sent forth to represent Him after His Ascension into heaven. The calling of an Apostle is to be a special witness of the name of Jesus Christ in all the world, particularly of His divinity and of His bodily resurrection from the dead (Acts 1:22; D&C 107:23). Twelve men with this high calling constitute an administrative council in the work of the ministry. When a vacancy occurred with the death of Judas Iscariot, Matthias was divinely appointed to that special office as a member of the council (Acts 1:15–26). Today twelve men with this same divine calling and ordination constitute the Quorum of the Twelve Apostles in The Church of Jesus Christ of Latter-Day Saints.

Atonement: The word describes the setting "at one" of those who have been estranged and denotes the reconciliation of man to God. Sin is the cause of the estrangement, and therefore the purpose of Atonement is to correct or overcome the consequences of sin. From the time of Adam to the death of Jesus Christ, true believers were instructed to offer animal sacrifices to the Lord. These sacrifices were symbolic of the forthcoming death of Jesus Christ and were done by faith in Him (Moses 5:5–8). Jesus Christ, as the Only Begotten Son of God and the only sinless person to live on this earth, was the only one capable of making an atonement for mankind. By His selection and foreordination in the Grand Council before the world was formed, His divine Sonship, His sinless life, the shedding of His blood in the garden of Gethsemane, His death on the cross and subsequent bodily resurrection from the grave, He made a perfect atonement for all mankind.

Baptism: From a Greek word meaning to "dip" or "immerse." Baptism in water is the introductory ordinance of the gospel and must be followed by baptism of the Spirit in order to be complete. As one of the ordinances of the gospel, it is associated with faith in the Lord Jesus Christ, repentance, and the laying on of hands for the gift of the Holy Ghost. Baptism has always been practiced whenever the gospel of Jesus Christ has been on the earth and has been taught by men holding the holy priesthood who could administer the ordinances.

Conversion: Denotes changing one's views, in a conscious acceptance of the will of God (Acts 3:19). If followed by continued faith in the Lord Jesus Christ, repentance, baptism in water for the remission of sins, and the reception of the Holy Ghost by the laying on of hands, conversion will become complete and will change a natural man into a sanctified, born again, purified person—a new creature in Christ Jesus (see 2 Cor. 5:17). Complete conversion comes after many trials and much testing (see Luke 22:32; D&C 112:12–13). To labor for the conversion of oneself and others is a noble task, as in Ps. 51:13; Dan. 12:3; James 5:19–20; Alma 26; D&C 18:15–16.

Conversion: Denotes changing one's views, in a conscious acceptance of the will of God (Acts 3:19). If followed by continued faith in the Lord Jesus Christ, repentance, baptism in water for the remission of sins, and the reception of the Holy Ghost by the laying on of hands, conversion will become complete and will change a natural man into a sanctified, born again, purified person—a new creature in Christ Jesus (see 2 Cor. 5:17). Complete conversion comes after many trials and much testing (see Luke 22:32; D&C 112:12–13). To labor for the conversion of oneself and others is a noble task, as in Ps. 51:13; Dan. 12:3; James 5:19–20; Alma 26; D&C 18:15–16.

Covenants/Ordinances: An agreement between God and His children. God gives the conditions for the covenant, and we agree to obey Him. God promises certain blessings for our obedience. A sacred, formal act performed by the authority of the priesthood. Examples include baptism, receiving the Holy Ghost, and the sacrament. Ordinances are often a means of entering into covenants with God.

Duty to God Award: All of us are in debt. God has given us our lives, all that we have on earth, and the hope of returning to live with Him. In return, our duty to God is to keep His commandments and live lives worthy to return to Him. To earn the Duty to God Award, young men will need to complete the duties and goals outlined in the guidebooks, as well as choose goals of their own. These include: 1. Priesthood duties and standards 2. Family activities 3. Quorum activities 4. Personal goals 5. Service projects 6. Keeping a journal.

Eagle Scout Award: The Eagle is the highest recognition that Scouting offers to Scouts. It is earned through the advancement program, and only a small percentage of boys who begin in Scouting receive this honor. The wearer of the Eagle Award is the epitome of Scouting's best efforts and beliefs.

General Authorities: The Church of Jesus Christ of Latter-Day Saints follows the same pattern as the church that Jesus Christ established during His mortal ministry, restored in modern times. He remains the head of the Church and directs His chosen servants as they lead. The leaders of the worldwide Church are known as General Authorities and General Officers. General Authorities include the First Presidency, the Quorum of the Twelve Apostles, the General Authority Seventies, and the Presiding Bishopric. General Officers include the General Presidencies of the Relief Society, Primary, Sunday School, Young Women, and Young Men organizations. The First Presidency is the highest governing body of the Church. Along with the Quorum of the Twelve Apostles, members of the First Presidency are special witnesses of Jesus Christ. They seek the Lord's guidance as they oversee the affairs of the Church. General Authorities, General Officers, and other Church leaders likewise seek divine guidance as they love and serve specific groups of Church members throughout the world.

Gospel: The word gospel means "good news." The good news is that Jesus Christ has made a perfect Atonement for mankind that will redeem all mankind from the grave and reward each individual according to his or her works. This atonement was begun by His appointment in the premortal world but was worked out by Jesus during His mortal sojourn. Therefore, the records of His mortal life and the events of His ministry are called the Gospels; the four that are contained in our Bible are presented under the names of Matthew, Mark, Luke, and John.

GODHEAD: Heavenly Father (God the Father), The Son (Jesus Christ, Savior), and the Holy Ghost—The supreme Governor of the universe and the Father of mankind. We learn from the revelations that have been given that there are three separate persons in the Godhead: the Father, the Son, and the Holy Ghost. From latter-day revelation, we learn that the Father and the Son have tangible bodies of flesh and bone and that the Holy Ghost is a personage of spirit without flesh and bone (D&C 130:22–23).

Grace: Divine help and strength given through the mercy and love of Jesus Christ. Through His grace, made possible by His Atonement, all mankind will be resurrected. Through His grace, those who continually repent and live according to His gospel will feel an enduring closeness to their Heavenly Father in this life and live in His presence after this life.

Jesus Christ: Faith is a strong belief that motivates a person to act. Faith that leads to forgiveness of sins is centered in Jesus Christ, whose Atonement makes forgiveness possible. Faith in Jesus Christ is more than a passive belief in Him. It means believing that He is the Son of God and that He suffered for your sins, afflictions, and infirmities. It means acting on that belief. Faith in Jesus Christ leads you to love Him, trust Him, and obey His commandments. LDS scriptures (*Bible Old/New Testaments, Book of Mormon, Pearl of Great Price, Doctrine and Covenants*)

Melchizedek Priesthood: King of Righteousness. A notable prophet and leader who lived about 2000 B.C. He is called the king of Salem (Jerusalem), king of peace, and "priest of the most High God." Unfortunately, information concerning him in the Bible is relatively scarce, being limited to Gen. 14:18–20; Heb. 5:6; 7:1–3. Mention of the priesthood of Melchizedek is given in several other instances, primarily in Psalms and in Hebrews. However, the latter-day revelation gives us much more about him and his priesthood (see JST Gen. 14:17 [Gen. 14:18 note d]; JST Gen. 14:25–40; JST Heb. 7:3 [Appendix]; Alma 13:14–19; D&C 84:14; 107:1–4). From these sources, we realize something of the greatness of this prophet and the grandeur of his ministry.

Mission: The Church of Jesus Christ of Latter-Day Saints' missionary program is one of its most recognized characteristics. Latter-Day Saint missionaries can be seen on the streets of hundreds of major cities in the world as well as in thousands of smaller communities. The missionary effort is based on the New Testament pattern of missionaries serving in pairs, teaching the gospel, and baptizing believers in the name of Jesus Christ (see, for example, the work of Peter and John in the book of Acts). Mission leaders refer to a mission president, who holds priesthood keys, and his wife. A mission president and his wife, who serve together as mission leaders, are called by God and set apart to lead the mission. Together they love and serve, help fulfill missionaries' purpose, and help keep missionaries safe and happy.

Missionary Training Center (MTC): The purpose of the MTC is to train missionaries in classes or large meetings. Skills include language training and teaching gospel principles. The biggest blocks of time are scheduled for classroom instruction. Classes are very interactive, and two teachers, both returned missionaries, share their enthusiasm and testimony. At least two to three hours of classroom time each day is discretionary, so missionaries get help just where they need it. MTCs are located in 10 locations around the world.

Patriarch/Patriarchal Blessing: Every worthy, baptized member is entitled to and should receive a patriarchal blessing, which provides inspired direction from the Lord. Patriarchal blessings include a declaration of a person's lineage in the house of Israel and contain personal counsel from the Lord. As a person studies his or her patriarchal blessing and follows the counsel it contains, it will provide guidance, comfort, and protection.

Priesthood blessing: Priesthood ordinances are sacred acts given by the Lord and performed by the authority of the priesthood. Priesthood blessings are given by the authority of the priesthood for healing, comfort, and encouragement. Brethren who perform ordinances and blessings should prepare themselves by living according to gospel principles and striving to be guided by the Holy Spirit. They should perform each ordinance and blessing in a dignified manner and comply with the following requirements; the ordinance should be: 1. Performed in the name of Jesus Christ. 2. Performed by the authority of the priesthood. 3. Performed with any necessary procedures, such as using specified words or using consecrated oil. 4. Authorized by the designated priesthood leader who holds the proper keys, if necessary.

Prophet: A prophet is a man called by God to be His representative on earth. When a prophet speaks for God, it is as if God were speaking (see D&C 1:38). A prophet is also a special witness for Christ, testifying of His divinity and teaching His gospel. A prophet teaches truth and interprets the word of God. He calls the unrighteous to repentance. He receives revelations and directions from the Lord for our benefit. He may see into the future and foretell coming events so that the world may be warned.

Repentance: The Greek word of which this is the translation denotes a change of mind, a fresh view about God, oneself, and the world. Since we are born into conditions of mortality, repentance comes to mean a turning of the heart and will to God, and a renunciation of sin to which we are naturally inclined. Without this there can be no progress in the things of the soul's salvation, for all accountable persons are stained by sin and must be cleansed to enter the kingdom of heaven. Repentance is not optional for salvation; it is a commandment of God (D&C 18:9–22; 20:29; 133:16). The preaching of repentance by John the Baptist formed the preparation for the ministry of our Lord. See Matt. 3:2; 4:17.

Resurrection: The Resurrection consists in the uniting of a spirit body with a body of flesh and bones, never again to be divided. The Resurrection shall come to all because of Christ's victory over death. Jesus Christ was the first to be resurrected on this earth (Matt. 27:52–54; Acts 26:23; 1 Cor. 15:23; Col. 1:18; Rev. 1:5). Others had been brought back from death but were restored to mortality (Mark 5:22–43; Luke 7:11–17; John 11:1–45), whereas a resurrection means to become immortal, with a body of flesh and bone.

Revelation: The English word "revelation" is translated from the Greek word "apocalypse," meaning to make known or uncover. This is in contrast to "Apocrypha," which connotes covered or concealed. Divine revelation is one of the grandest concepts and principles of the gospel of Jesus Christ, for without it, man could not know of the things of God and could not be saved with any degree of salvation in the eternities. Continuous revelation from God to His Saints, through the Holy Ghost or by other means, such as visions, dreams, or visitations, makes possible daily guidance along true paths and leads the faithful soul to complete eternal salvation in the celestial kingdom. The principle of gaining knowledge by revelation is the principle of salvation. It is the making known of divine truth by communication with the heavens and consists not only of the revelation of the plan of salvation to the Lord's prophets but also a confirmation in the hearts of the believers that the revelation to the prophets is true. It also consists of individual guidance for every person who seeks for it and follows the prescribed course of faith, repentance, and obedience to the gospel of Jesus Christ.

Seminary: The purpose of seminary is to help youth and young adults deepen their conversion to Jesus Christ and His restored gospel, qualify for the blessings of the temple, and prepare themselves, their families, and others for eternal life with their Father in Heaven.

Temple: Uniting families for eternity is part of the work of salvation and exaltation. Ordinances performed in temples make it possible for families to be together for eternity and experience a fullness of joy in God's presence. For Heavenly Father's children to return to Him, each of them must repent, become worthy to receive the ordinances of salvation and exaltation, and honor the covenants associated with each ordinance. The ordinances of salvation and exaltation are Baptism, Confirmation and the gift of the Holy Ghost, Conferral of the Melchizedek Priesthood and ordination to an office (for men), The temple endowment, and temple sealing. Heavenly Father knew that many of His children would not receive these ordinances during their mortal lives. He provided another way for them to receive ordinances and make covenants with Him. In temples, ordinances can be performed by proxy. This means that a living person receives ordinances on behalf of someone deceased. In the spirit world, deceased persons can choose to accept or reject ordinances that have been performed for them (see Doctrine and Covenants 138:19, 32–34, 58–59).

Tithing/offerings: The Bible indicates that God's people followed the law of tithing anciently; through modern prophets, God restored this law once again to bless His children. To fulfill this commandment, Church members give one-tenth of their income to the Lord through His Church. These funds are used to build up the Church and further the work of the Lord throughout the world.

Ward/Stake – bishop/bishopric, stake – stake president: Congregations of The Church of Jesus Christ of Latter-Day Saints are organized geographically and members attend worship services near their home. Each member belongs to a ward or branch. The lay leader of a ward is called a bishop. He is a member of the congregation who has been asked to serve as a volunteer in this position. Bishop is also an ordained office in the Aaronic Priesthood (D&C 20:67), and a bishop is a common judge in Israel (D&C 107:74). The desirable qualifications of a bishop are listed in 1 Tim. 3:1–7; Titus 1:7–9. Each ward has classes and activities for different ages, including children, youth, and adults. The substantial time and effort required to administer a ward and meet the needs of the members is carried out by the members themselves. Most members are asked by local leaders to contribute in specific capacities. Duties include local administrative, teaching, or service-oriented positions. These responsibilities are changed from time to time, according to the needs of the congregation. Members of a ward worship together on Sundays and hold activities during the week. A ward is a community where Latter-Day Saints can develop friendships and support their fellow church members in their efforts to worship and follow Jesus Christ. Several wards make up a stake, which is similar to a Catholic diocese. The leader of a stake is called the stake president. In areas where there are fewer church members, Latter-day Saints are organized into districts and branches in place of stakes and wards. The lay leader of a branch is called a branch president.

Youth Programs: The Church of Jesus Christ of Latter-Day Saints provides a comprehensive program for youth through its Young Men and Young Women organizations. Youth ages 12 through 17 meet in classes on Sundays for religious instruction and several times during the month for social activities including service projects, sports, camping, and dances. Young men and women are also given leadership positions within the organization in which they learn leadership skills such as setting goals, planning group activities, and problem-solving.

About the Author and Reader Questions

ABOUT MATTHEW HARRISON

In *Unraveling Wrongful Conviction and Miscarriage of Justice*, Matthew Harrison bares his soul in a compelling narrative that unfolds against the backdrop of a life shaped by the dichotomy of faith and despair. In the close-knit community of The Church of Jesus Christ of Latter-Day Saints, Matthew's early years were marked by achievements as an Eagle Scout and recipient of the Duty to God award. His athletic prowess, particularly in high school basketball, hinted at a promising future.

Yet, beneath the surface, the specter of divorce cast a long shadow over Matthew's formative years, leaving him grappling with feelings of unlove, unworthiness, and an innate reluctance to trust others. The remarriage of his mother introduced a stepfather whose broken promises and subsequent abuse forced Matthew into a defensive posture, vowing to safeguard his heart at all costs.

Undeterred by early setbacks, Matthew embarked on a journey that included a mission to Portugal, marriages, fatherhood, and successful ventures in business. However, his world crumbled when a wrongful accusation led to a conviction and subsequent incarceration, with an unsuccessful appeal prolonging his time behind bars to nine years and counting.

Unraveling Wrongful Conviction and Miscarriage of Justice lays bare Matthew's struggles, his descent into a double life, and the pivotal moment when false accusations threatened to unravel everything. In despair, he turned to God, experiencing a spiritual rebirth that illuminated a path toward healing and transformation. Despite the confines of prison, Matthew's life continued to be infused with blessings—food, clothing, family support, and a newfound sense of safety and well-being.

Throughout four years of writing, Matthew unraveled the layers of his tumultuous life, aiming to expose the truth concealed by the judicial system and media. Chapter by chapter, he reveals the pain, the choices that led him astray, and the unwavering faith that ultimately guided him toward redemption.

Readers have responded with five-star reviews, captivated by Matthew's resilience in the face of adversity and the remarkable redemption that emerged from the crucible of his experiences. *Unraveling Wrongful Conviction and Miscarriage of Justice* is a testament to the strength of the human spirit, the capacity for change, and the profound impact of faith in the face of life-altering challenges.

As Matthew looks to the future, he trusts God with his faith and life, finding peace in repentance and a resolute commitment to move forward, no matter the twists and turns that lie ahead.

READER QUESTIONS

During the last four years of writing and publishing, I have been asked several questions answered in this portion of my book.

What inspired you to write this book?

My book is a true story of my youth into adulthood that left me scarred with unresolved issues that hurt and were painful. Growing up and rarely feeling loved and accepted, I chose not to trust to protect my heart. That led to living a double life that I hid from everyone. Eventually, that double life came to light when I was accused of a crime I did not commit. Facing the prospect of prison and being afraid of losing my entire life, I turned to God and had an experience that showed there is a way to heal and change. My family was supportive and stood by my side throughout the entire ordeal and helped make this book a reality. I have read over 500 books since being incarcerated and felt my story, like others I have read, might inspire others to change and never lose hope in the face of incredible adversity. I still believe the truth will set me free one day.

What happened when you were accused?

I lost the most important people in my life when I was accused of a crime I did not commit. I lost my job, reputation, family, and freedom. Being falsely accused and sentenced to a lengthy prison term, I began to seek ways to help others avoid the painful consequences of poor life choices and lead people to the greatest source of healing and change—God. Against all odds, I not only survived but also changed in my prison environment. Writing my story is one of many ways I hope to help others find the path to self-discovery and change and avoid the path that leads to incarceration and misery. Part of my survival was having a supportive family who stood by my side throughout the entire ordeal and has made writing this book a reality.

What inspired you to start writing?

My book was inspired by family members who were familiar with my life story and felt that it had value for those who might go through similar circumstances. I also felt that the truth needed to be told and that the myths that the justice system always gets it right or is about truth and justice being served could be uncovered for the misconceptions they are.

What was the writing process like?

Writing is painstaking for me because I cannot access many of the tools authors need. That is where my family comes in as a supporting cast. For four years, I wrote my story to them through emails; my family compiled and formatted all the emails into book chapters. It was a great learning experience for all of us.

What is your advice for aspiring writers?

My advice for those wanting to write is simply to begin writing whatever you are passionate about and then go back over it to fine-tune and make it what you want it to be. For me, that is how I found the inspiration to write and not to be too overwhelmed by trying to write it perfectly from the start. Also, writing in the mornings while my mind is fresh and rejuvenated was a great help.

What is the most important thing about a book?

The most important thing about a book is its theme or main message. You must constantly stay on track to shape the narrative to express your message fully. In my book, the theme of choices shaping decisions and decisions bringing consequences is reiterated time and time again in the examples I use. My life thus far results from bad choices that opened the door to others using me to shape their narrative.

What kind of research do you do and how long do you spend researching before beginning a book?

My true story is replicated throughout the prison as new prisoners come in and others leave. Some are guilty, but some are not. When I learn by watching them or listening to their stories, I can soon discern those who should not be here. Their stories support my own wrongful conviction experience.

Do you have a set schedule for writing, or do you only write when you feel inspired?

Because of the prison routine, my time is not my own; consequently, I have to look for a few opportunities to be alone and write. That will vary depending on the day and events. I also run some of my narratives by other prisoners in my situation, so my story reflects that of others here with me.

Do you read much, and if so, who are your favorite authors?

I love to read and have read over 500 books this year. Since COVID, our educational opportunities and outdoor exercise have become infrequent; reading has become my favorite pastime. Reading also led me to discover what triggered my reactions to feeling unwanted and unloved. Once I understood why I chose to do what I did, that opened the door to those who would mistreat me or lie about me. I was then able to move forward to being in a better place. I read many spiritual books because I believe the Lord has blessed me while I have been here, forgiven me, and given me personal inspiration to find new and positive directions.

When can we readers expect to read more wonderful books from you?

I am working on another book to help others navigate the legal system and jail-prison. For those like me who had never experienced the legal process before coming to prison, I was shocked at how things were done and the injustices that take place behind these walls. I want others who might face legal battles, especially those who are innocent, to know how to find a good attorney, their basic rights, and how to ensure their rights are protected during the process. They also need to be aware of what happens in jail and prison to protect themselves and the jail-prison culture. I wish I had known the things I shared in my book while going through the process because I think things would have turned out differently. I want to advocate for those with few rights under the current judicial system.

New Book Preview

PEOPLE CHANGING BEHAVIOR

Here is my sage advice, which was not in this first book but will be emphasized in my second book, *Judicial Misconceptions Shattered*. In the meantime, you may find this information useful in creating more positive relationships.

From the time I was arrested until this day, many of the people in my life and those around me still find it hard to believe I have changed. The world generally has difficulty accepting that people can change their lives. It is often said that once someone does something or acts in a certain way, they will always do or act in those same ways in the future. So why are people so skeptical of others and their ability to change? I want to share what I have found to be the greatest obstacles that undermine our faith in others.

PRIDE

First, pride. Pride comes out in many ways, all pitting us against others. When prideful, we compare ourselves to others and often see them as adversaries rather than equals. This leads to us competing to be better than they are and less likely to recognize their accomplishments. Pride is the opposite of humility, leading us to be combative and skeptical because we do not want to see others be better than we are. For these and other reasons, pride is a major obstacle because some cannot fathom that others can overcome weaknesses and improve their lives. They do not want them to succeed at all because, in their hearts, what they want is to be better than that person.

Others Resist Change

Another reason others question real change is their inability to change themselves. Their reason may be that they have failed to overcome some other weakness, so how could someone else possibly do what they cannot? Or perhaps they have not had many examples of people who have overcome weaknesses, so they doubt others can either. For some, seeing is believing; however, for others, doubts persist because they allow their pride or inability to change themselves to project doubt on everyone else.

Lack of Forgiveness

For all these reasons and many others, people generally are hesitant to believe a person has changed his or her life. There is one last thing that I have found impedes a person's ability to change—a lack of forgiveness. Those who cannot forgive others will not allow them to move forward and change. As long as people hold onto the past and refuse to forgive, they will never be able to allow others to be anything other than what they envision them to be. In my life, I held onto past hurts for 30 years, and doing so totally retarded my ability to let go of the past and allow those who hurt me to be different than they were 30 years ago. Once I was willing to forgive, I could see some I held grudges against for who they are now, not who they used to be. Lack of forgiveness is a key reason many struggle to believe others can change.

Making lasting changes is hard to do, but entirely possible. In my own life, I tried many times to change behaviors and failed before finally succeeding. The key for me was asking for God's help and believing He would give me the strength and courage to overcome. It has now been many years later, and I have not returned to my previous lifestyle choices. I continue to overcome this daily to ensure I keep on the right course. Real change is possible, and many truly experience this lasting change. Though the world tends to doubt and be skeptical, those who have experienced real change know that it is possible and are the ones who encourage and have faith in those who are trying to change.

As a Christian, I believe in real change—a change that originates in our hearts and changes our desires. The power to overcome, change hearts, and heal souls is available through the Atonement of Jesus Christ, which is why I am who I am today. Those who believe in God and ask for His help to change become new people who lose all desires to be less than who they can be. Instead, they become the person they were meant to be.

Topics Covered in *Shattering Misconceptions*

- Myths About Criminal Justice

- Finding A Competent Attorney

- Talking With Police

- The Arrest and Investigation

- County Jail and Prison

- Commissary and Prison Environment

- Judicial Procedures and Hearings

- Judicial Process and Bail

- Diagnostic Testing

- Private vs. State Prisons

- Prison Life

- Preparing to Re-enter Society

- Conclusions

DEDICATION

This book is dedicated to my children, family, and good friends. Without their love and support, this book would not have been possible. I love you all more than words can express.

Matthew Harrison

ACKNOWLEDGEMENTS

While confined, I've relied on the support of numerous individuals to bring this book to fruition. A multitude of remarkable people—from cherished family and friends to unknown readers—have enriched my life. To every one of you, my heartfelt gratitude!

Creating a flawless narrative eludes any writer, especially me, regardless of the number of revisions undertaken. The process of receiving suggestions, compounded by the constraints of email or mail communication only, was an arduous journey spanning four years. Throughout this odyssey, I am indebted to a dedicated team: family members and friends who meticulously compiled each chapter and provided invaluable insights, diligent proofreaders who unearthed our oversights, talented designers responsible for crafting captivating artwork, Chris Baird for his invaluable marketing expertise and prompt responses, and my resilient children who provided unwavering encouragement through countless challenges. Lastly, but certainly not least, I extend my deepest gratitude to my Heavenly Father and Savior for their constant presence that sustained me throughout the writing process and the resulting blessings they provided.

Matthew Harrison